D1156690

the
undervalued

self

Also by Elaine N. Aron, PhD

The Highly Sensitive Person

The Highly Sensitive Person in Love

The Highly Sensitive Child

The Highly Sensitive Person's Workbook

the
undervalued
self

Restore Your Love/Power Balance,

Transform the Inner Voice That Holds You Back,

and Find Your True Self-Worth

Elaine N. Aron, PhD

Little, Brown and Company
New York Boston London

Little, Brown and Company
Hachette Book Group
237 Park Avenue, New York, NY 10017
www.hachettebookgroup.com

First Edition: March 2010

Little, Brown and Company is a division of Hachette Book Group, Inc. The Little, Brown name and logo are trademarks of Hachette Book Group, Inc.

The persons portrayed in this book are composites of different individuals, with all names and some characteristics changed so that the confidentiality of each is completely protected.

Library of Congress Cataloging-in-Publication Data
Aron, Elaine N.
   The undervalued self : restore your love/power balance, transform the inner voice that holds you back, and find your true self-worth / Elaine N. Aron.
      p. cm.
   Includes bibliographical references.
   ISBN 978-0-316-06699-0
   1. Self.   2. Love.   3. Interpersonal relations.   4. Self-actualization (Psychology)   I. Title.
BF697.A724 2010
158—dc22   2009018351

10 9 8 7 6 5 4 3 2 1

RRD-IN

Design by Meryl Sussman Levavi

Printed in the United States of America

To Art

Contents

the
undervalued
self

Introduction

We all have an undervalued self buried deep inside, a part that can make us feel worthless. It may rise to the surface now and then or, for some of us, it may be a constant companion. It makes us doubt ourselves or feel shy, anxious, or even depressed. It often interferes just when we most need to be accurate in our estimation of our value. It results in "low self-esteem," the most common problem addressed by psychotherapists and self-help teachers and the root of most other psychological issues. However, despite all of our work on improving self-esteem in the past decades, the undervalued self is still with us, tagging along and causing trouble. This is largely because, as research has now shown, positive thinking and self-affirmations can make those with low self-esteem feel even worse about themselves.[1]

I never planned to study the undervalued self, but it kept turning up in my patients. In fact, it was what they all had in common. They ranked themselves against others, even if others were not thinking about rank, and they ranked themselves too low.

In addition to being a psychotherapist, I am a social psychologist specializing in the study of love and "linking," our natural, innate tendency to like and support one another. I knew that my patients needed and wanted more linking and less ranking. But I also knew that the ranking I was seeing represented another innate behavior, one with the directly opposite effect of linking, namely, a sense of being seen as a competitor and not supported. As a result, I began to think about that problem of low self-esteem in quite a different way.

First I saw that the very phrase "low self-esteem" implies ranking—a judgment that we should climb from low to high. The problem really is inaccurate self-valuing, or undervaluing the self. Second, if low self-esteem is so hard to change, perhaps there are good biological reasons for why we jump so readily to the wrong conclusion about our value compared to that of others. What might those reasons be, and could understanding them help us stop this widespread self-undervaluing?

THE GIANT TASK I UNDERTOOK BY CHANCE

I began to wonder whether seeing ranking as an innate aspect of our behavior could help with the problems created by the undervalued self. Fortunately, I knew from my study of high sensitivity that being aware of what we are born with allows us to adapt better to it. In the case of the undervalued self, it seemed that the problem could be that we need to gain control over built-in reactions associated with ranking conflicts and defeats.

Taking control of innate behaviors is actually something we do all the time, so it is not impossible. For example, some of us have innate fears of heights, blood, snakes, or spiders, fears that evolved because they are valuable for survival, but most of us can control these reactions if we must. We all have strong innate sexual impulses, which are essential for survival to the next generation, but we control these remarkably well. So perhaps we can also learn to control our tendency to undervalue ourselves.

4

It was a big task, in that in my quest to explain the undervalued self, I had unknowingly embarked on the task of explaining most of our daily behavior—the part with love and power at its root—and how it can go wrong. Further, I wanted to explain some complicated ideas clearly enough to be useful and to present truly effective ways of dealing with the undervalued self. Knowing that superficial affirmations would not work, I had to help readers recognize and deal with their unconscious, automatic responses.

In some cases simply becoming conscious of what was usually unconscious would be enough, but some readers would have personal histories of defeat and trauma that dramatically reinforced their undervalued selves. Doing something about that would require methods thought to work only in deeper, and therefore lengthy and expensive, psychotherapy. But could a mere book help these readers? I believed it could.

After ten years the giant task is done. I have tried to be as scientific as possible about the innate factors that contribute to the undervalued self without wasting your time with undue explanations. I have outlined how you can explore your personal history so that you can take it into account. And I have provided the kind of deeply layered approach used by the best psychotherapists because I believe you can make use of this even if you are working on your own. Some of you may be in psychotherapy already or may turn to it as a result of reading this book, but I know many of you cannot or will not. I think you can do a great deal of healing on your own under the right conditions, which I have tried to provide.

By the way, I, too, have an undervalued self. Indeed, it has been a hefty, pushy one and has caused me trouble most of my life. I recall giving a lecture early in my career and having some students come up afterward to tell me that although they found the lecture fascinating, my delivery was extremely distracting. They said I spoke as if I thought that I, and what I had to say, was worthless. Eventually I had to do something about my undervalued self.

Fortunately, I found excellent help, and what helped me will help you, too.

You will achieve immediate payoffs from simply reading this book. But some of you, like me, will work for years on healing the undervalued self. I am not a wizard, and this book is not an instant solution. If the roots of your problem are many and deep, it will take real effort to bring your undervalued self under control. But this book, with its unique approach and careful guidance, should make your task much, much easier.

HOW TO USE THIS BOOK

This book will be helpful if you simply read it through. But you will gain much more from it if you follow the suggestions in each chapter. Since you will be writing quite a bit at times, buy a journal just for using with this book or start a new folder on your computer.

You will also have to be patient. This book is rich, complex, and deeply layered. Learning from it will be like baking a birthday cake from scratch. Each chapter is an ingredient, but you cannot dump them all into the bowl at once. You have to prepare one set of ingredients and then another, then combine them carefully in stages. Still, it is worth the effort when you are going to celebrate the birth of someone as important as yourself.

How does this recipe work? Chapters one and two are like the eggs and butter that you blend together at the start of making a cake. Chapter one describes our innate tendency to rank and link; chapter two discusses the self-protections we all use to avoid the painful feelings of defeat in a confrontation about rank, protections that keep us from seeing the full extent of the undervalued self.

To those two we add chapter three, the flavoring, your own personal reasons for undervaluing yourself, some of which may be so traumatic that they have been kept out of your memory until now.

Just as you add milk to the cake batter alternately with flour, chapter four and chapter seven add the milk of human kindness, the affectionate linking that must balance ranking in a skillful way. But these skills have to alternate with deeper work on the undervalued self, which you learn in chapters five and six. They help with our innate defenses against defeat and trauma, which keep us safe from further trouble but also keep us trapped.

The mixture of all the ingredients in these seven chapters will require baking: you will need to reflect and work on the material contained in them, probably going back to each chapter often. Chapter eight is the frosting on the cake: the application of what you have learned to your closest relationships. This frosting does not just add sweetness; it is essential for holding the layers together. Healing the causes of the undervalued self will greatly improve your close relationships, and those relationships are the best places to heal the undervalued self. But chapter eight takes a careful, thoughtful approach to these relationships, because otherwise the opposite of healing can occur: the undervalued self can ruin your closest relationships, which can then add to the problem of the undervalued self.

When you can gracefully apply what you learn in chapter eight to your life, you will have a reason to celebrate indeed. Your undervalued self will no longer interfere with what you want, whether in relationships, career, or anywhere else. More important, you will feel better about yourself and the world around you every day.

CHAPTER ONE

Ranking, Linking, and the Undervalued Self

Much of what we do every day is to compare ourselves to others and to strive for respect, influence, and power. That is, we rank ourselves among others. Equally often we link with others by expressing affection, caring, and love, to feel connected and secure. At times we combine the two, for example, by using our rank in the service of a link when we want to improve another's life, as when we teach or advise someone or parent our children. Ranking and linking are always with us.

Sometimes we are conscious of these activities and sometimes not. Either way, ranking and linking play a role in almost all of our personal relationships and problems, including the problem of undervaluing ourselves.

When we undervalue ourselves, we are ranking ourselves too low. Often we drop into an all-or-nothing feeling of worthlessness or shame as we identify with a part of our personality we would otherwise avoid—the undervalued self. This self is out of touch with reality; it is inaccurate in that it underestimates. Whether we are trapped in that self for a moment or for a lifetime, we lose opportunities and suffer greatly.

While ranking is the source of the undervalued self, the right balance of ranking and linking offers the best solution for it. As you become more aware of how you rank and link with others and see the deeper, mostly unconscious and instinctual reasons why you undervalue yourself, you can often avoid tapping into this self with surprising ease. And when you cannot, this awareness is even more essential for dealing with the undervalued self.

Ranking and linking have been observed in the behavior of all higher animals, but researchers have only very recently begun to recognize these activities as the two primary innate systems guiding all of our social behavior. The phrase "linking and ranking" captures the breadth of what we sometimes mean by "love and power." Love is one part of the broader behavior called linking; ranking is what actually determines power. "Ranking and linking" was first used as a term in political psychology in 1983 by Riane Eisler and David Loye, and the importance of the ranking-linking interconnection was picked up again in the early 1990s in social psychology, but since then the term has rarely been used.[1]

Separately, however, topics related to power and love have always been a major focus of research on human and animal behavior. I myself have researched them separately. But I woke up to their intimate connection as I addressed the problem I see in almost all of my therapy patients: low self-esteem, leading to a lack of healthy close relationships. I realized that although my patients wanted love or linking, they were always seeing power or their rank in relation to others.

While ranking is an integral and even valued part of our lives—for example, we enjoy sports and friendly competition, and we willingly compete for jobs, promotions, and even future life partners—it has the potential to make us feel bad about ourselves in a variety of ways if we let it color our entire social viewpoint. We must all deal with defeat eventually, and, as you will see, defeat naturally affects our overall sense of self-worth and triggers a temporary depression. So if we see life as a series of competitions and comparisons, we are going to suffer more downs than ups. If we mostly rank high, the inevitable defeats will only feel worse.

Of course, we do not want to eliminate doing well or being on top, but our drive to rank high can blind us to ranking's other aspects. Besides depression, we feel other negative "self-conscious emotions" after a failure or defeat, such as shame, and these are highly unpleasant. Support from friends and family helps, but the more you rank inappropriately, the fewer strong links like this that you will have.

Many of us do rank too much, partly because of our social environment but largely because of serious defeats in our pasts that amounted to trauma. These bias us toward being vigilant to prevent future defeats and humiliations, so we often see ranking even when it is not present. We cannot heal the effects of these traumas without the tools that come with a full understanding of ranking and linking. Whatever the cause, most of us need more linking and less ranking in our lives, and we cannot create the right balance without being able to see ranking and linking clearly.

WHO MAKES YOU FEEL GOOD? WHO MAKES YOU FEEL BAD?

Throughout this book you will find exercises and self-tests to help you understand how ranking, linking, and the undervalued self operate in your life. Keep a journal just for this purpose, in which you record your answers for easy reference. The first exercise is to make two lists: one of the people who usually make you feel good when you are with them and another of people who make you feel bad. (A person can also be on both.) Leave space between the names, because you will return to these lists to make notes.

Notice that almost all the people who make you feel good are those with whom you have a link—anything from a warm, friendly hello or occasional talk on the phone to a link of love that is central for both of you. Almost all the people you feel bad around are those by whom you feel ranked—encompassing everything from a vague sense of being judged to an acknowledged all-out competition that feels as if it is about deciding who is the better person. Linking relationships leave us feeling good about ourselves and others. Relationships that are largely about ranking tend to make us more anxious about our worth and far less happy. Your lists illustrate in a personal way how much ranking can be associated with unhappiness.

THE DANCE OF LINKING AND RANKING

Ranking refers to our place in a social group or hierarchy. Power is closely related to ranking in that it results from high rank. A gentler way to think of power is as influence over others, which can take many forms, including being respected by others.

Linking is our innate balance to ranking. We are drawn to others, enjoy them, want to know and help them if we can. Love is simply linking amplified.

All day we try to strike the right balance between linking—giving and receiving friendliness or concern—and ranking, working to gain others' respect through our influence, competence, business acumen, fame, fortune, or the quality of our friends and allies. Others seek a higher rank through their appearance, possessions, or membership in a respected group. We often feel that the balance is not right in ourselves or others, and usually there seems to be too much ranking. In some situations we are constantly thinking about our rank or are expected to know it. At other times we may not consciously think about it. In some settings we would prefer to believe there is no ranking. But in any group of two or more people, ranking is always present, even if only in the background. To strike the right balance rather than be pulled by circumstance requires conscious effort.

Even without conscious intent, most of us try to counteract the potential unpleasantness of ranking by maintaining a sense of equality. For instance, in competitions we try to remain good sports and follow fair rules. In business we honor contracts and stay cordial.

In friendships, too, ranking has to be dealt with. We know who has more money or a more respected job. But we share rather than compare. We split the bill rather than adding up who had what. If one gives a compliment, the other tries to return it soon afterward. In time, close friends may lose track of who owes what, and priority is simply given to the one with the greater need. That's the essence of linking.

Important Definitions for Linking

Linking: Your innate tendency to be drawn to and affectionate with others, to be interested in them and want to help them when you can.

Love: A more distilled form of linking based on a powerful attraction to someone, which leads to a desire to be near the person, know him or her intimately, meet the other's needs as much as possible, and enjoy the other's efforts to meet your needs. It is as though you include the other in yourself.

Altruism: A selfless love for others whom you may never meet, sometimes extended to all of humankind and felt as compassion when others are in need.

Linking and ranking dance together in many ways. Ranking can sometimes serve the goals of linking. Parents, teachers, supervisors, and politicians have high rank and the power that goes with it, but ideally they use their power in the service of linking, love, and altruism. We do not mind those people of higher rank enforcing certain rules or going off to meetings to talk about us because we know they are trying to help. But we consider power to be abusive if it gives no consideration to the needs of others. Ranking also serves linking when we use it to add spice to a compliment: "You were clearly the most intelligent of the bunch."

Linking can serve ranking, too, as when we form alliances to gain what the group wants, with no intention of having the link last. Linking can be hidden behind ranking, as when a professor and student, employer and employee, or even guard and captive try to ignore their attraction to each other. And ranking can hide within linking, as when one person controls the lives of others "for their own good."

A common and troubling aspect of ranking occurs when it creeps into your attempt to link and triggers the undervalued self. For example, you meet a friend for lunch and receive the good news of her promotion. You want to feel joy for her, and perhaps you do, but you also rank yourself against her, perhaps quite unconsciously, and feel miserable at the realization that you have not been promoted in five years. In a sense you are no longer having lunch with your friend. You are having lunch with your undervalued self.

Important Definitions for Ranking

Ranking: Your innate tendency to see and improve your position in a social hierarchy, to be a separate and distinct individual, and to try to demand fairness.

Power: The influence you have over others according to your rank in a hierarchy. Power can be exerted physically or psychologically in ways that are harsh or gentle, obvious or sly.

Power in the Service of Linking: Using your rank and power to meet the needs of others as well as or instead of your own needs.

Abusive Power: The use of power for entirely selfish purposes.

Linking in the Service of Ranking: Forming friendly alliances purely to raise your rank and gain more power for yourself or for all involved.

YOUR INNATE TENDENCY TO HAVE AN OVERALL SENSE OF SELF-WORTH

I have said that too much ranking leads directly to the undervalued self, and knowing exactly how that happens will help you avoid that path. As social animals, we have evolved to live in groups to better ensure our survival and well-being. Groups transmit knowledge from generation to generation so that each person does not have to reinvent the stone axe or the computer. A group protects all of its members, sees that everyone gets what he or she needs to survive, and keeps selfishness in check. Those of our ancestors who spontaneously reacted in ways that kept them in good standing within their group were better off than those who did not so react. We still have those spontaneous reactions, even when they occasionally no longer serve us or others well. We can learn to override them, but first we need to know what they are.

If you lived in a single group, as our ancestors did, you would have a particular status in a defined pecking order. The higher you were, the more influence you had in group decisions. If someone challenged you or wanted to rise above you in the hierarchy, there would be a confrontation. One of you would win; the other would have to back down. To avoid dangerous mistakes, you had to have an instant, often unconscious sense of your overall strength, social support, confidence, skill, intelligence, and other traits.[2] Further, if you had been defeated recently or often, it was far better to err on the side of undervaluing yourself. After all, the best bet is that the future will repeat the past. Better to save your energy and not fight. So your overall sense of self-worth often errs on the low side.

However, today we live in many groups—family, groups of friends, colleagues, teammates. In each of these we are ranked on different qualities at different moments and rarely need to decide if we are in some *overall* sense better than someone else. In these groups the innate tendency to have an overall sense of self-worth has become a handicap, in that within any one situation it will always be inaccurate to some degree.

Definitions Regarding the Undervalued Self

Overall Self-Worth: Your sense of your capacity to win in a confrontation, regardless of the specific abilities needed in a particular competition.

Defeat Response: The tendency to respond to defeat with depression and shame, making it more likely that you will accept a low rank rather than continue to compete.

The Undervalued Self: The part of you that develops from the tendency to avoid defeats. The more past defeats you've had, the more vigilant this part of you is. You see ranking even when it is not there, and then you rank yourself so low that you are not a contender.

Your Innate Response to Defeat

Along with the strategy of taking defeat seriously and erring on the side of undervaluing ourselves, we have another innate tendency, the defeat response.[3] You can see this response in animals: when they lose, they slink away, looking depressed and ashamed. They seem to feel hopeless and to have lost interest in life, and their bodies show all the physiological indicators of depression. This sudden drop in enthusiasm means that they will not continue to care about their rank, feel confident, or endanger themselves with further fighting.

You have the same innate response to defeat: shame and depression. When you lose, you tend to feel down. You lack energy, enthusiasm, and confidence. You also tend to feel ashamed, to believe that your core self is no good. When you lose big, you may feel depressed and ashamed for days. If you felt you were rejected, your shame and depression can take the form of shyness. That is, you fear additional social judgment and defeat.

If you have lost very heavily or very often or when you were very young and impressionable, you feel powerless, worthless, ashamed, shy, and unenthusiastic most of the time. Feeling that it all must be your fault, you undervalue yourself chronically. Such feelings are the essence of a major depressive disorder, which is often the result of the "self-conscious" emotions[4] that arise in ranking situations.

The Self-Conscious Emotions

As social animals, we come equipped with self-conscious emotions, which determine how we behave around others in specific situations. These emotions make us act quickly to secure or resecure our place in a group. Pride, guilt, anxiety, the depression just described, and shame are called the self-conscious emotions because they arise from our view of our overall self-worth. Of course, anxiety and depression can arise in nonsocial situations, but we feel them most often as a response to social interactions.

These emotions vary according to individual temperament and upbringing, but we all feel them to some extent. Often they are not very adaptive, again because we no longer spend our entire lives in one group. Maybe you live with a roommate (even two people constitute a group), work in another group, play basketball in another, and so forth. Yet we often take the strong emotions that developed in one group into the other groups.

These feelings often arise from a much earlier group, the family or a play group. Or they may come from a group in which you recently suffered a defeat. Maybe you text-message someone for a date and she declines. Soon afterward you walk into a job interview, not feeling very good about yourself. You think it goes poorly. Then, in an evening softball game, your impulse is not to risk swinging your bat, and you strike out. You did not want another failure, yet that is just what happened because unconsciously you took your anxiety about defeat from one place to another.

Pride

Pride is the positive self-conscious emotion, what we feel when we have a high rank or move up in rank. When we feel proud, our self-worth sparkles and we feel confident about any future confrontations about rank. When others see our pride, our rank may rise even more or help to maintain a high rank.

However, pride has a downside. If pride contributes too much to our overall sense of self-worth, it can lead to overconfidence, causing deep depression and shame when we eventually overstep and fail at something. In fact, shame is particularly intense when pride precedes failure. Another potential problem is that when we feel proud we have less empathy and compassion for others. In research studies, those who felt proud rated themselves as similar to others of high rank but saw little in common between themselves and those who were lower or weaker.

Guilt

We feel guilt when we know we have done something wrong but have the potential to undo it, make it up to the other, be forgiven, offer a good excuse, or otherwise limit the results of our action. In the moment, guilt can lead to feeling worthless and undervaluing ourselves, a necessary reaction that will motivate us to do all that we can to make up for our error. Once we act, the group will accept us again and we can stop feeling worthless. Guilt usually does not last long because it is about our actions, not our very being.

Guilt was a very important emotion for our ancestors. If group members who were strong and good hunters did not feel guilty about taking the best meat for themselves, the mothers, children, and elderly would have gone hungry. Thus groups with members who felt guilt survived. Today, too, family members are usually made to feel guilty if they do not call home or show up for weddings. But when a member is in trouble, a strong family will take care of him or her. Guilt will see to that if love does not.

Anxiety and Shyness

Most anxiety occurs when we are worried about being defeated. Even when we fear snakes or tornados, we are in a sense fearing defeat. The most debilitating and unreasonable anxiety is usually social, however, and specifically about ranking, our status in a group. Are we about to drop in rank? Are we at risk of being confronted and defeated? Might we face total rejection?

Shyness is one manifestation of social anxiety. Shyness is the fear of being observed and judged, which could lead to a drop in status. Both anxiety and shyness are increased by an undervalued self, and being anxious or shy can then cause us to undervalue ourselves more. "I'm too shy — I totally lack confidence."

Anxiety and shyness can become permanent contributors to the undervalued self: 40 percent of people say they are shy in almost every social situation.[5] Again, we take these social emotions from one group, where we probably were defeated or judged, to groups in which we have not yet been judged. Hence we are mostly anxious when we have no reason to be. However, anxiety and shyness can be self-fulfilling in that people do tend to rank others lower if they seem anxious or shy. These social emotions have become maladaptive.

Depression

I have said that depression is often a response to defeat (although it can occur in other situations, since it involves the depletion of neurotransmitters, which can occur due to any stressful experience). Again, depression after defeat serves to keep us safe from physical injury or the loss of rank that might occur if we continued to fight. Today, however, the risk of physical injury during a ranking conflict is small. In contrast, the risk of damage to health and relationships through depression is large, making this response far less adaptive now.

If you think about the times you have felt depressed, you may be surprised to observe that most of them did involve a sense of defeat. It has been known for years that both depression and general anxiety are more likely to occur after stressful life events, but new research finds that depression in particular is associated with humiliation.[6] Also, the high levels of cortisol associated with stress and anxiety are found only when the stress or fear is of being negatively evaluated by others.[7]

Many people who have experienced a number of defeats and separations, especially in childhood, suffer from chronic depression. The cause may be defeats by other children, but more damaging are defeats by adults with whom children should feel a secure link but don't. In that case, the adult's high rank and power will not be experienced as being in the service of linking and helping the child, so when the adult has his or her way, the child repeatedly experiences defeat and depression. These defeats can lead to a lifelong sense of hopelessness and worthlessness — a truly undervalued self.

Shame

Along with depression, shame occurs instinctively after a defeat, but it also occurs in other social situations. Shame is the sense that our core self is worthless, flawed, and no good, so it is the emotion that most reinforces the undervalued self. Like depression, it causes us to accept the lowest rank, stay there, and be glad just to be included.

Shame is the most potent and painful of the self-conscious emotions; our brain registers it as if it were physical pain.[8] Because it is so painful, shame is the greatest protection against allowing ourselves to be thrown out of a group. A brief moment of shame, like the zap from a cattle prod, shapes us up very quickly. We go back to behaving the way others expect us to. Embarrassment, a milder, short-lived feeling akin to shame, gives us a similar sense of being out of sync with social expectations and forces us to change quickly so as to get back in line with the group.

When our ancestors lived in a single group, shame kept them safe from engaging in useless fights or being exiled. But these days, when we operate in multiple groups, shame can actually decrease our safety, because feeling totally worthless in all situations and all groups causes anxiety, lack of confidence, and poor performance. For example, research finds that people who focus on doing well perform better than those who focus on not doing badly.[9] And performing well and feeling good are what keep you included in many of the groups you belong to.

Carol Fails an Exam and Feels Utterly Ashamed

Carol had studied for weeks to pass her social-work licensing exam. Part of it was an essay, and because a wrist problem made it difficult to write by hand, she was allowed to use a personal computer cleared of any files related to the exam.

She thought she did a good job, but a week later she received her score: 21 points out of a possible 100. Carol plunged into such despair that she could not eat or sleep. She just wanted to be numb. She was so ashamed that she could not tell anyone for some time.

After she finally confessed to a friend and then to her family, she felt a little better. When she was around people who believed in her, she was reassured. However, being alone was truly unbearable. All she could feel was the pain and horror of how awful she was because of her poor performance. She was the only one in her study group to fail, so she was sure that this proved she was extremely incompetent. She felt totally stupid and worthless.

As her therapist, I knew this woman to be very bright, highly conscientious, and, in particular, well prepared for this exam. How could she have scored so poorly? I finally convinced her to go through the humiliating ordeal of asking to see her test.

The exam committee e-mailed her what she had written. The essay began well, but after a few paragraphs it became jumbled. Carol immediately realized that early on she had saved her rough draft on the disk they had given her, but she had mistakenly saved the much longer final version on her computer's hard drive. The committee could see this was what must have happened. Once she submitted the correct version, her revised score was 96.

In Carol's experience we see so well how the defeat response of depression and shame can put us through completely unnecessary torture. Carol belonged to at least five groups besides the group that took the licensing exam. She had a group of friends, a family group, a work group, the group of all the people who breed and show Labrador retrievers (her passion), and, with me, a group of two. And as a therapist, I knew her well enough to promise her that she was not worthless or stupid. Those were five groups in which she ranked high. Yet she felt completely defeated, depressed, and ashamed because of one "failed" test in one group. These feelings caused her to give up rather than explore why she failed the test and to withdraw from those who loved her because of her sense that she should be excluded from all human contact for her shameful performance.

It would never occur to anyone who knows Carol to shun her for her score on this exam. However, the truth is that when faced with a similar failure *in one important area of our life,* we might all react as Carol did. Do we have to react this way? At least we can react less intensely if we learn to recognize the effects of the innate aspects of ranking and linking.

LINKING AND LOVE

Linking can be automatic, little more than good manners. "Good morning, how are you, have a nice day." It serves to show that you are not feeling hostile, that you are ready to cooperate with the other person. This sort of linking greases the wheels of social life and helps us work together with few ranking conflicts. Or linking can be more focused, for example, an upsurge of genuine joy at seeing or being with someone you adore. You want to know what is going on with this person, to be helpful, and to allow the other to help you. Love is an intense version of these same reactions to another person.

Countless studies show that linking relieves group tension, reduces stress, and increases well-being and longevity.[10] Often the only reason that people work is to continue providing for and linking with those they love. And the camaraderie found in linking with coworkers can be the only joy people receive from their work. In fact, in study after study, the biggest factor in job satisfaction is the quality of the social relations at work.[11]

Love, again, is more intense and mysterious. We use the same word for desperate, obsessive love; passionate sexual love; companionate married love; unrequited love; love between parent and child; love between friends; and selfless love for all beings. But when I talk about love in this book, I have something specific in mind. First, I mean love between two people who know each other, which often begins with a sudden strong attraction. As yet, no one knows for certain how we choose the particular person we do, but it does seem to be innate to focus on one person at a time.[12]

However love comes about, a desire develops to know this person completely, to be part of the other and have the other be part of you, so that you can revel in his or her reality. You spontaneously want to fulfill the other's needs as much as you can, as if the other's needs are yours, and you are comfortable letting the other meet your needs.[13]

Notice the phrases "as much as you can" and "as if." There are still differences between the two of you — different preferences and therefore potential conflicts. There is a clear boundary where you leave off and the other begins. In these ways, at least, ranking is present. Like overlapping circles, you are each inside the other, yet separate.[14] This type of love is almost always mutual, and it involves both giving and receiving. (Even between parent and child this reciprocity occurs over their lifetimes.)

Ultimately, linking and love lead to a variety of feelings — joy, guilt, pleasure, grief, frustration, curiosity — but primarily they lead to feeling very good. They give us the pleasure of connecting with others through joking, compliments, and exchanges of concern. They truly make life worth living.

Jake Wakes Up to the Linking and Love in His Life

Jake was a levelheaded guy, brilliant with computers, but not particularly skilled at linking. He was seeing me in therapy because he had recently moved to our area and did not make new friends easily. Above all, he wanted to marry, but he was anxious when it came to dating. Although he was trying, he was either being rejected or having to reject. As both types of rejections mounted, I noticed he was going out less and less, and I worried that he was moving from anxiety to a sense of depression and shame. When we discussed it, he admitted that he didn't think anyone he liked would ever be attracted to him.

I noticed that Jake often talked about Cheryl, who lived in his building. They had met when a fire alarm went off early one evening, and they were the only two residents clutching cats and wearing bathrobes. They found it funny and started greeting each other in the hall.

After a few more months I heard Jake say he had looked after Cheryl's cat and plants while she was on vacation. He even joked that he had introduced her cats to his and that they got along surprisingly well. And one time she had come to his door at five in the morning to borrow milk because she could hear he was up. He described Cheryl's stopping him on the stairs to ask how he was and their spending an hour talking. I mentioned that he seemed to enjoy these encounters, but Jake said it wasn't "like that." He even thought they "just used each other." He was seeing ranking instead of the linking that was actually happening.

Still, a few months later he referred to her as "my friend Cheryl." Jake was beginning to see linking. Hoping to nudge this along, I asked him later in the year if he found Cheryl attractive.

He said, "She doesn't think of me that way. She goes out on a lot of dates."

I asked him, "Is it that you're afraid to think of her 'that way' and spoil whatever you have?"

He nodded glumly. I hoped I had helped him see how ranking stood in the way of his growing link.

One day Jake was looking ecstatic for a change. He had been chatting with the building manager when Cheryl passed them. The manager whispered to him that Cheryl had told a neighbor that one of the best things about the building was Jake. In fact, Cheryl had said she had a crush on Jake. As he told me this, I could see him finally allowing himself to risk falling in love.

A year later Jake and Cheryl were married, and, yes, the building manager was invited to the wedding.

RANKING AND POWER

For many of us, the subject of ranking and the power that results from high rank seems less charming than linking and love. However, both linking and ranking will always be with us and, when used appropriately, ranking can be enjoyed. Ranking and power fulfill our desire to be separate, stand out, get our share, be noticed, enjoy the respect of others, and have some influence. We all have those innate desires, and fulfilling them brings pleasure that can be measured physiologically.[15]

The higher your rank, the greater your influence or power. Power covers an enormous range.[16] We may have power because, for example, we are in a certain position, either earned or assigned; because we are physically more threatening than others; or simply because people find us knowledgeable or nice to be around.

Of course, power and rank can change. If we are challenged or we challenge another, we may win or lose. Or we may be promoted or demoted by others. In some groups ranking changes often because rank is very flexible, earned or deserved according to the situation. Sometimes we drop in rank because we have poor ranking skills. For example, if we try but fail to make a person who is lower in rank do something, our own rank drops.[17] And even if we succeed, we may drop in rank if we had to use harsh methods. When a high school teacher punishes an entire class with extra homework because a few kids are continually acting up, the teacher finally feels in control again, having regained her "proper" rank. However, her true rank has been diminished, not improved, because she could not manage the disruptive class members in any other way.

Although ranking does not create as many general good feelings as linking, knowing our rank does spare us the unpleasantness of having to learn again and again who stands above us. Imagine going to work and having to begin every day by figuring out who is in charge. In the case of sports, ranking actually becomes a source of great pleasure. We gladly strategize and sacrifice for the chance to feel the thrill of a quick change in standing, and fans obviously love doing all of this vicariously. Gambling, making risky investments, and dating provide similar high excitement for some people. "How'd you score?" "What's he betting?" "What's it selling for today?" "Who's she seeing now?"

Ranking in the Service of Linking

In spite of their natural drive to enjoy power, many people feel uncomfortable when they have power or think about seeking it. People who are basically altruistic, cooperative types especially avoid power. When these people gain or are given power they usually become more altruistic instead of more selfish.[18] They want to use their rank in the service of linking of others, whether they know these others or not. In fact, this tendency holds true for most of us while we are in roles such as parenting, teaching, managing, counseling, or mentoring.

Perhaps more than any species, humans simply love one another a surprising amount of the time. They love enough to give others their time and energy and even their lives. It is common to see people using their resources, and whatever other influence they gain from their rank, to help those who are not kin and who could not possibly help them personally. Scientists now offer an explanation for this type of selfless love.[19] They have shown that very often groups survive better if they have mostly altruistic members. As I said when discussing guilt, in the old days altruistic behavior—behavior that helped everyone survive—meant sharing your meat. Today group survival is about teamwork on the job and family loyalty at home. Altruism can be passed down genetically or culturally as moral values, but however it happens, it helps survival. Groups made up entirely of freeloaders and obsessive rankers are less likely to make it to the next generation.

Most groups include a mixture of altruists and selfish types. So the group in which altruists can control the freeloaders and the selfish high-rankers will have the best chance of survival. For millions of years, the majority of people have been trying to control the few selfish individuals in their midst in order to elevate the welfare of all.[20]

Altruism need not end with members of our own group, however. Our ability to be altruistic and to feel compassion for those who are weaker rests on our ability to empathize, to grasp how another person feels. Altruism can extend to everyone, because we all can imagine how others feel even if they are on the other side of the world. Of course, ranking can extend far, too. We can feel superior to people we have never seen. In fact, thinking that our own group is superior to other groups has led to most of the world's ills. Thanks to the media, however, we know so much about what is happening to others across the globe that I like to think empathy is pushing us toward seeing all people as part of our group.

Abusive Power

If the power resulting from ranking is not tempered by linking or a cultural tendency toward altruism, it becomes abusive. The powerful person pursues goals that take no account of the needs of others and often controls people without their realizing it. Because ranking is an innate response, we all have the potential to abuse the power of high rank. For example, in experiments, when a person is merely given a seat behind a desk and expects another person yet to arrive to be seated in the chair of lesser status, the person behind the desk will make decisions that are not good for the person not there yet, such as who will be given the easier tasks.[21]

Power without concern for others is often wielded through harsh methods: ridicule, cheating, even physical threats or injury. But some of the worst cases occur when an abuser uses "gentle" methods, such as being sweet and beguiling to get his or her way, or makes "rational" arguments that shame people into ignoring their feelings. "All you have to do is give up your petty self-interest." Abusers of power may want you to see linking by saying "I'm doing this for your own good" when it is really for their good.[22] A favorite method of the tyrant is to persuade the citizens that only he can protect them from attack by some other group, focusing everyone on this outer threat while he and his cronies enjoy the resulting power.

However abuse happens, it is pure selfishness, and when it causes great harm and is cold-blooded—not the result of a momentary desire for revenge or a passion to win—then we think of it as evil.

Why do some people go berserk with power? They may have a genetic tendency toward psychopathy. If this tendency is seen during childhood, very skilled parenting and teaching can probably prevent its full expression except in the most extreme cases.[23] Even more often, people who abuse power have learned from their parents that giving love is weak or risky, so power fills the void left by an absence of linking. Or, siblings are not taught to manage their jealousy, so that one dominates another brutally and abusive power becomes an obsession for both. At school, abuse occurs if bullies are not controlled by teachers. Their victims may become so focused on revenge that when they do gain power they go crazy with it, sometimes with a gun.

Some situations will bring out abusive behavior in almost anyone, as when an abusive leader uses coercion or the fear of exclusion if those lower in rank do not conform and be equally or more abusive to those below them. This happens in instances of genocide and in prisons where guards are encouraged to mistreat prisoners. The usual norms that insist on the appropriate use of power disappear, and people are suddenly capable of massive evil, although in a sense they are committing evil deeds because they are afraid of losing their link with others in their group.[24]

Linking in the Service of Ranking

Linking is sometimes used constructively in the service of ranking. For example, you might declare solidarity with your coworkers and join a union to raise your rank in relation to management. Or two people might join forces to help each other study for an exam. They share knowledge generously while they do this, but during the exam itself they strive individually to do as well as possible.

It is invaluable to learn to recognize when linking is being used in the service of power, whether for good or ill. If it is for good, you should be prepared for the linking to lessen or end once the goal is achieved, which may seem sad, but it's very natural. If the linking is really for the other's selfish purposes, you can see beneath the veneer and refuse this fake link.

Personal Boundaries

Our rank is our own, determined by who we are, separate from all others. We have our own attitudes, preferences, and possessions. We have our own schedules and our own work. We have our own personal space. In short, we have boundaries, which we want to keep as they are. The higher our rank, the more we are able to maintain our own boundaries rather than having to give way to others' attitudes, preferences, schedules, or demands. Those who undervalue themselves naturally have trouble keeping their boundaries.

The lower your rank, or the lower you think it is, the more those with higher rank can ignore your boundaries and influence you to do what they want. If they ask for your time and energy, you will probably feel you have to give it. You feel that you must show them respect, but they do not have to do the same. They look at you directly, but you may feel the need to lower your eyes.

Anger is the emotion we feel when our boundaries or wishes have been violated. Those who undervalue themselves usually express their anger too little, when in fact, if they did express it, their boundaries or wishes would be respected. It can be unpleasant to feel angry, and often counterproductive to express it fully, but it can have many good effects when used well. Showing anger reminds others to obey the rules expected of everyone. It lets someone you care about know when he or she is distressing you. And it helps you stand up for yourself in a conflict, so that the resolution will be a good one for all involved. Expressing anger is futile, however, if you rank very low, because others will usually ignore your demands. In fact, being angry and demanding when it is inappropriate or ineffective can lower your rank even further.

Melissa Wakes Up to Ranking and Power at Work

Melissa, freshly graduated from college, was very angry about a situation at work. A photocopier had been installed near her cubicle, and its loud noise and the talking that inevitably went on around it were driving her crazy. She wanted to complain, but when a coworker who was a friend of hers had complained about a similar situation, not only had nothing changed, but his complaining was mentioned in his next performance review. She was shocked and angry that their company was so inconsiderate of its employees.

I pointed out gently that business is by nature competitive. The company she and her friend worked for would not treat her with the same consideration as her wonderful family did. Rather, it would attend to the bottom line and do only what was needed to keep their best employees happy and productive. From what I had gleaned, she was one of their stars, but her friend was not.

I suggested that Melissa, who frequently undervalued herself, might get better results if she made her request in the context of her most recent achievements, highlighting her high rank among her coworkers. I coached her to point out that maintaining her current level of quality work would require considerable concentration, and thus, to keep her work error free, it would probably be best to move her away from the copier.

After having this talk with her supervisor, Melissa was moved to a quieter space, and she happily realized the power that comes with high rank.

Linking Trumps Ranking

Although ranking and power are important factors in our daily lives, and they definitely dominate in many situations, in the end linking trumps ranking because of its biological, emotional, and spiritual importance. The big advantage of being a social animal is that we bond, helping one another stay safe, rear young, find good food, recover from sickness or injury, play or practice, and think things through. As I have said, altruism can be even more important to survival than "survival of the fittest."

Look around you. We cooperate in order to live in communities, make things, and govern ourselves. The ultimate linking phenomenon may be the Internet, with its e-mail, chat rooms, blogs, friendship networks, dating services, and free idea exchanges. The Internet certainly can be a competitive place in many ways, but we can't deny that its essence is linking, not ranking.

Our day-to-day efforts, too, are usually not just for ourselves but for the sake of those we love, as well as those we do not even know. Our love for others can transcend all ranking. Spiritually, selfless love is at the center of all the great religions, which teach that doing for others is its own reward. No religion and few philosophies have ever suggested that ranking, thinking of your own needs first, is the path to happiness.

THE VALUE OF ATTENDING TO RANKING AND LINKING TOGETHER

By now you are probably seeing ranking and linking everywhere, and they *are* everywhere. Every member of a group understands unconsciously how each member ranks and who is linked to whom. But to heal the undervalued self, you must become conscious of ranking and linking. By understanding how they intertwine, you can see which of the two is at work in a situation. If someone speaks as if in one mode but is actually in the other, you need to recognize that, rather than seeing ranking—or linking— when it is not there. If you see the two as having nothing to do with each other, you are far less free to choose between them.

It takes a little effort to keep both ranking and linking in mind as possibilities, because we tend to see each one as a separate force operating in one broad class of situations but not in any other. We try to resolve ranking and power issues at work in order to do better in our careers, but our problem there may be failing to link or to see offers to link coming from others. Away from work, our focus is on linking to improve close relationships and make friends, but your particular relationship issues may be more about your own low rank—feeling unattractive or unintelligent, failing to stand up for yourself, or feeling controlled by another.

Humans can be quite subtle about linking and ranking. We can use "I love you" to control someone, while "Do what I tell you" can be an expression of love. We also do a lot of ranking and linking in our heads, which especially leads us to undervalue ourselves. Often subconsciously, we imagine and play out our fears over and over, seeming to validate all sorts of wrong assumptions about our worth based on past experience or simply inadequate information. Putting the focus on ranking and power at the wrong times, whether you do this a little or a lot, can spoil the good things in life, such as connecting with others, living up to your full potential, and being successful. You are designed to link, to love. And you are designed to have appropriate influence, take pleasure in competition, and feel comfortable when given authority. Above all, you are designed to choose what will work best in a situation, so learning to recognize accurately the ranking and linking in your own life is the first step to correcting problems created by the undervalued self.

WORKING WITH WHAT YOU HAVE LEARNED

Having learned how ranking and linking make up the foundation of the undervalued self, you are ready to look at how you approach these two. Read the following lists and place a check mark next to each statement that is true for you.

Linking

☐ I know how to help people express their deepest feelings.

☐ I often surprise the people I like with gifts and favors.

☐ I know how to get people to stop feeling self-conscious.

☐ It's very easy for me to let someone else help me or take care of me.

☐ I know how to make a relationship more intimate.

☐ I know how to stop arguments.

☐ When I meet people, I expect we will like each other.

☐ When I am the only one with food, I either offer to share or do not eat in front of the others.

☐ There are several people in my life with whom I can have deep, intimate, honest conversations.

☐ When I am speaking to people, I look them in the eye and smile if it is appropriate.

☐ When I disagree with or do not like someone, I still fully understand the person's perspective and know what he or she is feeling.

☐ When I feel bad, I can count on certain people being able to make me feel good again.

Ranking

☐ I do not fear failure when I begin something.

☐ I have a clear sense of when someone is using power over me for my own good.

☐ When I do well, I can really feel proud of myself.

☐ When I fail at something important and feel worthless, some part of me knows I am not *really* worthless.

☐ I don't think I get any more depressed than the next person when I fail at something important.

☐ I have ways of getting over my depressed feelings after a failure.

☐ If someone says or does something nice, I can usually tell whether it is sincere or just to get me to do something.

☐ I can take criticism gracefully.

☐ I can speak up in a group of strangers if I have a good idea.

☐ I can manage public speaking.

☐ If I'm well prepared for a performance or competition, I feel confident.

☐ I am able to speak up and defend the boundaries I have set.

☐ I can recognize, at the time, when someone is using me without concern for the harm it may do me.

☐ I can form alliances to ward off abusive power.

☐ I can leave an abusive relationship before I am damaged by it.

The fewer items you checked on the linking and ranking lists, the more you have to gain from this book. If you checked a disproportionate number of items on one list compared to the other, this book will also help you correct your ranking-linking imbalance.

Choose the Right Company

Fortunately, no innate or learned tendency, even the defeat response, is beyond remedy. Just as you can suppress a reflex like blinking your eye when putting in eye drops, you can learn to be flexible in engaging your self-conscious emotions when you choose to do so, and you have one way to do that right now.

Go to the journal that you began for this book and look at the two lists you made at the start of this chapter, of the people who make you feel good and those who make you feel bad. You might want to use your contact list or address book to add anyone you may have missed. Cover up the list of people who make you feel good. Now you are looking only at the people who make you feel bad about yourself, the ones who create a ranking mood in you. Notice how your mood drops. Now cover the list of people who make you feel bad about yourself so that you see only those with whom you link. See how your mood and your confidence lift. This shows one way that you can consciously shift out of an innate response—in this case by shifting the people you are with or are thinking about.

Looking More Closely

Beside or under each name on the two lists, make notes of your ranking and linking observations about these relationships. Do any of your ranking relationships feel abusive? Or does the person use power to do what is really best for you? How many of your linking relationships are at the level of love? Within a linking relationship, do you see some ranking? Within a ranking relationship, do you see some linking? Your goal is to become better at seeing the ranking or linking beneath the surface of relationships.

Think about some exceptions to the usual pattern of feel-good goes with linking and feel-bad goes with ranking. For example:

1. Is there someone on your feel-good list with whom you have a ranking relationship? Why might this be? A person higher in rank can make you feel good about yourself by praising you or simply reporting accurately on your work. You might be enjoying an alliance that is working for you, even though you know it is not a lasting friendship but is only in the service of both of you gaining a higher rank. Or you might be in a ranking relationship in which you have the higher rank and are enjoying another's respect or your own power or influence.

2. Is there anyone on your feel-bad list with whom you thought you had a good linking relationship but now realize it is actually mostly about ranking? For example, does the person often make you feel inferior, ashamed, or powerless? Or do you not enjoy the other's company because you feel superior, bored, or unable to respect this person's ideas or beliefs?

3. Does anyone seem to belong on both lists, making you feel both good and bad? Is this a case of you or the other person

using ranking in the service of linking? Or linking in the service of ranking?

4. Focus on those you love. Presumably they are on your feel-good list. But do you ever rank yourself with them in the sense that you worry that you need or love them more than they need or love you?

5. Would you like to strengthen your link with anyone on the feel-good list? How might you do that, even today?

6. Looking at the ranking relationships you have with those on your feel-bad list, does anyone abuse his or her power over you? If you rank higher than someone on the list, why does this person make you feel bad? For example, is your higher rank too much responsibility, is the other too needy, or does it bother you generally to have power?

Choose the Right Groups

Make a list of the groups you belong to: family, clubs, teams, social groups, coworkers, and so on. Include two-person groups such as friends or life partners. You can also include important groups from the past, such as your high school class, and those in which you do not know all the members, such as your organization, your generation, or your ethnic group. In other words, list all of the groups that have a strong influence on how you see yourself. Now underline the groups that make you feel good about yourself. Next, circle the one that is most influencing your overall self-worth today. If that influence is negative, focus your attention on the group that makes you feel best about yourself right now.

Identifying Ranking and Linking in a Typical Day

Think back to yesterday. Choose a few memorable interactions and describe how much linking and ranking you felt in each, using rough percentages. The numbers don't need to be specific but should express how much linking or ranking you felt in each interaction. Also, if it was a ranking situation, consider whether you were undervaluing yourself.

For example, when you woke up and greeted the person with whom you live, perhaps you felt 90 percent linking. This is always a good start to a day. It would be 100 percent linking if you didn't always worry a little that he thinks you look awful when you first get out of bed. You know this is probably undervaluing yourself—he doesn't look that great either.

Next, when you drove to work, you had mostly competitive feelings or conflict with other drivers—80 percent ranking—although you slowed down for one person desperate to change lanes and later someone did that for you. You did not undervalue yourself.

At work you exchanged greetings with a coworker who is still hurt that you replaced him as the boss's favorite, through no fault of your own—70 percent ranking. Although you have the higher rank now, you feel a little guilty, even ashamed, so there is some undervaluing of yourself here.

You had a meeting with your boss. The two of you get along terrifically—50 percent ranking, since he's your boss, and 50 percent linking. You did not undervalue yourself when with him.

You spoke with a client you thoroughly enjoy—60 percent linking, but 40 percent ranking because you cannot afford to lose this account, so you tend to act as if you agree with her much more than you actually do. But you felt successful and did not undervalue yourself.

You had lunch with a close friend—90 percent linking. It would be 100 percent linking except that you felt a little uncomfortable afterward. The two of you take turns paying, but you could not recall who had paid last, and she joked that you always conveniently forget. You often feel ashamed in some way after seeing her. You now wonder if this relationship isn't more about ranking than you thought, because she regularly triggers your undervalued self.

You went to the gym after work and felt like the most unhealthy, unfit person there. You felt 100 percent ranking and can see that you were undervaluing yourself.

CHAPTER TWO

The Six Self-Protections
We Use to Deny Low Rank

It is not always easy to know when we have fallen into ranking and undervaluing ourselves even to the point of feeling worthless, because we each employ largely unconscious self-protections to keep us from feeling shame. The shame that follows a social defeat is, as the last chapter explained, registered in the brain in the same place as physical pain. No wonder we say that it hurts to be rejected or to fail and that we have found ways not to feel that pain. To know when we are undervaluing ourselves and by how much, we first have to remove our blinders.

We have six main self-protections: minimizing, blaming, non-competing, overachieving, inflating, and projecting. These self-protections sometimes allow us to stay unaware of, or avoid, our worst feelings. But these mechanisms can cause as much trouble as the defeat response and the negative self-conscious emotions they are designed to protect against. For example, blaming others for our failings *when they are not to blame* will make us feel good only until we are faced with contrary evidence, as we almost surely will be.

Usually we are not aware that we are using self-protections. If we were aware of them, they wouldn't work. They are attempts to fool ourselves, and perhaps others, about our rank. "Who, me? I'm not feeling powerless and shamed." But because these self-protections have covered over some of the times when you have felt undervalued, you will have to strip them away before you can see, feel, and eliminate your feelings of worthlessness. As a bonus, not only will you be more aware of when you are using self-protections, but you will be able to identify when others are doing so. This awareness will help to keep you from assuming blame or feeling inferior to someone who is inflating his or her rank and from carrying the burden of others' undervalued selves.

ASSESSING YOUR SELF-PROTECTIONS

Since you are not normally aware of the six self-protections you may have developed to protect you in ranking situations, you will need to establish some guidelines to answer the questions in the list below.

• Mark "*T*" for any statement that is true of you now or at any time in the past, no matter how irrational or unpleasant the view may seem.

• If you marked "*F*," take time to reflect whether it is in fact true of you, even if you hate to admit it. Your goal here is to try to be aware of what you normally do not want to be aware of.

• Answer each question independently. Do not worry if you seem to be contradicting earlier answers. Instead, think of this as an opportunity for all the parts of yourself to respond, including the undervalued self. Different aspects of you use different self-protections.

• Withhold judgment. Admitting something is true may only mean that you had the thought without acting on it or that you acted on it, but the action was understandable at the time.

• If you want to ensure your privacy, write your answers on a separate piece of paper rather than in the book. But keep your answers handy, because you will return to them.

1. I believe that everyone is looking out only for herself or himself.

2. Deep down I know better than to trust people.

3. When I'm told I've done well, it just does not sink in.

4. I think the odds are high that someday I will be robbed, raped, or murdered.

5. When something is cut in half and shared, I can't help but notice which piece is larger.

6. It drives me crazy that others do the things I am very careful not to do, like being selfish, weak, lazy, or needy.

7. Rather than feel guilty or ashamed about an action I took or a remark I made, I try to think that it just doesn't matter and forget about it.

8. If I had to choose, I would find it better to spend the rest of my life making others happy than making myself happy.

9. I feel powerless.

10. I can't get ahead because I have been treated so unfairly.

11. Even when people love each other, they are also probably using each other.

12. My enemies are evil.

13. When I fail at something that matters to me, I pretend it doesn't matter.

14. I find myself deeply and thoroughly disliking people for no obvious reason.

15. I am often disappointed with myself, but I strive to do better.

16. No matter how much trouble someone causes me, if I were perfect I would still respond with love.

17. When I fail, I often just chalk it up to bad luck.

18. If people were honest about it, they would admit that some people should be treated better than others.

19. Most of my life I have been seen as second best.

20. I work so hard that I don't bother to take care of my health.

21. I find most people terribly disappointing.

22. I always want to cause others as little trouble as possible.

23. When I am driving, I am very aware if someone tries to cut in front of me.

24. I'll do almost anything to avoid a conflict.

25. I am willing to break the rules if it probably won't hurt anyone else very much.

26. When I don't think I can win at something, I tend to think the whole thing is silly or trivial.

27. Others tell me that I let people take advantage of me.

28. When I am part of an ongoing group or organization, I refuse to pay any attention to the "politics."

29. I have been completely wrong about someone more than once or twice.

30. I think people make too much of a big deal out of everything.

31. I think there are a lot of bad people in the world.

32. I'm not going to stop on my career path until I have proven myself.

33. If I want people to keep liking me, I will have to continue to impress them.

Most of the items in this assessment are meant to capture the ways that we all try to avoid feeling or being undervalued. Some—1, 2, 5, 11, 18, and 19—also capture how much you tend to see ranking as a life philosophy. Generally people who answer *true* to these answer *true* to quite a few of the others. Some of these items may seem more like plain reality than self-protections.

For example, maybe you *do* think that people are only out for themselves—it is a very common assumption. And, of course, in some cases people *are* only out for themselves. But to think that this is *always* true signals a self-protection at work.

There is no "normal" when talking about seeing ranking or using self-protections—we all do it at times, and your task is to acknowledge that and see it in yourself. Further, I have asked you to be scrupulously honest. It would not be fair to you or good for your undervalued self to now tell you that your "score" shows that you are abnormal, so shame on you. Use the following guidelines simply to help you see the self-protections you rely on most.

If you use the "minimizing" self-protection, you probably answered *true* to questions 7, 13, 17, 26, and 30.

If you use the "blaming" self-protection, you probably answered *true* to questions 1, 2, 4, 9, 10, and 19.

If you use the "noncompeting" self-protection, you probably answered *true* to questions 8, 16, 22, 24, 27, and 28.

If you use the "overachieving" self-protection, you probably answered *true* to questions 3, 15, 20, 32, and 33.

If you use the "inflating" self-protection, you probably answered *true* to questions 1, 11, 18, 21, 23, and 25. (1 and 11 project a ranking focus onto others.)

If you use the "projecting" self-protection, you probably answered *true* to 6, 12, 14, 29, and 31.

THE SIX SELF-PROTECTIONS

Every one of us uses all six of these self-protections—minimizing, blaming, noncompeting, overachieving, inflating, and projecting— at times. But recognizing our self-protections and reducing their use will result in a more peaceful and happier life. Further, if you checked more than eighteen items on the assessment, you probably feel a need to protect yourself a great deal, see ranking almost everywhere, and surely undervalue yourself often or even always. While you may feel vulnerable at first, by casting off these self-protections as much as you can—as you will learn to do in this book—you will improve your ability to deepen your relationships and let go of the anxiety caused by ranking yourself against others—all the results you've been trying to achieve through using self-protections.

The Six Self-Protections

Minimizing: Making light of or denying your role in a negative situation or what can be expected of you in a positive one.

Blaming: Accusing others of being unfair in order to explain a failure, when in fact there is no unfairness.

Noncompeting: Denying any interest in or perhaps even awareness of ranking and striving to link at all costs.

Overachieving: Working endlessly to reach a high rank yet never feeling good enough.

Inflating: Feeling you are the best or should be seen that way and doing almost anything to keep yourself in the spotlight.

Projecting: Denying your own flaws while seeing them in others when they are not there.

The Minimizing Self-Protection

Minimizing or denying is almost the essence of what most of us think of as defensiveness. For example, any of us might explain that our tennis game today was poor because we had a hard day at work. The poor score cannot be distorted, but we minimize our own role in it. Or we might minimize our effort: "I wasn't really trying today." Or we minimize the game's importance or even deny having any interest in it: "I've never been that into tennis anyway."

Another mild way we minimize our own role is by attributing the larger role to chance or fate: "Luck was against me today." Or, after failing a swim test, "I just was not meant to be a lifeguard."

Another way we minimize is to announce ahead of time that we are not very good: "Putting is the weakest part of my golf game, but here goes." Or "I'm basically shy, but I'll go to the party anyway." That way very little is expected of us. If we fail, everyone will understand why and know that we did not overestimate ourselves, which is another potential source of shame.

One problem with minimizing is that it is so easy to do and so common that everyone recognizes it as a self-protection; thus you almost inevitably sound defensive. It also signals that you are in a ranking mode. For example, as you and a friend put on bathing suits for a swim, you might say, "You look great. This looked better on me last year. I've gained a little weight. It will come off once I start swimming regularly again." All that may be true, but who was comparing anyway? Now, when you have those thoughts, you will know that they mean the undervalued self has taken over as it tries to avoid shame.

Minimizing at Work

Stewart has been working for years at the same level. He's competent at what he does and takes all the courses that would allow him to be promoted, yet he never takes the proficiency exams that would move him to a higher level. He says he doesn't care. He finds it humorous to see how everybody sweats to chase after a higher rating "just to make a few more bucks and have harder work to do."

The fact is that Stewart has a learning disability and has always done poorly on timed tests. When he was a boy, no one diagnosed his disability, and after years of receiving the lowest test scores, he stopped trying. However, Stewart is actually very smart, as a few teachers discovered. They helped him enter a field where his disability would not be a problem. Still, Stewart does not ever want to put himself in the humiliating position of taking a timed written exam again. Just about anything would be better than that, even a lower salary. Stewart continues to minimize in order to protect his fear of being shamed, as he was when he was a boy.

Minimizing in Relationships

For years, Claudia heard from Ron that he wished she was "just a little more fussy." He wished she would lose weight and dress better and would make sure that they both kept the house cleaner. Claudia minimized the problems behind his wishes. "I just love good food. Heck, I just have no self-control. At least I don't shop all the time."

Sometimes Ron minimized how much he was bothered, too. "That's just Claudia. She's not the type to stand in front of a mirror all day and worry about her looks. And we have better things to do on a weekend than clean house."

Claudia knew she had an eating problem and was deeply ashamed that she could not control herself. Because she was overweight, she saw no point in trying to look attractive. Her general despair spread to the rest of her life, but she always minimized it. Her parents had been alcoholics and had treated their addiction like a joke, so Claudia had learned to minimize from experts.

Then Ron's job changed. He had to travel more. While visiting an old college friend in another city, he met a different kind of woman. Sue Ellen was attractive and so was her home. Moreover, she was serious, thoughtful, and able to talk about her own faults, including those that had caused her to choose the wrong husband. Sue Ellen was now single.

Ron saw new possibilities for his life—if he could be with someone like Sue Ellen. He hated feeling that he was betraying Claudia, even in his heart. It frightened him to realize how unhappy he was at home and how the relationship might go on like this for his entire life. As soon as he walked in the door after his trip, he tried to talk to Claudia about what he was feeling. He asked her to go to couples counseling.

But Claudia laughed. "Us? We're not the type."

When Ron persisted and received the same minimizing reaction, he knew it was over.

The irony is that after Ron left, Claudia did change. She could no longer make light of her weaknesses, and she sought help. To her surprise, it was not as difficult as she had thought to become someone she could admire.

Signs of Minimizing

Unconscious assumption. "Being ranked low can't hurt me if I make the ranking or my effort seem trivial."

Common statements. "I wasn't really trying today — it was just for practice." "I've just been too busy to give this my full attention." "I don't know why people take this sort of thing so seriously." "I'm really having a run of bad luck."

Other possible signs:

• When discussing your performance, you make excuses such as being under the weather today or having had too little sleep.

• You think and talk as if fate or luck decides much of what happens in your life.

• You try to ignore the things you don't like in yourself or those close to you.

• You deny that something is important to you when deep down you know it probably is.

• You deny you have a problem when you know you do.

The Blaming Self-Protection

"I fell because she tripped me." "I lost because there was some cheating going on." Of course, it can be true that someone tripped you or cheated. Sometimes you are right to blame others rather than to falsely see yourself as the cause of a situation. But if you feel wronged often, then it may be a self-protection.

The blaming self-protection is frequently triggered by an internal switch from linking to ranking that you are hardly aware of. For example, you offer to help your closest friend move. Halfway through, you realize that she did not plan well. The boxes aren't packed, and there's no one to move the big stuff. You feel rightly annoyed. Instead of recognizing that you need to sit down with your friend and talk, state your limits, and help develop a realistic plan, you feel that she has taken advantage of you. You feel undervalued. Now a ranking perspective has replaced linking. You assume that your friend must feel she can order you around, as those higher in rank can do to those who are lower. Whether you think of it in this explicit way or not, you feel used and possibly ashamed that you allowed anyone to do this to you.

You don't want to be an unloving, selfish, and petty friend, but you feel as if you are all of these. The only self-protection in this situation is to blame your friend. By extracting justice from her—an admission of guilt or an apology—you will stop feeling undervalued. But now your friend will be the lower-ranking person. This blaming self-protection does not help your friendship.

Whatever your reason for suddenly feeling bad about yourself, if you have a credible target, you can use the blaming self-protection to shield yourself from shame. I call this the shame ball. We often toss shame to someone else as soon as we see it coming: "You did it, not me." "You have the problem—I don't have any problems." "Yes, I did it, but you do it all the time, too." When we're in this state of mind, it never occurs to us to just set the shame ball down. Our fear of shame is too great.

When Blaming Was Justified in the Past

Blaming can become chronic if it has been justified in the past. If you have been badly hurt by prejudice, for example, you can hardly be expected to link or avoid ranking when you are face-to-face with someone from a group that you know is prejudiced against you. In fact, you are completely right to be suspicious. Yet this mistrust, seeing every situation through a ranking lens, makes it very difficult to live a normal life. You feel hopeless about trying because everything seems rigged against you. This leaves you on the outside looking in. And when people do try to help or offer friendship, you feel you have to protect yourself by rejecting them and maybe blaming them for what you see as their ulterior motives.

If you have been subject to prejudice, you have been vastly underranked. In order to build a realistic view of ranking and linking, you must acknowledge that the prejudice happened and that it hurt badly. If you don't, you will suppress the negative self-conscious feelings associated with prejudice and the reality of your overall diminished self-worth. You will hardly be aware of your undervalued self. As a result, you will keep the blaming self-protection active and inflexible, often seeing ranking where it does not exist.

When you do acknowledge the prejudice, you will have to feel all of the negative self-conscious emotions — guilt, anxiety, depression, and shame — as well as the anger that you have been unable to express openly because of your enforced low rank. But in the short run, this acknowledgment is necessary to heal the damage and become open to linking. Fully acknowledging the extent of prejudice and its effects usually requires some group consciousness raising, that is, linking with others who understand what you have been through. Being in a group will give you the security you need to express your anger and other negative feelings honestly. Other self-protections often used by those who have experienced prejudice are noncompeting and overachieving.[1]

Blaming and Prejudice at Work

Maude is an African-American lesbian who admits that she will always have to be alert to her blaming self-protection. She most emphatically wants to blame the people who should be blamed—but not behave as if the entire world were guilty until proven innocent. The prejudice she has experienced, from whites for her race and from both blacks and whites for her sexual orientation, has become the subject of her life's work. As an undergraduate she was fascinated by some social psychologists who were uncovering prejudice by using people's unconscious reactions to subliminal cues. They found that almost everyone in the United States is prejudiced against African Americans—including African Americans.[2] The same result has been found to be true for women. For example, both female and male students will rate the transcript of a lecture lower if they are told it was given by a woman.[3]

Maude applied to do graduate work with one of the professors involved in this research. Soon after entering graduate school, she received an anonymous note warning her that the chairperson of the department hated lesbians and she'd do well to hide her sexual preference. She had been open about being lesbian in her application. Still, she knew departments had minority quotas to fill. She wondered if she had been accepted because of her race even though they disliked her sexual orientation. She now remembered little signs she'd gotten from the chairperson—failing to show up for events she was at, certain looks and tones of voice.

Maude was furious and fumed for days about how to respond. She had become friendly with two high-spirited graduate students, and she often bantered with them. They kept asking her now what was wrong, but she wouldn't say. These two white women teased her about losing her cool and pestered her to find out what was the matter, but she just clammed up even more.

Finally, Maude could not stand it any longer. She marched into the chairperson's office and demanded to see him immediately. When his assistant protested, she threatened to punch her out. Maude went in, slammed the note down on his desk, and said, "You explain yourself, or I'm going to be sure that every psychology department in the country knows about you." Fortunately, the chairperson ignored Maude and read the note.

"Who wrote this?" he demanded.

Maude admitted she didn't know. In that moment, she also remembered that this man had always been friendly and had acted toward her with great kindness. Why did she trust an anonymous note more than his goodwill?

In the open doorway behind her, she heard the voices of her two friends saying, "Thank goodness we heard you finally popped and we got ourselves in here." They admitted that they had written the note as a joke.

Again Maude felt rage. And it was obvious who to blame: whites who create and then underestimate the shame due to prejudice at the core of every person of color or lesbian, even if the person looks confident. But these white friends had meant no harm, and she could accept some blame for not seeing through the silly note and their teasing and questioning. To put it in our terms, her undervalued self was so intense that without plenty of self-protections against her shame, blaming being only one of them, she would not have achieved what she had. And she had been almost too successful in that these whites, like all the others, had taken her to be simply a strong, bright, confident, and resilient woman. For her own good she had to see herself that way, too, and moderate her blaming.

Maude is now famous for her own contributions to the study of prejudice. She's a wildly popular lecturer, and people fight to get a place in her courses. But she admits that she still has to battle her blaming self-protection, which can go up in an instant.

When the Wrong in Your Past Happened at Home

Maybe it is prejudice you experienced in your own family that has led to the blaming self-protection. Don was a huge disappointment to his parents because in their eyes he was not talented enough athletically or academically to be a member of their prestigious family. In fact, his parents joked that he must be illegitimate.

Don blamed himself for his "shortcomings," as children do, and naturally expected to fail as he went through life. When he started college, he was barely conscious of this expectation. Rather, he saw college as a place to make a fresh start where no one knew him. He worked hard at first and in some areas did quite well because he was actually very smart. But nothing took away his feelings of worthlessness, which would flood him whenever he received a less than perfect grade. To handle these feelings, Don used the self-protection of blaming, saying, "This instructor had it in for me from the beginning."

In protest, he refused to take the assignments seriously, finding fault with their underlying assumptions—and he was excellent at finding fault. Or he would proclaim with certainty that his work was too "outside the box" for the instructor to understand. To signal his superiority, he would skip classes or arrive late. With all of this self-defeating behavior, Don really did disappoint teachers, but their inevitable disapproval only proved his point.

Initially his friends sympathized with him. It's not cool to side with instructors, and Don's friends could see how smart he was. But in time his friends realized that something was amiss. They began to spend less and less time with Don. Unfortunately, Don found it easier to blame his friends than to face his greatest fear: that he was unteachable and unlovable. He was building his entire life around the blaming self-protection.

Signs of the Blaming Self-Protection

Unconscious assumption. "If my failures are not my fault but are the result of someone else's unfairness, then I'm not worthless."

Common statements. "Someone wants me to fail." "Everyone is against me." "People are lying about me, undermining me, making me look bad." "Fate is against me."

Other possible signs:

• Others hint that you "feel a little sorry for yourself" often or raise valid questions about whether you are distorting facts.

• You repeatedly end friendships or change jobs because you feel mistreated.

• You sometimes feel a bit guilty because you suspect you have blamed some people for mistreating you when you know they did not mean to do so.

• You are passive-aggressive, doing little things to obstruct the desires of someone you feel is mistreating you.

• You intensely hate (or willingly accept) being called a "victim."

The Noncompeting Self-Protection

When we use the noncompeting self-protection, we unconsciously try to deny the very existence of power. We fear the entire issue of ranking because it raises the possibility of a terrible defeat. This self-protection is not about a conscious religious or moral decision to rank one's own needs lower than all others' in order to serve the common good. That would not be a self-protection, but an altruistic value. Nor is noncompeting about accepting a low rank to please people, as that implies accepting ranking itself. Instead, the noncompeting self-protection is not only about *not* seeing ranking but about feeling you are above it. If you are using this self-protection, you might say, "Who's keeping score about a thing like that? Not me." "I'm the one who keeps things peaceful around here." "I just don't care what others think." "I don't want any credit. I just want to be helpful."

Alas, as much as you try to deny ranking with this self-protection, others may see you as simply willing to accept the lowest rank. Hence they may pile more work on you, let you do all the chores, and ignore your ideas. Another potential problem with using the noncompeting self-protection is that you will hesitate to exert power over others when it is in fact your job to do so. Due to your lack of leadership, all sorts of abuses and conflicts can happen among those you are trying to help.

When Someone with a Noncompeting
Self-Protection Is Given Power

A person who tacitly accepts a low rank by denying all ranking is in real trouble when given power. This was Weston's challenge. Being a father to his adoring young son, Bud, had helped alleviate Weston's feelings of worthlessness, but he was ill prepared for a twelve-year-old who belittled him, did not want to be seen with him, and attacked him in every possible way to try to get what he wanted. Bud was out every night until the wee hours, and Weston had no idea where he was. Bud had certain chores to do, but Weston was doing them secretly because he would have been embarrassed to have his wife know that he was not able to make Bud do them. There were no consequences for any of Bud's negative behaviors.

Weston explained that he was using a "child-centered" style of parenting, allowing Bud to express his authentic feelings and make his own choices. In fact, the research is clear that an overly permissive parenting style is as bad for children as an authoritarian style. Simple, caring authority works best: setting realistic limits that demonstrate concern and love and explaining them in ways a child can understand. Instead, Weston used his noncompeting self-protection out of fear of a confrontation, during which his son would certainly say horrible things about him. Weston might even lose more control over Bud. But because Weston could not face his fear of defeat and act, his noncompeting self-protection was doing his son great harm.

The Extreme Noncompeting Self-Protection

"Funny, sunny Sharon," fifty-five, had been employed by the same company, with the same boss, since she was thirty-one. She often said that the people at her office substituted for family. She never compared or cared about who got credit. As her boss's executive assistant, she worked as tirelessly as he to see the business succeed. She said that working nights and weekends was almost fun for her. It was better than being alone at home. But then her boss sold the company for a huge profit and retired to Hawaii. He gave her a bonus and recommended her glowingly to the new owners. She was grateful for his generosity and prided herself on not being greedy. All she really wanted was to own her own home, and she had saved for a down payment.

The new owners of the company, however, decided to restructure, and Sharon was among the first to be let go, as she was "not a good match" with the aggressive new CEO. The changes were wrenching for everyone, and in the general mayhem no one paid much attention to Sharon's particular plight. Everyone promised to keep in touch with her, but she knew they were all busy with their families and probably would not. That chapter of her life ended.

Sharon did not find another position for a year and a half. She lived on unemployment and then her savings before finally accepting a job that paid one third less. Feeling insecure financially, she was never able to buy a home. She had looked out for everyone but herself, trying to ignore the fact that ranking is a major part of any organization, especially a business, and if she did not move up in the ranks she would suffer for it.

Signs of the Noncompeting Self-Protection

Unconscious assumption. "I'm worthless, so better never to compete; no one will want me or stay with me unless I show them that I would never challenge them about anything."

Common statements. "I just like making other people happy." "I don't do that comparing stuff." "I don't mind not winning." "I'll do whatever you'd like."

Other possible signs:

• You have an unwritten rule with friends that you will not criticize them and would be distressed if they criticized you.

• You want to believe that people doing wrong will eventually learn their lesson without your saying anything.

• You insist that you do not care how others view you.

• You discover after many years that you were following a leader or being controlled by someone who did not have your well-being in mind.

• You regularly have sex to make another happy, even though you do not want it just then.

The Overachieving Self-Protection

Those who use the overachieving self-protection have learned that the sense of being completely no good disappears when you are being praised. Usually you adopt this self-protection early and use it most of your life, but sometimes it is temporary. For example, you are jilted by a lover and, even though you know you are not ready to be in another relationship, you feverishly start dating just to prove you can still attract someone.

Often this self-protection begins in childhood with parents or teachers. If a child has had trouble at home or at school that has led to a chronic sense of defeat and to feelings of depression and shame, his or her ability to please a series of kind, appreciative teachers can stimulate this self-protection. Teachers often encourage overachieving, even love it, not realizing what they are doing to a child in this situation, who will grow up always trying to prove her worth rather than being okay with who she is.

Other situations that can bring out this self-protection are having a handicap, being a member of a minority, or feeling flawed in some way. The pain is assuaged by overachievement in one area, such as academics, music, sports, computers, or whatever talent you have that you can nurture to the point of exhaustion. If you have this self-protection, you think you can prove yourself and regain power. You can be triumphant rather than defeated. The problem is that the fix is only temporary. It does not lead to an accurate sense of your overall self-worth. You think you are valued only for what you can do, and if you stop doing it, you will be without value. So you remain driven, even to the point of literally killing yourself with overwork.

Overachieving is not always a self-protection, of course, even if others say you overwork yourself. Maybe you work so hard because you just love what you are doing. You can determine if you are using the overachieving self-protection if your ability to take care of yourself, take time off, and stay close to those you love is hampered.

Siblings and the Overachieving Self-Protection

We often overlook the rivalry between siblings that, if mismanaged by parents, can leave one sibling feeling defeated for life.

Chelsea and Cameron are fraternal twins, the youngest of five children. As is the case with all twins, one has always been larger and more dominant, even in the womb. That is Chelsea, who has always been seen as the prettier, more coordinated, and more outgoing twin. Cameron, who is quieter, was the tag-along when girls came to play with her sister and was chubby until puberty. Their parents tried to help by being scrupulously fair, but Cameron needed more than equal treatment to keep from undervaluing herself.

In junior high school one math teacher noticed Cameron and praised her abilities. She loved this teacher's recognition and worked night and day to please him. When she graduated, she cried because she would not see him anymore.

In high school Cameron struggled socially. Her shyness increased because she was so often compared to her sister, "the pretty, fun, outgoing one." But again she found shelter in the encouragement of her science and math teachers. Cameron especially shone in chemistry and decided to major in this field in college. Secretly fearing she would never marry, she wanted to be able to support herself well, so she studied chemical engineering and became a professor, while Chelsea graduated in liberal arts and had a semiprofessional acting career.

When Chelsea married and had two children, Cameron, still single, could not help deeply envying her sister. Suddenly she hated chemical engineering and all the men who saw her as a colleague and friend but nothing more. When some students asked her to help them identify toxins in a local water supply, she was seized with a determination to become an environmental activist. In the back of her mind she thought that fighting for a healthy environment was even more important than what her sister was doing, "just being a mother." She became so dedicated to the causes she took on that others were in awe of her boldness, the health risks she took, and her general lack of interest in her own needs. She prided herself on requiring only a few hours of sleep a night. Eventually, she won prizes for her groundbreaking work, but by then she was suffering from a chronic stress-related disorder.

Meanwhile her sister had become a well-known children's book author, and she volunteered in schools serving low-income students. Without noticing any connection, Cameron decided to write books about her experiences fighting big business. When Chelsea became a national figure in the fight for better education, Cameron ran for public office, campaigning as an environmentalist. However, as always, Chelsea maintained a happy balance in her life, while Cameron was better known for her selfless dedication in spite of her private struggles with various illnesses. People said of Cameron, "she just works so hard at everything she does." Anyone who had known these sisters from childhood, however, would have said that the "hard" part was Cameron's need throughout her life to prove she was even half as good as her sister.

Signs of the Overachieving Self-Protection

Unconscious assumption. "If I work hard enough, then someone will love me, no one can say I am no good, and I will finally stop feeling worthless."

Common statements. "However you want it done, I can do it—I'll find a way." "I'm devoting my entire life to this work—nothing else matters." "I'll feel a lot better about myself once I get that face-lift [lose weight, earn my doctorate]." "People say I've accomplished a lot, but to me it seems like nothing."

Other possible signs:

• Somehow, no matter how much success you achieve, you are not impressed with yourself.

• You feel like an impostor even when others see you as an expert.

• When others offer criticism or work on a project similar to yours, you find yourself attacking them or their work with surprising vehemence.

• You hear complaints that you work all the time and do not leave enough time for your friends or family.

• When you are not working, you feel ill at ease, but when you are working you usually feel good about yourself.

The Inflating Self-Protection

The inflating self-protection does not strive to achieve some impossible state beyond the reach of shame, as the overachieving self-protection does, but instead takes you directly to the castle on the hill. You are more attractive, smarter, or better educated than others, you are the best salesperson ever, on top of whatever hill you have chosen, above the competition and beyond any risk of feeling worthless. Don, who mainly used the blaming self-protection, also employed inflating, as when he considered himself too creative to be appreciated by his instructors.

We have all met narcissists who blatantly inflate themselves either in one area or in general, usually as a self-protection, although some may simply feel entitled. But sometimes this self-protection can be hard to see. We all use it occasionally. Studies find that when threatened with failure, some people adjust their self-worth upward without knowing it.[4] Perhaps you are in a situation where showing any sign that you doubt or undervalue yourself is cause for instant shame. You have to exaggerate your rank and believe the exaggeration to protect yourself from defeat.

Sometimes we inflate ourselves when any other self-protection would sound too defensive. For example, you've been playing cards with your boss and the other honchos at work, and you lose badly. You fear that you will only look worse if you use the ordinary self-protective excuses — it must be your unlucky day, winning isn't that important to you, or you are taking online poker lessons and will beat them next time. You feel you simply must say something that puts you back up near the top, even if it isn't quite true: "Well, good thing my sales are going so well that it's no problem paying you guys off."

As always, there are times when a statement that sounds like self-protection is not that. Sometimes bragging is not inflating but just healthy pride or good public relations. Maybe you simply need your boss, boyfriend, or parents to hear about your success. "Yeah, they gave me first place." Other times, however, it is purely defensive. Which is it when you say "You guys may have MBAs, but I've been in this business for thirty years"? It might be wise to say that, or you might be covering up a terrible sense of inferiority and shame about your lack of education.

When using the inflating self-protection, we are not comforted by actual achievements or scores. We still feel ashamed of who we are. What soothes us is the favorable impression others have of us or, rather, the feeling that we have successfully covered up our worthlessness. We not only have to have money, we must display our wealth. We not only have to be well read, we must spout off about what we know. We not only have to stay thinner than most people our age, we have to fast for three days before an intimidating event to get into that certain dress.

Another way the self-protection shows itself is in pulling rank. You are chair of a committee or winner of an award, and when you start to feel worthless around someone, your undervalued self makes you slip your important position into the conversations even when it is superfluous. Or you refer to your general status when feeling inept in a specific situation. "True, I'm new to this country and don't have your experience, but I'm a doctor, and this illness looks the same the world over."

Another example is making a purchase to impress others. We have to have the best car or best home, take the best vacation or be seen walking the best dog. We may fight too hard to stay attractive or competitive in a sport, as if falling behind would destroy us. Or, when we feel most insecure, we act flamboyantly or make crazy jokes to ensure that everyone's attention is on us.

In each of these examples, the inflating self-protection serves to bolster feelings of superiority in order to avoid the opposite: the anxiety, shame, depression, and sense of defeat that would arise if you allowed yourself to fall under the strong spell of your undervalued self.

The Inflating Self-Protection in Parenting

Even when our efforts seem intended to help others, they may not be so positive in the long run if our primary unconscious goal is to maintain a high rank to protect ourselves from shame. For example, we may insist on helping someone who no longer needs help so that we can maintain our superior status. We may suffer from even the smallest failure of the person we seek to help and must make excuses for any deviation from perfection. This is especially a risk for parents who undervalue themselves and use being the best parent or having the best child to avoid any moment of defeat or shame.

Do you feel ashamed when your son is passed over in Little League, your daughter has low SAT scores, or your toddler is late in toilet training? There is nothing wrong with striving to be the best parent possible (or the best employee, team member, or whatever). And there's no problem with feeling pride in your kids, or seeking praise. Raising children is a hard job, and dedicated parents deserve praise. But problems arise when we sacrifice our children's best interests. For example, a mom who has to have a popular child may try to override her child's deeply introverted nature.

Marilyn and Steve met in graduate school. As soon as they married they started a family, so as Steve rose in their shared field of work, Marilyn was forced to wait to earn her doctorate. The sexism she had absorbed as a girl and her natural competitiveness added to her feelings of worthlessness as "just a mother." She often felt deeply depressed. But being a strong woman, she overcame these feelings and focused on giving her daughter, Darren, what she needed to be a leader in whatever field she chose. With this exclusive focus on ranking, by age four Darren was an outstanding reader, gymnast, singer, and swimmer and a paragon of good behavior—a champ at everything she tried. But after a month in kindergarten, parents and teachers complained that Darren was bossy and was making the other girls cry. Hearing this, once again Marilyn became depressed, feeling defeated by those making these accusations. Her parenting efforts were really about seeing that Darren would rank very high in the eyes of others to make up for her own sense of having no rank at all, at least not yet, in her chosen profession.

The Inflating Self-Protection on the Job

Ray's top position in his organization gives him high rank and enormous power. However, he has an exaggerated fear of competition from certain young people rising quickly from below. Rather than show true leadership by controlling his insecurity and mentoring the rising stars for the benefit of all, he has begun inflating himself so much that others have started to doubt his self-confidence and their own confidence in him. Not only does he criticize ideas that are actually very good and speak ill of those who are becoming highly respected, but he constantly brags about his past accomplishments. He needs to trust that his real wisdom and experience, uninflated, will continue to earn him the influence he naturally desires.

Signs of the Inflating Self-Protection

Unconscious assumption. "I must make clear to myself and others that I am highly qualified or the best in order to cover up the fact that I feel worthless."

Common statements. "I find it hard to find people who are good enough to keep up with me or don't bore me." "I seem to know things that others don't." "People tend to find me hard to resist." "You'd be wise to support me if you want the best."

Other possible signs:

• You're obsessed with staying thin, youthful, or well muscled and prefer to be seen only with those who meet these criteria.

• You exaggerate your own achievements and minimize those of others.

• You pull rank or bring up your superiority when threatened.

• You consider ending a close friendship when the other person has slipped in a way that could reflect poorly on you.

• You feel significantly less love for someone you are supposed to love because you can't help feeling superior.

The Projecting Self-Protection

The projecting self-protection is extreme, but it is very common. What psychologists call "defensive projection" is the hardest to recognize although the easiest to stop. With this self-protection, instead of seeing in ourselves whatever makes us feel worthless, we see it in others. It's amazing how well we can do this feat of mental gymnastics. Simply saying "I really hate snobs" could be a sign that you're a bit of a snob yourself. Perhaps the reason you hate this trait so much, focusing on it everywhere, is that at one time someone made you deeply ashamed of acting like a snob. You have become obsessed with snobbishness as a real sin and need to believe that you never commit it. Or you might say "I can't believe how critical she is" when you are obviously the one being critical. It is something you learned to hate about yourself so much that you are obsessed about it, but only see it in others, constantly. If you worry constantly about being unattractive but feel you shouldn't, you may say without a thought, "Those people are so vain—all they think about is how they look."

The best way to catch yourself projecting is to consider honestly the people whom you especially dislike (for reasons other than their mistreatment of you or others)—people for whom your dislike is irrationally intense. Now think of the one thing about them that you most dislike, a character trait or behavior, such as arrogance, helplessness, deviousness, greed, jealousy, or gullibility. Examine this particularly detestable characteristic honestly. Isn't it something you simply would not tolerate in yourself, something that, if you admitted to it even a bit, would leave you feeling ashamed? You know rationally that no one, including you, is entirely free of that behavior; yet you have learned to feel very bad about yourself when you act that way.

We may also project our own good traits onto others if we have deep feelings of shame and worthlessness, because we feel these positive traits couldn't possibly belong to us. We are able to see others as happy, fortunate, or talented, but we cannot possibly see ourselves in these ways, even when those others do not feel as fortunate as we think they do.

The Projecting Self-Protection in Rejecting a Potential Partner

Rosanne was a tough young woman, the oldest of six children. Her father was an ambitious self-made man from a developing country who brought his family to the United States when Rosanne was five. Her mother was self-effacing, sickly, and depressed, always overwhelmed by her children and trying to adapt to a country she did not like. So Rosanne took charge of things early, following her father's orders in everything, and was proud of her role.

When Rosanne was a junior in high school, her father was reassigned to their homeland. At her father's urging, Rosanne did not return with the rest of the family. He wanted her to stay and gain every advantage she could. She had a terrible senior year. She missed her family and felt unwanted by the family her father had paid to care for her. The following year was even worse: she had to either accept a scholarship to a college in a strange city or go back to her homeland.

Rosanne did accept the scholarship. Further, after completing college, she became a citizen, found an excellent job, and rose rapidly in her company, much as her father had done. That is when she came to see me. She wanted a relationship, but nothing was working out. She attracted men, yet none of them pleased her. They all seemed to be slackers, just wanting to live off her money, or they were too clingy.

Then Rosanne had a dream about a man in her life whom she was about to reject for those same reasons. The dream involved her meeting him in her senior year of high school. After sharing the dream with me, Rosanne recalled for the first time those nights by herself when she had been completely overwhelmed by feelings of grief, insecurity, and loneliness. Being separated from her family and being alone had both terrified her and undermined her faith in herself as a tough, independent person. Rosanne saw how very much she still wanted to be taken care of.

Being taken care of, however, would make her too much like her mother. Her father had taught her that needing others was always weak. So she had projected her desire to be close and supported by another onto the men she was meeting, suspecting them of wanting *her* to take care of *them*. Very often, as was true of Rosanne, the trait we despise and project is one that our parents deeply disliked in us, or that we deeply disliked in them. In this case, Rosanne despised her mother's weakness, and her father would have despised it in Rosanne if she had dared show it.

Projecting in the Workplace

Burt grew up poor. His teachers saw his unkempt appearance as a sign of inferior intelligence, and he was never encouraged to take courses that would have led to a college education. So he poured his energy into repairing cars. He liked to invent gadgets, and he came up with an ingenious tool that made it easier to replace brake linings. With the help of an interested librarian, he applied for a patent. Another interested bystander, a business-woman, loaned him some capital, and he began manufacturing the tool. Now, years later, thanks to his intense ambition and desire to prove himself, he owns a company employing several hundred people.

Burt loathes unfairness. He prides himself on giving the ordinary guy a break. But his employees do not see him as fair at all. Although he hires "ordinary guys," he then watches them constantly for signs that they are trying to take over, and he refuses promotions to those who "push themselves forward too much." In fact, he is the one who has spent a lifetime pushing forward and taking over. Having experienced so much unfair ranking and so little linking as a child, he became obsessed with getting ahead. He sees ruthless ambition in everyone around him while disliking it so much that he could never admit to it in himself.

Signs of the Projecting Self-Protection

Unconscious assumption. "I can't bear my feelings of shame and worthlessness. Certain things about me are especially bad, so I have to get rid of them. Yet they haunt me. I see them everywhere, in everyone."

Common statements. "I don't know why, but I just *hate* that person." "I'm not upset at all by what you said to me. You're the one who's upset." "I'm not planning to take over [although unconsciously you would like to], but watch out for those guys...they'll fool you with their niceness and then suddenly grab control of everything."

Other possible signs:

• You see in others what you consider the most unacceptable behaviors but rarely see these in yourself.

• You see others as all good and yourself as all bad (you are seeing your own good qualities in them instead of in yourself).

• You often criticize others for being so critical, ignoring the fact that you are doing just that.

• You think you know that someone is dishonest or selfish and then find that your view of him or her is utterly baseless.

• You attribute evil to those on the other side but none to your own side.

WORKING WITH WHAT YOU HAVE LEARNED

In this chapter you assessed which self-protections you tend to use. Now that you know more about them, go back to the self-assessment and see if some of your "false" items are actually "true."

You are now prepared to explore how you have used these self-protections in specific situations and how you could avoid using them in the future. Do not expect too much of yourself, however. You will become better at doing without these self-protections as you proceed through the book and reduce the force of your undervalued self. But you can begin reducing that force right now. When you forgo a self-protection, you will start ranking yourself and others less and improving your links with them instead. Start by seeing what you have been doing and then imagine how you could respond differently.

Identify Times When You Have Used Self-Protections

In your journal write down each of the six self-protections—minimizing, blaming, noncompeting, overachieving, inflating, and projecting—on a separate page. Now, looking back at your lists from chapter one of the people who make you feel good and those who make you feel bad, write down three specific times in the last week when you used each of these self-protections with people on your lists. Sometimes it can be difficult to recall a moment when you felt ashamed or were trying to avoid that feeling. (Forgetting is another self-protection, but it's hard to assess if you do not remember doing it.) Stay with the exercise until you do remember, going further back in time if you cannot recall three instances in the last week.

Be sure to list only those times when a self-protection really was that rather than, say, minimizing because whatever happened really wasn't a big deal; blaming because you really were wronged; choosing to ignore ranking rather than running away from it; striving to do your best without overdoing it; letting others know your abilities without having to inflate them to avoid feeling inferior; or not projecting because it really was the other person's problem, not yours.

Imagine What You Could Have Done
Instead of Using a Self-Protection

This exercise is very important. It will help you see how you have used the self-protections in particular relationships, let you imagine the good feelings that might come from not using them, and practice thinking of ways to avoid needing them. For each of the eighteen incidents listed above (three for each of the six self-protections), reflect on the following questions and imagine how you might have handled things differently.

• How do you think the other person reacted to your self-protection?

• What might you have said instead? Suppose you had shown even a little of your honest fear of feeling like a failure or a bad person?

• In that case, what might the other person have thought or said in response?

For example, maybe you went ahead alone on a project you were supposed to do with a coworker, and she found that out. You felt that others underestimated your abilities, so you wanted to demonstrate that you could do the job without her. You were pretty sure she would not like this, so when she found out, you felt ashamed. You were caught doing something that you, she, or both of you would have to say reflects poorly on your character.

Before she could be angry, and perhaps even before you felt ashamed, you said, "It just never occurred to me that you would mind." You used the minimizing self-protection, denying that it was a big deal. There may have been some blaming here, too, if you were implying that she should not have minded. So now your task is to imagine what happened in her mind and what you could have said instead by answering the questions listed above.

• *How do you think the other person received what you said?* She didn't believe my denial.

• *What might you have said instead?* Perhaps "I'm sorry—I guess I knew you would mind. I wanted to show them I could do it myself, without your help. I'm truly sorry I went ahead without you and traded the opportunity to work with you for a chance to make myself look good."

• *If you had said that, what might the other person have thought or said in response?* She might have been impressed that I could be so honest in such an uncomfortable moment. She might have been angry too, as she had a right to be. But because I admitted that I knew it was wrong and sincerely regretted it, she could not hold it against me for long. And at least I would not have added a new reason to feel bad about myself, that I had lied to cover my mistake.

How Your Use of the Self-Protections Masks the Undervalued Self

Using the self-protections less will be an important goal for you. But the main purpose of this chapter was to identify the self-protections you use and to help you see through them to how much you really are ruled by the undervalued self. Reflect on and write about this. Do you use these self-protections more than you thought? Can you see how often you are in ranking mode and trying to avoid feeling defeated and ashamed? If you are not sure yet, that is all right for now.

CHAPTER THREE

Reasons from Our Past for Ranking Ourselves Too Low

At times you really know you are seeing the world through the eyes of the undervalued self, and you may have more of those moments of knowing now that you are beginning to see through your self-protections. The hallmark of those times is that you think you are just generally no good. You tell yourself, "I'm a loser and worthless. No wonder people don't like me." Yet you *know* this is irrational.

Sometimes the undervalued self can grip us so completely that we can't see our way through the murky mess until some external event finally *shifts* our perspective and we realize we were significantly, even drastically, undervaluing ourselves. Have you ever met someone for lunch and been sure you were a bore and would never hear from the person again? Then you receive a message the next day that she sincerely wants to get together again soon. That's the kind of shift I mean.

To help you make the shift sooner rather than later, you need to uncover your personal reasons for undervaluing yourself so much. Identifying the causes of your feelings of shame and worthlessness will give you a better idea of what triggers those feelings so that you can more easily recover from undervaluing yourself. Also, reviewing your particular history will diminish the sense that you are somehow to blame for these feelings of worthlessness.

TWO FACTORS CONTRIBUTING TO THE UNDERVALUED SELF

You already know from chapter one about the first factor, that the undervalued self partly results from innate tendencies: to have an overall sense of self-worth that errs on the side of undervaluing (so that you avoid situations where you might be defeated and shamed), as well as an innate defeat response and strong social emotions. Yet these tendencies can be activated only by the personal defeats you have experienced, and that is the second factor. The more defeats you have had, the more crucial it will be to explore your personal history as you use this book. In this chapter you will learn how to do that. Along the way you will see why almost any type of trauma (any experience that leads to overwhelming, seemingly unbearable emotion) profoundly influences how much you undervalue yourself.

Our innate tendency to rank ourselves low is difficult enough to handle, but if past traumas have reinforced this undervaluing, it becomes chronic and the consequences become even more costly. For example, maybe you have not spoken up in a group at work because of past defeats that caused you to assume, for safety's sake, that you were not as good as the others. So you stayed quiet even though an original idea was percolating in your head about how to solve some of the company's problems.

However, you also grew up with a critical father who sometimes raged at you for making small mistakes or for arguing back. Being young and in awe of your parent, you found his rages almost unbearable to endure. So it is not just that you fear making a less than brilliant contribution, you have a true terror that someone will decimate your ideas, in particular your boss, who even looks a bit like your father. You keep your idea to yourself, only to hear someone else present a solution that is similar to yours but not as good and receive accolades.

These two factors, innate tendency and personal history, can hammer us over and over. Maybe you are always shy on a first date if the guy is especially handsome. You rank yourself too low to interest him. But added to that, a boyfriend you trusted recently left you for another. So when your date is as quiet as you are, you think he hates you, only to find later that he thought it was you who lacked interest in him. Or a supervisor suggests a way to improve your project. He has ranked your work—not you but only your work—as beneath your capabilities. You struggle not to take it as an overall statement of your worth but to simply make the changes he suggests. However, your sixth-grade teacher used to tear apart your work in front of the entire class, and you still expect your work to be the worst. So you look over the edited project, see it and yourself as a hopeless mess, and entirely rework it. Your supervisor is distressed by this, since he liked most of what you had done. At your next review he tells you that you "overreact to criticism" and thinks it might be best to delay your promotion.

Very often, if these two factors are at work in you—the innate tendency to undervalue plus serious defeats in your life—you will undervalue yourself chronically and decline all sorts of opportunities and relationships that might have turned out well. And you may be depressed or anxious.

These results of the undervalued self can also become self-fulfilling, leading you to keep declining opportunities until your skills are rusty and your lack of confidence is so obvious to others that they, too, rank you low. Your low value has become a reality.

To avoid these losses and begin your healing, it is essential to identify the past traumas that have intensified the ever-present instincts to undervalue yourself when defeat seems possible. But first, let's assess just how much you undervalue yourself. You can do this more effectively now that you have learned about the self-protections, because you are more aware of the feelings hidden behind them.

HOW MUCH DO YOU UNDERVALUE YOURSELF?

Before you begin the assessment, you will need some guidelines.

• Mark *S* for any statement below if it is *ever* true of you or if you have ever held this view, no matter how irrational or unpleasant the view may seem. *S* stands for a "state" you may get into now and then.

• Mark *T* for any statement below if it is *often* true of you. *T* stands for "trait," a more fixed part of your personality.

• Take time to reflect on each item so that you can look past your self-protections and see whether it might be true of you. If your initial response is that the statement is true, stick to it even if you don't like it.

• Answer each question independently. Do not worry if you seem to be contradicting earlier answers.

• If you want to be sure of your privacy, write your answers on a separate piece of paper rather than in the book. But keep your answers handy, because you will return to them.

1. You do not believe people when they say they like you.

2. You look down or away when face-to-face with another person.

3. You think about who's better than whom—prettier, richer, brighter, has better ideas or a nicer car—even when you are fairly sure others are not thinking that way.

4. You have to please others and keep them happy at all costs.

5. You see yourself as inferior even when you know objectively that you could be seen as an equal.

6. When you're criticized, you hardly consider the source. Your day is ruined.

7. You fear speaking out even when you know you have a good idea.

8. Your posture is head down, shoulders rounded.

9. In a restaurant you have trouble complaining about a problem any reasonable person would be unhappy about.

10. You feel like an impostor.

11. When you are the appointed or natural leader (parent or teacher, for example), you expect to have trouble getting respect.

12. When someone says, "We have a problem," you immediately fear that you caused it or will be blamed.

13. You cannot see how you could have stood up for yourself in a difficult situation until later.

14. You expect to lose before you begin.

15. You worry about losing your job even when there is no objective reason for your fear.

16. People say you lack confidence.

17. You expect people not to be interested in you when they meet you.

18. You feel jealous or insecure around a best friend or committed partner even though you know you come first.

19. You easily feel ashamed of what you've just said, your appearance, your family, your past, or the person you're dating.

20. You have sex mainly because you fear the person will not like you if you refuse.

21. When you want someone to stop doing something, you cannot bring it up with the person.

22. You hesitate to ask for what you need.

Scoring

Add the number of statements you marked with an *S* for a state you get into now and then. Add the number of statements you marked with a *T* to acknowledge a trait, a fixed part of your personality. There is no normal score here, but ten or more *S*s and two or more *T*s would indicate considerable undervaluing.

TRAUMA AS A CAUSE OF LOW RANK
AND AN UNDERVALUED SELF

When we say someone has had a traumatic physical injury, it means the body has lost its wholeness in some way: the skin has been deeply cut, a bone has been broken, or an organ has been injured. Trauma happens to the mind as well, either with or without physical trauma. It occurs when emotions are not just overwhelming but in some real sense unbearable. With enough stress and a sense of powerlessness to prevent more stress, the mind loses its wholeness and "falls apart," "breaks down," or "goes to pieces." The brain goes through changes that, although often reversible, are the equivalent of an injury. Trauma can be acute, an abrupt experience, or chronic, something that grinds you down over time.

Most life traumas involve other people in some way. Someone abandoned, defeated, hurt, or rejected us. Or, during a physical trauma, we feel that a person did not help us or did not help enough. As a result, most traumas automatically lead to the innate defeat response of depression and shame and an overall low sense of self-worth.

When a trauma involves an experience so bad that we can't look at the whole thing, the mind must break it up for us, meaning that we dissociate. We may separate entire events from our consciousness so that we have no memory of them at all. Or we may separate feelings about a trauma from our memories of it, so that we do remember what happened but have no feelings about it. Meanwhile, we experience upsetting feelings, including chronic anxiety and depression, for "no reason." And we behave in ways that surprise us because we do not see the connection between what we are doing now and the trauma in the past.

While some parts of our mind are falling apart due to trauma, other parts are taking over without our being aware of it, so that we can survive the ordeal and avoid anything like it in the future. These "other parts" are those innate responses you already know about, such as lowering your overall sense of self-worth and staying depressed and shamed. These responses assume that the best predictor of the present is the past, so they lock us into using the self-protections, becoming depressed, and, consciously or unconsciously, ranking ourselves very low, all in order to avoid further social trauma.

It is important to remember that the decision to accept a low rank due to trauma is often unconscious. Because it is too painful to think about all the time, you may not be aware that you expect every human encounter to lead to a ranking defeat. This is why it is essential to learn about the traumas of your past in spite of the dissociations that may be keeping you from fully appreciating them. Recognizing the amount and type of trauma in your life is the next step to healing the undervalued self.

Rank and Traumatic Events in Childhood

Unless you were very well protected as a child, you were probably exposed to far more trauma than adults usually are. Why? You were physically smaller. You were usually not able to escape from a situation, a possibility you now take for granted. You were surrounded by people who were larger and ranked much higher, so you often experienced defeat or else feared and avoided it. And a great many experiences were new and potentially scary to you.

Further, a child's mind dissociates more in response to traumatic events because the sense of self is just developing. The younger you were when the event happened, the fewer self-protections and other coping methods you had that adults readily use to keep from feeling traumatized by a defeat. For example, if someone behaves horribly toward you now, you can probably stop yourself from feeling that you deserved it. But a child treated horribly is likely to feel very defeated, powerless, and at fault, leading to the need to dissociate.

In most families a very young child ranks high. The entire household may revolve around a newborn, and the mother's first concern is for her baby. But a very young child may view his or her situation differently. Even the most devoted parents must, for example, let their child be restrained for a vaccination. How traumatic is that? I know a man whose loving mother stood by while he was held down for his first shots by a very angry pediatrician who actually hated kids. Today that man still avoids doctors.

Childhood experiences of abusive power are traumatic, but almost any trauma in childhood is experienced as an abuse of power in the sense that the adults who are supposed to be taking care of you in fact left you helpless. For example, if you are five years old and your house burns down, unless your parents are quick to attend to your terror that such a thing could happen and to the bewildering loss of everything you had the day before, you will in effect feel abandoned with these unbearable—traumatic—feelings. This is not what an adult would see as abusive power, because there was no intention to ignore the child's needs. But for children, big people are either there for them or not.

A particular trauma for children that involves an innate response is separation from the person who is supposed to take care of them. When children are separated from their caregivers, first they protest (cry loudly), then they despair (curl up and whimper), and finally they detach and appear to act almost normal, except for signs of depression.[1] They have been defeated. The defeat response saves their energy but leaves a sense of depression and shame.

Besides the temporary shame that always comes with defeat, if the child feels there is no linking, or the parent feels no regret about separations or having to mete out punishment, then the child can come to feel that his or her core self is truly unlovable. This apparently innate tendency to blame yourself rather than putting the blame where it belongs, on the adults, makes it more likely that you will change how you behave until you find the formula that keeps you reasonably well taken care of.

Bear in mind that as a child you were highly vulnerable to traumas involving separations that seem barely significant to adults. For example, your parents may have given you a time-out for a period determined by them. Since we all innately dread social isolation, this is a terrifying situation. You might as well have been locked in prison, as you see it. Your power to stop it? Almost none. Your rank was too low.

Parents can also tease, shame, or ridicule a child almost without realizing it, especially if they were teased or shamed as a child. They can drive a child to compete and win with such force that the child is constantly anxious, afraid that failure will lead to abandonment. Of course, parents can also neglect a child or be physically abusive.

So as you look at your own traumas in childhood, keep in mind that a psychological trauma happens inside a child's mind, not outside. Your mother's going into the hospital for a few weeks when you were two years old might seem trivial to you now, but it may not have been then. It depended upon how secure you felt during that experience. Similarly, a house burning down might not be traumatic for a child well supported through the experience, while a balloon bursting could be a nightmare for another.

The younger you were, the greater the likelihood that any distressing event was experienced as traumatic. Prior to age four, you were especially vulnerable because you lacked the coping methods and the strong sense of self that adults have. When you were a little older, say between four and twelve, you were still strongly affected by experiences that might be manageable for someone older, especially because adults were not always around to protect you from siblings and peers.

Whatever your age, the amount of support you had from parents or others during a stressful event also determines a great deal. If your mother goes into the hospital but your beloved grandmother has come to stay with you, you will manage far better than if your father spent all of his time at the hospital and you were left alone with your fears.

In addition, a repetition of the trauma or an additional trauma soon after the first can more than double the distress, because the first made you more vulnerable to the effects of the next. Your mother going into the hospital and your father becoming unavailable as well leaves you not just with two losses but with a sense of having no support whatsoever, and that is a huge trauma.

Finally, some traumas stand out in a child's mind so vividly that the total number of other traumas is irrelevant. That would be the case, for example, if your mother went off to the hospital and died there. Again, a trauma that was life-altering for you might not have been for another person. You do not want to exaggerate your traumas, of course, but generally people do the opposite and underestimate them.

Although most of your childhood traumas probably resulted from the actions of others, this exercise is not about blame. Nor is it about abdicating responsibility: you are not responsible for what happened to you in the past, but you are responsible for healing your undervalued self. To do that requires that you *remember* past traumas—again, not to assign blame about the past or feel sorry for yourself, but to correct problems in the present.

As you look at the following lists of childhood and adulthood traumas, first acknowledge which ones happened to you, *adding any that occurred for you that are not listed*. And consider your age, level of support, and level of stress at the time; simply being on the provided list does not automatically mean that the experience was traumatic for you, and an experience that seems minor could still have been very traumatic. Think about how the event affected you personally.

Common Childhood Traumas

• Being bullied frequently, to the point that you felt afraid or helpless or had to arrange your life to avoid the bully

- Being shamed in the classroom or on the playground
- Being excluded by those with whom you wanted to be friends
- Being held back a grade
- Having no friends for more than a few days
- Having as your only "friends" people you were ashamed to be with
- Being dominated by a sibling
- Having unreasonably strict parents
- Being harshly criticized by a parent
- Being threatened with abandonment: "If you don't stop crying, I'll take you to an orphanage."
- Being overweight, underweight, having bad acne, or another condition that made you feel unattractive
- Feeling guilty about something you could not discuss with anyone
- As a teenager, having unusual trouble with dating

Less Common and Usually More Serious Childhood Traumas

- Experiencing the death or permanent serious injury of a parent or sibling
- You or a family member having a life-threatening or serious chronic illness
- Having mental illness, alcoholism, or addiction in your family
- Living through a period of extreme poverty, or stressful poverty lasting throughout childhood
- Moving frequently or losing your home because of eviction, fire, or natural disaster
- You or a family member being the victim of a violent crime
- Feeling discrimination, whether overt or subtle
- Experiencing or knowing of neglect, physical abuse, frequent verbal abuse, or sexual abuse by any family members
- Having a divorced or absent parent or caretaker
- Finding out your parents did not want to have you

• Knowing that a parent does not like you because of your basic personality, for example, being seen as "over" active or "too shy"

• Constantly having to take care of a parent emotionally

• Being frequently criticized by family members for your appearance or for normal child behavior

• As a teenager, being especially troubled, abusing drugs or alcohol, or feeling suicidal

Charting Your Childhood Traumas

Use the two lists of childhood traumas to remind you of these or any other traumatic events you experienced. Remember that a trauma, whether it is being bullied or having your house burn down, can have a variety of effects according to the circumstances. For example, when Audrey was five, her home burned down because a Christmas tree caught fire. She was not home at the time, and her parents carefully prepared her for the news and helped her deal with her fears and losses. Her grandparents lived across the street, and her family moved in with them until the house was rebuilt just as it had been. Audrey remembers the experience as an adventure. She especially liked seeing the new house rise from the ashes just as she remembered the old one, but better.

Mel's house also burned down, and her experience is a good example of a life-altering childhood trauma that triggered additional traumas and caused feelings of depression and shame. In Alabama in 1954 the Ku Klux Klan burned down Mel's house because her father tried to vote that year. As a result, her father had to go into hiding and her mother was fired from her job. Mel was only eleven, but she had to quit school and work to help provide for the younger children. Others feared being associated with her family and shunned them; the gap between her and her former friends widened as her clothes became shabbier and she fell behind in education. As an adult, Mel still undervalues herself chronically, even though she graduated from college later in life and understood that she should be proud of her father's courage rather than ashamed of herself.

Using Mel's chart as a guide, fill in the Childhood Trauma Chart in Appendix II for yourself. Write down the traumatic events in column 1. Place a check mark in column 2 if this event occurred before you were four or in column 3 if it happened before you were twelve. (If it occurred when you were two, you would check both columns, since it happened before you were four and, obviously, also before you were twelve. A younger age is thus weighted more by having check marks in both boxes.)

Place a check mark in column 4 if you received very little or no help recovering from this traumatic event. Check column 5 if this traumatic event happened two or more times. Check column 6 if more than one traumatic event happened at the same time. Column 7 allows you to indicate how bad this trauma was for you. Put a check mark or even two in column 7 if you feel the trauma had a huge impact on you, making it one of the defining events behind your feelings of worthlessness. Do not hesitate to check column 7 even for items on the list of "common" childhood traumas—it all depends on how the event affected you personally. Check column 8 if the trauma made you feel depressed or ashamed for more than a few days.

Mel's Chart

1	2	3	4	5	6	7	8
Childhood trauma	Before age four	Before age twelve	Received little or no help	Happened more than two times	More than one at a time	Life-altering or profound impact	Felt depressed or ashamed
House fire	✓	✓				✓	✓
Father went into hiding		✓	✓		✓	✓	✓
Mother fired		✓	✓		✓	✓	✓
Forced to quit school		✓	✓	✓	✓	✓ ✓	✓
Shunned by others		✓	✓	✓	✓	✓ ✓	✓

Rank and Traumatic Events in Adulthood

Our personal histories of trauma do not stop in childhood, of course. Adults have plenty of traumas, and they are almost always around ranking. For example, some workplaces overly emphasize competition, creating an environment in which harassment and bullying can easily grow. You may think you have gotten used to such a work climate, but prolonged experiences of abusive power are almost always traumatic. If you do not feel its effects, then you have probably simply cut yourself off from those feelings. When an animal is left in a small cage with its opponent in a ranking conflict, the loser, not surprisingly, becomes intensely stressed and depressed.[2] If you cannot escape or win in a situation of abusive power, it has the same effect on you.

The same factors that turn a stressful event into a trauma for children are at work in adults as well: age, number or repetition of traumas, and level of support. For adults, your absolute age matters less than your level of innocence. If your childhood was relatively free of loveless, abusive ranking, then your first traumatic experience of the abuse of power may be in adulthood, whether at work or in a relationship, and it will have a more profound impact than if you had become used to the world being a rough place sometimes.

A number of traumas at once or the repetition of one will similarly increase the impact. Because your life as an adult is more complicated than it was in childhood, a trauma now can have an especially large ripple effect. For example, when a long-standing relationship ends through death or divorce, the grief can lead to your feeling depressed and to others not understanding why you cannot "get over it." It can also lead to performing poorly at work and then to feeling worse about yourself professionally. It may even lead to job loss and a financial crisis and a sense of shame that you cannot manage your life better.

Social support or the lack thereof often dictates how traumatic an event will be. If you have support, a disaster can become an opportunity to learn how much others care. But social support may fall away when you need it most, especially if you are in a crisis for a long time. Such abandonment can be even more traumatic than the original trauma and leave you feeling even deeper depression and shame, as well as fear for your future.

Common Adulthood Traumas

- Being betrayed by a close friend or lover
- Having the person closest to you move far away
- Being rejected repeatedly while dating or looking for work
- Getting a divorce
- Having a serious or chronic illness
- Losing your job or being fired
- Being forced to leave your home through foreclosure or an unwanted move or having to move to a long-term-care facility
- Going bankrupt or being deeply in debt for years
- Suffering a serious professional or personal failure or the loss of your reputation
- Being diagnosed with a serious illness
- Still being ridiculed or rejected by parents or siblings
- Being addicted or having someone you love be addicted
- Being harassed verbally, physically, or sexually
- Experiencing the serious illness or death of someone dear to you

Less Common and Usually More Serious Adulthood Traumas

- Being a political prisoner or victim of terrorism
- Living in a war zone
- Being a victim of a serious crime or having someone close to you be a victim
- Witnessing another's death or coming close to death yourself
- Getting arrested or jailed

- Being named the defendant in a serious lawsuit
- Being the subject of cruel public gossip or written slander, damaging your reputation perhaps forever
- Becoming disfigured or handicapped
- Causing an accident, fire, or other catastrophe to yourself or others
- Being badly hurt by another's mistake

Charting Your Adulthood Traumas

Adult traumas can also lead to an undervalued self. Again, for adults it is especially easy for one bad event to lead to others. For example, sometimes a marriage breaks up under the stress of losing a child. What is traumatic is the breadth of the devastation.

Sam was working on contract for a software firm. He loved the job, knew he was doing well, and hoped to be hired. At twenty-four, he was making far more money than he ever had in his young life, so when he received a small inheritance after his aunt's death, he bought a condominium. He also began dating a very attractive woman, whom he hoped to marry.

Sam tended to ask questions in order to do his job better, as his supervisor had encouraged him to do. Working to meet a deadline while his supervisor was out sick, Sam called his supervisor's boss, Ted, who had been very friendly to him. Ted answered Sam's question, but later Sam learned that Ted had viewed the question as a sign of incompetence and an inability to work independently.

When it came time to fill the permanent position Sam had been counting on, he was not only passed over for someone who happened to be a friend of Ted's, but he was told that his services were no longer needed. Sam knew that the accusation and the higher-up's promotion of a friend, using a flimsy excuse, were utterly unfair, and he was shocked. He kept his undervalued feelings at bay by reminding himself that this was not his fault. However, he then learned that his supervisor had not supported him but instead had agreed with Ted that Sam was not really qualified for the position.

Sam's feelings about himself plummeted. He examined everything he had done over and over, finding fault with himself at every point. Making it all worse, he was now unemployed and had a mortgage payment due; the attractive girlfriend suddenly lost interest in him; and in his distracted state, he ran a red light and caused a serious car accident.

After Sam recovered he applied for other jobs but was rejected several times. When he finally called home to ask for a loan from his parents to meet his mortgage payment, his insensitive father said something typical: "I told you so. Take a contracting job and you just get used and then thrown away. After that, other companies wonder why you weren't hired on and won't touch you."

Sam eventually found another job, but not in time to prevent losing his first house and the first girl he had wished to marry. This series of traumatic events left him feeling like a failure for many years. Even when no one around him knew he had suffered these losses early on, he carried a secret sense of shame until he began to resolve this shame in therapy. In the meantime, he turned down several opportunities for both love and professional advancement.

You are about to chart your adult traumas, as you did those of your childhood. Again, this exercise is not about blaming others or abdicating responsibility. Rather, it is part of the path toward taking full responsibility for healing your undervalued self.

Use the lists of common and less common adulthood traumas to remind you of any traumatic events you may have experienced, and add as many others not on the list as have occurred to you. Then, using the Adult Trauma Chart in Appendix II, record in column 1 whatever traumas you have experienced. Check column 2 if this event occurred in early adulthood and you were relatively innocent. Check column 3 if the trauma happened more than twice. Check column 4 if more than one trauma was happening at the same time.

Check column 5 if you had no social support at the time of the trauma or felt you could not tell anyone or if others were unhelpful. Check column 6 if it was "less common," if you know the trauma has been an unusually strong cause of your undervaluing yourself or has had a ripple effect, creating other traumas in its wake. Check column 7 if the trauma left you feeling particularly depressed or ashamed.

Finally, for all "less common and usually more serious adult traumas" that you choose from that list or add to on your own, put a second check mark in column 6 beside the one you already put there, in order to give that event more emphasis. You will have to decide what traumas are more serious, but the list should give you an idea. In Sam's example in the following chart, the trauma of being ridiculed repeatedly by family members and losing his job, from the "common" list, caused a ripple effect of traumas, including causing a car accident, for him a less common and more serious adulthood trauma.

Sam's Chart

1	2	3	4	5	6	7
Adult trauma	Happened while still "innocent"	Happened more than twice	More than one at a time	Received little or no help	Life-altering or ripple effect	Felt defeated or ashamed
Lost job	✓			✓	✓✓	✓
Girlfriend left	✓		✓	✓	✓	✓
Lost condominium	✓		✓	✓	✓	✓
Still being ridiculed by family members		✓	✓	✓		✓
Caused a serious car accident	✓✓		✓✓	✓✓	✓✓	✓✓

WHY ANY TRAUMATIC EVENT CAN LEAD TO THE UNDERVALUED SELF

You know from chapter one why traumas involving defeat or failure lead to an overall sense of worthlessness. But to some degree all experiences of abuse will have this effect. You might think that if someone else is entirely to blame—if you were robbed, raped, or hit by a drunk driver—you would realize that it is the other person who has the personality problem, not you. But in fact, as a prisoner of war will tell you, the experience of powerlessness leads to that same defeat response of depression and shame, even if you could do nothing about it. This defeat response in this case probably keeps a prisoner of war from fighting back and thus may save his life. But after an experience of powerlessness, you may feel that somehow you should have been able to handle the situation better. That feeling, too, is useful in that it motivates you to learn from your experience and be more careful, but it also leads you to feel bad about yourself—that is, it leads to the undervalued self.

Even a flood, an accident, or an illness can lead to a sense of powerlessness and failure and then to the innate defeat response of depression and shame and lower overall self-worth. Blaming yourself gives you a sense that you can have some potential control over the future by buying more insurance or following a healthier lifestyle.[3] However, there is a price, in that now you must deal with the shame of having "let" the current situation happen. And even if there is truly nothing you could have done differently, you may feel shame for having had "bad luck" or "bad karma." You may sense that others treat you with pity or just differently from a person with "better luck."

You may also have some specific reasons for being vulnerable to undervaluing yourself as a result of a trauma. If your charts were full of check marks, you already tend to undervalue yourself because of past traumas. And three additional factors—prejudice, sensitivity, and insecurity in childhood—also make you more vulnerable.

The Special Problem of Prejudice

Racial, ethnic, and other types of prejudice can have a huge impact on self-worth, especially when the prejudice is experienced early in life. In this case, the child probably saw his or her parents subjected to prejudice, too. Since we are all designed to care deeply about being excluded from the group and to feel shamed if we are excluded, the abuse of power exhibited in prejudice is particularly insidious. Prejudice itself is infuriating, and it can increase every other negative emotion, including grief, anxiety, and depression. Members of minorities are less likely to associate their group with something positive, and this affects their overall sense of self-worth.[4] In fact, prejudice has such a profound impact that those who experience a lot of it tend to have shorter life spans.[5]

Prejudice greatly compounds the effects of trauma in someone's life. You will recall the story of Mel, whose childhood home was burned down by the Ku Klux Klan. The impact of losing her home, her father, her family's financial security, and her status in the community and among her friends was strongly increased by the prejudice she was subjected to all of her life for being African American.

Further, she felt the same sense of powerlessness, depression, and shame when she later experienced traumas having nothing to do with her race or her competence. For example, she broke her arm when a tree limb fell through the roof of a guest room where she was sleeping. When she went to the emergency room, she could not help feeling ashamed of her injury, as if her broken arm were caused by her personal bad luck. She certainly didn't feel she deserved the attentive care she received. Even at the time of her mother's death, she felt the same sense of powerlessness, depression, and shame. She kept thinking that she should have taken better care of her mother and that she had no right or reason to grieve for more than a few months.

Turn to your childhood and adulthood trauma charts and add another check mark next to all the ones already there if you experienced prejudice early or often in your life. This will give you a visual representation of the impact prejudice has had on your experience of traumatic events.

The Effect of Innate High Sensitivity

Another factor that increases the impact of trauma is the inherited trait of high sensitivity. Before I became focused on problems related to love and power, I researched and wrote about innate high sensitivity. In the past, high sensitivity has been mislabeled as shyness, introversion, or neuroticism. It is none of these things. Highly sensitive people constitute about 20 percent of the population—a minority.[6] As many men as women have this innate trait, which has been observed in infants at birth and is found in most and perhaps all species.[7]

You are probably highly sensitive if you notice more subtleties in your environment, have a rich inner life, need more downtime than others, are more sensitive to caffeine and to pain, startle easily, and are easily overwhelmed by loud noise or chaotic environments, deadlines, or changes in your life. On average, highly sensitive people tend to be more creative, conscientious, cooperative, and aware of consequences. For example, sensitive people were probably among the first to worry about climate change. They do not like risk, so they spot dangers, carry enough insurance, and take care of their own and their loved ones' health.

Although this trait can be a great asset, most highly sensitive people do not feel good about themselves for a number of reasons. First, although no one performs well or feels good when overstimulated, highly sensitive people become overstimulated much more easily than others because they are so aware of everything going on around them. Thus, when taking a test or being observed, they may do worse than others and worse than they themselves expect. Unless they understand that they are highly sensitive, they will completely misunderstand these "failures."

Further, the highly sensitive are more affected by feedback. They observe and learn from their mistakes more than others do, and this requires them to care about their mistakes more than others. But sometimes they care so much that criticism causes their overall self-worth to drop drastically.

Also, being members of a numerical minority, the highly sensitive can be the targets of prejudice. They often hear "Why are you so super-sensitive to everything?" Unless they are raised to recognize their sensitivity as a gift, they absorb the culture's often negative view of it.

Finally, high sensitivity increases the impact of all emotionally tinged events, making childhood trauma particularly scarring. Being so affected by "so little" can be an additional source of shame. People say, "Why can't you just get over all that and put it behind you?" But that is not so easy.

Turn to your childhood and adulthood trauma charts and add another check mark next to all the ones already there if you are highly sensitive. As with prejudice, this will give you a visual representation of the impact of high sensitivity on your experience of traumatic events.

The Effect of Your Security as a Child

Attachments to your mother and father are the first links you know. The research on attachment makes it very clear that the security of these links affects the security of all your other links.[8] If your first links with your mother and father were not secure, you are probably insecure now. Approximately 40 percent of adults feel insecure in their close relationships.

Insecure links are probably the greatest predictor of an undervalued self. Secure links set you up to see the world in terms of linking. You expect other people to like you, and you see your world as reasonably safe because you can count on others for help. Insecure links, on the other hand, set you up to see the world in terms of ranking. You expect others not to like you, you rank yourself low, and you feel that no one will be your ally or stand up for you when you are facing a challenge.

Insecurity means that your first experience as a child was of ranking when it should have been linking. Adults always rank higher than children in that they control a child's life. But ideally the child senses that the power being exerted over him or her is in the service of love, and that makes all the difference. If there is no love behind the power, as is the case when a parent does not care to foster a secure attachment, the child feels only the parent's power, his or her own low rank and powerlessness, and a sense of continual defeat. Not surprisingly, chronic depression is a very common result of an insecure attachment. The feeling of defeat that very young children experience when their needs are unmet seems to send them into the defeat response of depression, which never goes away entirely.

Although you may not remember what your first link was like, you can get a strong sense of its nature from observing your behavior today. In considering your first attachments, especially an insecure one, remember again that you are not doing this to blame but to understand why you undervalue yourself so that you can correct this tendency. Maybe your parents were simply too busy or stressed — or were poorly parented themselves.[9]

There are two types of insecurity: anxious and avoidant. If you are insecure, you may find that your type varies from situation to situation. You will tend to feel anxious when you feel lower in rank and avoidant when you feel higher. Still, you should be able to identify your prevailing attitude.

Secure

If you are secure, as an adult you find it relatively easy to get close to others. You are comfortable depending on them and having them depend on you. You do not worry very much about being abandoned or controlled by those who say they love you. When you need to use a self-protection, you probably don't use blaming, inflating, or projecting, which tend to be most distressing to others.

Anxious Insecure

If you are the anxious insecure type, you tend to idealize those with whom you form links and fear they will lose interest in you. When you were a child, your parents were probably inconsistent or very conditional in their love, so your best recourse was to undervalue yourself relative to them and try to please them. As an adult you tend to rank yourself within a linking relationship and see yourself as having little power to decide whether the link will continue.

You find it unusually painful to say good-bye to someone you care about, even if you know you will see him or her again soon—or even immediately if you wished. Consciously or unconsciously, you feel you have no control over the separation and are powerless to prevent someone from abandoning you. Although insecure people of either type use all the self-protections more, you most often use noncompeting, for you try to avoid ranking and its dangers, even though it is so much on your mind unconsciously.

Avoidant Insecure

If you are the avoidant insecure type, it can be harder to admit to insecurity, because the essence of this strategy is to ignore your need to link. You may say that linking relationships are not that important to you. If someone does become important to you, you may try to be the one who controls the length of any separations. For example, when a friend calls wanting to get together, you may not return the call right away. You may not know why. That is simply the way you like it—not to seem to care as much as the other does. But you know you do care, because if this same friend has not called for a while, you are the one who makes the call. Once the other responds, however, you may back off from scheduling a time to meet. All of this can be unconscious, of course, but it is a way to have more power.

As an avoidant insecure person, besides avoiding links and trying to act as if you don't need others, you probably try to rank yourself higher in other ways. Your parents were probably almost entirely in ranking mode, using power without much love, so you may have been neglected or abused physically or emotionally. You often use the self-protections of overachieving and inflating to avoid the shame you felt and still feel unconsciously about having been treated this way. By focusing on having a high rank, you also avoid the danger of needing others. For you, others cannot be relied on and could even use any need you show in order to control you.

If you find that you have an insecure attachment of either type, you can still become secure in adulthood, although it is much harder and slower to make this shift after childhood. This book aims to help you become an "earned secure" adult.

If you have an insecure attachment style, turn to your childhood and adulthood trauma charts and add another check next to all of the ones already there. Again, this will give you a visual representation of the impact of an insecure attachment style on your experience of traumatic events.

Kit's Anxious Insecurity and Her Undervalued Self

Kit, twenty-nine, was sent to me by a psychiatrist who was treating her recurring depressions with medication but who thought that psychotherapy might help, too. Kit's biggest problem was persuading Dennis, the man she had lived with since she was twenty, to finally marry her. Dennis had never ruled out marriage, but he had never proposed.

Kit had been in love with one boy or another since starting kindergarten. She had had many crushes on teachers, camp counselors, and even doctors if they were unusually kind. Kindness seemed to trigger these crushes, followed by endless hours of anxious but exciting fantasies of being noticed by the loved one and having her love returned.

Life with Dennis was not all that blissful, however. Initially he had been very kind, but now he disappointed her. He drank a bit too much and spent a lot of time hanging out with his friends or going to sports events that did not interest her. But she had never seriously considered leaving him.

Kit told me she thought she had had a happy childhood and a close relationship with her mother, but she did admit that her parents had been on the verge of divorce when her mother discovered she was pregnant with her. The marriage lasted another two years but was never happy. Her mother was mainly stalling so she could finish a nursing program and be able to support Kit, who spent most of the day and many nights with her grandmother. That might have worked out well, but when Kit was nine months old, her grandmother was diagnosed with cancer.

At this point Kit's four aunts took turns having her at their home while her mother worked. They were all busy with their own families or careers, and Kit would have been a real burden had she not been "such a quiet, well-behaved child." The only problem was that she had nightmares.

Kit remembered longing to be alone with her mother in their studio apartment rather than at some relative's house. But those times with her mother were agonizingly rare because, although Kit did not know it, her mother was dating in the hope of remarrying. She did remarry when Kit was five, and by the time Kit was seven, she had new twin brothers.

While the birth of the twins might have been a happy event for another child, or at most a stressful one, it was a trauma for Kit. Her nightmares increased, and she recalled feeling either blank or anxious for no reason. But she could never admit her pain because she was expected to become Mom's Little Helper, even as she watched the babies receive that early, adoring love from her mother that she had never had. It became clear to Kit that what she had thought was a happy childhood filled with love had not quite been that after all. Her mother and her other caregivers had been absent or distracted most of the time.

Those first years had left Kit with an anxious insecurity about close relationships. Her early inconsistent mothering had left her starved for love, which she imagined receiving lavishly in her comforting fantasies. But this was not a realistic image of a close relationship, so she was easily disappointed by Dennis.

At the same time, Kit was so terrified of having no one that she could not express her disappointment. For her this was no longer a linking relationship but a ranking one in which she had the lower rank. Her undervalued self ruled her life, as if she were stuck in the time when she was very small and blamed herself, as children do, for the frightening fact that no one seemed to want her around.

Her undervalued self caused Dennis to undervalue her, too, and left her in no position to stand up for her rights. As we worked together, however, she allowed me to meet some of those early needs and grieve for the little girl whose suffering was never her fault. This gave her the courage to see Dennis more objectively. As it turned out, Dennis was quite ready to settle down once he saw a more confident and less critical Kit, who was ready to move on if he did not wish to marry. Today Kit's depression is under control, and she and Dennis have two children. As she says, "We are in a good place."

YOUR TRAUMAS AND EMOTIONAL SCHEMAS

How does all of this add up? How does your innate potential to undervalue yourself, your history of trauma, your sensitivity, the effects of prejudice against you, and your insecurity manifest in your daily life? For every past trauma you've experienced, you have developed an emotional schema,[10] the whole bundle of thoughts, feelings, memories, sensations, social emotions, self-protections, and innate response tendencies that gather around a trauma. When anything associated with the trauma occurs—a memory, a situation, a conversation—the entire schema comes up.

Emotional schemas serve to keep everything about a trauma

well organized in case of an emergency. As you now know, much of your life is devoted to avoiding the feelings of depression and shame associated with trauma, which lead to the undervalued self. You are highly prepared to avoid both the physical and the psychological pain of repeating a trauma. An emotional schema is the mechanism that helps you avoid such pain by turning anything that seems like that first trauma into a danger sign. An emotional schema is a huge defense.

Further, because the memories and feelings stored in your emotional schema are so painful, they are kept hidden. Out of sight, they can continue to grow and, like a black hole, assimilate more and more of your life without your knowing it. Experiences are added to the bundle if they seem to be even a little bit like the first trauma, and any of these experiences can trigger protective responses. These responses would be appropriate if you were about to be hurt, but that's usually not the case. And since most of your traumas involved powerlessness, defeat, or being abused by the power of those with higher rank, your emotional schema always switches you to ranking, the undervalued self, and the self-protections that have become part of that schema.

The nature of your emotional schemas depends on your traumas. Betrayal leads to jealousy, abuse leads to general mistrust, being powerless to prevent a separation leads to deep fears of loss, and so forth. The specific contents of your emotional schemas determine what will trigger them as well as the self-protections you typically employ when they are triggered. For example, you may fear betrayal when you are with two other women because in girlhood your two best friends turned on you. Your typical self-protections are minimizing, noncompeting, and projecting. Or you may feel particularly powerless about a separation because you were often left alone as a child, and you protect yourself most often with overachieving and inflating. In addition, insecure attachments, the experience of prejudice, and high sensitivity spawn emotional schemas of their own.

Emotional schemas are too wired in to ever go away completely. You can only hope that they will be triggered less often and stay in the triggered state for a shorter time. In fact, emotional schemas are the building blocks of your personality. They affect you deeply, so they account for much of who you are and what drives you. But they can be very damaging to linking. Since traumas usually involve relationships, emotional schemas are most often triggered in relationships, especially your closest ones. Here are some common emotional schemas generated by past experiences that may cause trouble in current relationships.

• *Jealousy.* It might be triggered when someone you care about merely mentions being fond of someone else or when you know he or she will spend time with others without you along.

• *Dread of separation.* It could arise from simply saying good-bye or watching someone you love pack a suitcase.

• *Fear of blatant physical, sexual, or verbal abuse.* This emotional schema may be triggered by raised voices, a sexual overture, or merely a sudden movement toward you.

• *Feeling controlled or exploited.* This schema may be triggered by someone giving you instructions, borrowing a possession and forgetting to return it, or using your good ideas without remembering to give you full credit.

• *Fear of not being a "real man" or "real woman."* If you are a man, this fear could be triggered by someone's comments about your sensitivity or by a woman's seeming indifference. If you are a woman, this emotional schema could be triggered by comments about your being unusually ambitious, unmarried, or childless, or having only one child.

• *Fear that another person will make it impossible to realize your dream.* This emotional schema can arise in a close relationship when, for example, the other wants to spend money that now cannot be saved toward your goal.

• *The absolute necessity of being submissive and pleasing others.* This can be triggered by the mere possibility of someone being irritated with you or having a need different from yours.

How bad can an emotional schema get? Well, I once called my husband, who loves me very much, "the embodiment of all evil." How is that for an example of confusing your current situation with an abuse of power in your past? I am extremely fortunate that our relationship did not end then and there.

What Does a Triggered Emotional Schema Feel Like?

When one of your emotional schemas is triggered, it can seem that you hardly know yourself. Because these schemas are the result of trauma, they are dissociated—not part of our day-to-day consciousness—until they are triggered. Even though they are a deeply personal part of you, they can take you by surprise. "Who, me? Jealous? Never." Later you may feel fresh shame about how you behaved and undervalue yourself for your "craziness."

For example, suppose you have identified that you were bullied as a child, a trauma that often left you feeling defeated and powerless. That trauma was the seed for an emotional schema that recorded every instance of social rejection, and even every time when you feared being rejected. At school you lacked confidence, so you were not especially popular. Your family moved several times, and while for some children that would not be a problem, for you those experiences of being unknown among strangers only added to your emotional schema of social rejection.

Now you are good at your job, have a strong social network of friends and family, and generally enjoy life. But every time you walk into a party full of strangers, you become so unbearably shy that you can't think of anything to say. You stand there like a statue. You might think you would stop going to such events, but each time, your shyness surprises you, given all your success and happiness now. It seems unlike you. You feel frustrated and ashamed afterward about the "silly" way you behaved.

As the example illustrates, emotional schemas can cause all sorts of specific troubles. One problem they all cause, however, is that when they are triggered they destroy any linking that could occur; what happens is that you stop being with the person you are actually with and enter a world in which the trauma is happening again, along with everything else that you associate with that first trauma. It began with bullying, but it spread to fearing defeat and rejection in many different settings. So when you enter the room, you are once again the new kid in school who was bullied and as a result lacked confidence and suffered more than most kids do. In this drama you are reliving, "no one wants to be friends with me." You have written a ranking script, and the other person is only an actor, even though many people in the room might like to link with you. But your role in this drama is to be silent, no matter how friendly someone is, and the other's role is to reject you, no matter how he or she really feels about you.

Not only can emotional schemas prevent links, but they can make people who are close begin to hate each other in the moment and possibly forever. This may happen when, for example, one person, who has been betrayed, develops a jealousy schema, and the only solution seems to be controlling the other's behavior at all times. It is amazing how thoroughly a schema can take over. But it all makes sense if you remember that the purpose of the schema is to be sure you avoid anything that could lead to further trauma.

WORKING WITH WHAT YOU HAVE LEARNED

In this chapter you assessed how much you undervalue yourself, identified the traumas in your past, and started to think about the emotional schemas that developed as a result. You have seen that these traumas and emotional schemas almost always involve defeat or powerlessness and the accompanying depression and shame. You also learned about and made note of whether prejudice, high sensitivity, or an insecure attachment increased the impact of your traumas.

Appreciating the Full Impact of Trauma on Your Undervalued Self

Take this opportunity to review what you have learned about yourself. You may need considerable time to reflect. As you do the following tasks, entering your answers in your journal, do not rush. Think before you write.

1. Look back at your score on the How Much Do You Undervalue Yourself? self-assessment near the start of this chapter. To what degree have you suffered and missed out on opportunities because of this undervaluing? Think about this systematically by considering how undervaluing yourself affected your childhood, both at home and at school. For example, was your physical development affected because you lacked social confidence or had a fear of being awkward under pressure and so did not play sports? Was your academic development impacted because you did poorly on tests or were afraid to ask questions? Was your social development limited because you were shy or angry with everyone? Be as specific as you can. Then turn to high school, romantic relationships, friendships, career choices, and career advancement. What would you have liked to do but did not because you undervalued yourself?

2. Consider the traumas listed and the density of check marks on your Childhood Trauma and Adulthood Trauma charts. What does this mean for you and your undervalued self? Generally people find that the "darker" their chart is with items and check marks, the more they undervalue themselves.

Handling Your Emotional Schemas

Although emotional schemas are too basic to your personality to ever go away completely, your goal is to prevent them from being triggered so often and, when they are, to be able to identify them as soon as possible. To do this you need to become very familiar with your emotional schemas. Schemas can be hard to see, so you will want to try getting to know yours in several different ways.

1. For each trauma in your life, look for the schema that resulted. For example, if you were suddenly laid off by a company you had been told was doing well, by management that seemed to give little thought to workers' needs, on the next job you will be vigilant and suspicious even when you have no reason to be. This schema has to be there, even if you have learned to avoid the trauma most of the time. In the above example, you might have even started your own business in order to avoid being dependent on an employer.

2. For each trauma, consider what situations are related to it and thus trigger a particular schema. In the last example, you may have avoided the original trauma by being self-employed, but now you are anxious about your biggest clients suddenly "firing" you. The emotional schema is still there, but it has broadened to include any situations that are remotely similar.

3. Think about the times when you behaved as if an emotional schema had been triggered, times when you were "not yourself." You became silent or argumentative, and your voice was intense, whether too loud or strangely soft. You spoke in absolutes ("always," "never," everything black or white) and could not understand why others did not see the situation as you did. You felt a wave of rage, fear, grief, or some other strong emotion that was more than the situation seemed to call for. You treated people unfairly or were too suspicious or fearful of them or loved or missed them to an absurd degree.

4. As you explore your schemas, ask for help from those who know you well. Once you explain the idea of emotional schemas, they will probably be able to tell you all about yours and what triggers them. But warn them to be gentle. And try to stay objective, like a scientist looking for answers, so that a schema is not triggered again.

When you feel an emotional schema being triggered, you now have conscious knowledge to counter the unconscious forces. You know what is happening. Sometimes it helps to think of the schema as an autonomous person inside of you, whom you want to meet and calm down before it gets all excited; you can even try closing the door on it. Give it a name, such as Mr. Silent Statue or the Jealous Nut. You can reason, bribe, beg, flatter, negotiate a compromise, or do anything else that will keep it from insisting on your doing or saying something you will regret later.

For example, if you are suddenly certain that your girlfriend has been seeing someone else, you can tell the Jealous Nut that you will ask your girlfriend about this again and will carefully watch her expression, but you will not permit snooping through her e-mails when she's not home. That is against your principles and would truly give her a reason to leave you.

A History of Your Undervalued Self

Write one or two pages of personal history summarizing what you have realized about how much you undervalue yourself and the type and intensity of trauma you have experienced, including the role of prejudice, sensitivity, or insecure attachment. What emotional schemas did you develop in response? This history will be important to refer back to in later chapters as you work in depth with the feelings that arise in you now because of these traumas.

CHAPTER FOUR

Healing the Undervalued Self by Linking

You now know the innate causes of your undervalued self and why it easily leads to a sense of defeat, depression, and shame. Because you understand the six self-protections you use to avoid that pain, you can see your undervalued self better. You have identified the traumas and emotional schemas that further contribute to your undervalued self and cause you to use these self-protections even more. You are now ready to take action to heal your undervalued self.

The typical approach is to *raise* your *low* self-esteem. However, you can see that this approach is based on ranking your self-worth against that of others. When you undervalue yourself, you are already relying too much on ranking to navigate through life, so focusing more on your rank is not the solution.

The solution is linking, which is as hardwired in our brains as ranking and undervaluing ourselves are, and it is right there inside of you as the antidote. To use it, you will learn to switch from ranking to linking in the moment. It will not always be easy, but it is the place to start.

Ranking has its place, even in healing the undervalued self. It drives you to compete when you ought to compete and helps you stand up for yourself in conflicts and maintain your boundaries, skills that are always important if you undervalue yourself. But while ranking is elemental, it does not *heal* an undervalued self. The rule for healing is: "Where ranking was, let linking be."

WHY LINKING HEALS THE UNDERVALUED SELF AS NOTHING ELSE CAN

Switching from ranking to linking takes the undervalued self entirely out of the picture, because it is only when we are ranking that we compare our overall value to that of others and rank ourselves too low. Once we are linking, we are primed to care and be cared for mutually, not unequally.

Sometimes you cannot end ranking and would not want to. But even in ranking situations you can still increase your linking; for example, you can make friends with your opponents in a tennis match or chat with the others waiting to audition. This kind of linking has a remarkable effect on the undervalued self. Generally, when you switch to linking, fear of failure moves to the background, because you are feeling connected, not judged. With victory and defeat irrelevant for the moment you will not slide into feeling the defeat response of depression and shame or alter your overall sense of self-worth downward. In fact, research finds that when people switch from ranking to linking, either in the laboratory or on their own, it has the following effects:

- Raises self-esteem.[1]
- Makes people more open-minded.[2]
- Reduces prejudice. In experiments, when people are made to feel inferior or superior (focused on ranking), their prejudice is above average, but when they are focused on linking, their prejudice falls below average.[3]

• Makes people under stress seek help from others rather than spend time blaming themselves for their situation.[4]

• Moves people to help someone they do not know, with less fear of being upset by getting involved.[5]

Isn't Linking a Matter of Introversion and Extroversion?

Most people think that extroverts care more about linking and are better at it, but linking is even more important to introverts, because they focus much more on the quality of their linking than on the quantity.[6] Introverts would rather have deep, open, one-on-one conversations with people they know well than meet strangers, spend time in large groups, or have many friends with whom they spend less in-depth time.

That preference, however, leaves introverts more vulnerable to feeling ineffective in groups or with strangers. Rather than linking in these situations, as extroverts do, introverts remain quiet or stand aside. Even if it is their choice, nonparticipation can quickly lead to feeling low in rank or even rejected. Introverts' social skills can become rusty, too, so they often feel defeated in larger groups or during first meetings, and the undervalued self firmly holds them in its grip. Introverts can and must learn to feel competent in linking, even in social situations they do not particularly enjoy, if they want to avoid undervaluing and make new friends as others are naturally lost due to moves or changes in interests.

If you are an extrovert yet you undervalue yourself, superficial linking may be relatively easy, but you still privately rank yourself low against others, including those silent, wise-looking introverts. As you know, a person can seem confident on the outside and yet be struggling and feeling worthless on the inside. You may chat away, appearing to link, and still be afraid that you have said too much, argued, been too pushy or overly friendly, or kept the conversation too superficial. At these times, you are ranking yourself even though you seem to be linking, so you, too, could use more confidence about your skills.

LEARNING TO LINK WITH SKILL AND GRACE

Linking may be innate, but when you feel unsure of yourself it helps to consciously keep some points in mind. Whether you are linking with a stranger, an acquaintance you want to be closer to, or an old friend, the process can be divided into getting started and strengthening. In both steps there are a few points to remember.

The most universal way to link is to offer food, drink, or gifts. You can do this to initiate a link or to maintain it. My husband offers a wrapped candy to his seatmate on a long flight. He's planning to work, not talk, but the candy is a small link that improves the trip.

Touching, if you are sure it will be appropriate, can also create an instant link. When you greet, try an old-fashioned, truly warm handshake and "I'm so glad to meet you" or "What a pleasure to see you again." When someone you like is having a hard time, think about how, in this person's place, you would welcome a sympathetic touch on the shoulder or arm, and risk doing this for your friend.

Today we most commonly link with words. Compliments work well, but inviting a self-disclosure may be particularly appreciated. For example, suppose you have talked before with a coworker about his worry over his teenage son. You can initiate or strengthen your next linking by simply asking, "How's it going with that teenager of yours? Is he still keeping you on your toes?"

Be alert to the questions you are asked and give a personal answer if one is invited. If you were the one with the teenager and were asked the same question, you might say, "I think a little better, although he has a birthday coming up, and my deepest, most hopeless wish is that he was turning thirty instead of seventeen." The more details you exchange in conversation like this, the more you activate each other's linking behaviors and become better friends.

Appropriateness is part of linking, too. In conversation, this means you care about the other's needs. Do not self-disclose when the other is rushing or otherwise not in the mood. Do not insist on giving a gift, doing a favor, helping with a move, hugging, or taking someone to lunch when she has declined, just as you would not insist that someone help you or do you a favor. Again, appropriateness is a gift in itself, showing that you are responsive to and respectful of the other.

Paradoxical as it may seem, linking is not helped by merging your interests with your friend's or by the two of you agreeing on everything and being shocked when you do not—for example, "I can't believe you don't like this—I love it." It's also not about letting the other always have his or her way, saying, "Oh, whatever you want. I don't care." Two people cannot link if they are not allowed to be separate individuals.

Linking Behaviors

- Offer food.
- Invite self-disclosure and listen attentively.
- Do a favor or offer help.
- Give a compliment.
- Ask for help without seeming generally helpless.
- Give a gift.
- Touch in a friendly way.
- Shake hands.
- Show sincere interest.
- Say something caring.
- Reveal something personal.
- Acknowledge the link. For example, "It's nice we're friends."
- Respect each other's different opinions rather than forcing agreement.

Initiating Linking

If you undervalue yourself, the first step in linking is often the hardest, because you naturally fear rejection. But the truth is, most of the time people want to link with you. Here are four things you can remember to do even when rattled or stuck in ranking mode. I call them SEEK: *Smile, make Eye contact, Empathize*, and *show Kindness*. A smile is a universal expression used to initiate a link, while eye contact, neither staring nor looking away, signals equality. On the phone, the equivalent would be using a cheerful voice initially and then matching the other's tone and intonations. These first two steps may seem obvious, but they are easy to forget when you are stuck in ranking and feeling worthless.

As you engage in conversation, show some empathy for the other's feelings. For example, if the other says, "I'm roasting," even before considering how to solve the problem, you might say, "Yeah, I can imagine. You had to wait in line in the sun, didn't you?"

You would *not* say, "So am I" or "Why don't you take off your coat, then?" Those remarks are not empathizing. The first shifts the attention back to you, and the second implies that this is the other's problem, not yours. Better to say, "Anything I can do?"

Finally, show kindness. Remember, part of linking is wanting to know and meet the other's needs if you can. So you must be attuned to the other's actual needs or ask about them; you should not assume you know and risk being inappropriate and controlling, which puts you right back to ranking. Instead you could ask, "Can I get you some water?" Again, it may seem obvious, yet it is easy to overlook opportunities to be kind.

How to Initiate Linking: SEEK

- *Smile*. Obvious, but so easy to forget.
- Make *Eye* contact. Not meeting another's eyes is a sign of low rank and signals ranking, not linking.
- *Empathize*. Try to understand the other fully and express your understanding.
- Show *Kindness*. Do something thoughtful or helpful.

To initiate a real link rather than a mere greeting, you should continue talking. Any conversation that is not about ranking is good, but some topics can provide a stronger link. People usually love to be asked more about their children, partner, profession, or childhood once they have mentioned any of these. Be sure to follow up a question with sincere interest. Asking another question also shows that interest. A question followed by indifference to the answer can give the sense that you were only acting interested for the sake of ranking.

Good Questions plus Follow-ups

- I see you're married [if you see a ring]. How did you two meet? So how did you know he was the one?
- Did you grow up around here? What was it like to be a kid here?
- I hear you like to travel. Been anywhere interesting lately? Would you go back there?
- I overheard that you own a [type of dog or cat]. What's its name? What are they like as pets?
- What do you do when you aren't at this convention [party, etc.]? [Avoid asking specifically about a person's profession, as some people do not have one.] What's it like, doing that?

Linking Through Giving

In all linking there are two modes: giving and receiving. One talks, the other listens. One offers food, the other eats. One compliments, the other feels good. These two roles are not about rank, even though the one receiving seems, for the moment, to be more important. But giving either alternates or is determined by the recipient's need to receive right now, not by rank.

The essence of linking is giving something specifically meant to please the other person or meet his or her specific needs. Sometimes we give for ranking reasons: pleasing others because we want to gain status in their eyes or because they rank higher. Giving to link is different.

For example, suppose you and a coworker are stuck working on a Saturday. You initiate linking with SEEK, by smiling, looking into her eyes, noticing she is a little upset, and empathizing when she says she's missing her son's soccer game. As an act of kindness, you bring her a cup of coffee made just the way she likes it.

Having made this successful initial link with your coworker, if you want to make a deeper connection, you'll have to GIVE: *Get emotionally involved, develop Insight, Verbalize that,* and *Empathize.*

In this case the first step, getting involved emotionally, would mean reflecting a moment on how you feel about your coworker's situation. You might think, "Gee, she's got her kid on her mind. She's really missing being at that game. That's sad. I know how that feels—I have to travel all the time and miss my kids' events." You move on to insight. "I'll bet she'd at least like to talk about her son the soccer player."

All of this has gone on in your head — this is what we mean when we say someone is "thoughtful." Now you verbalize your sense of what is happening to her: "That must feel pretty lousy, not being at the game. How long has he been playing? How's his team doing?" Expressing your insight that she needs to talk is a very important step. Often you may feel emotionally involved, have insight, and truly empathize, but if you do not show and say all of this, you lose your chance to deepen the linking, a risk for introverts, especially.

Finally, there can be no successful giving without empathy. To empathize is to identify with the other and understand what he or she is going through and feeling but without shifting the attention to yourself. So empathizing simply means understanding how someone feels. Fortunately it's easy—it's in our genes, as is the desire to help. When we want to link, we can never empathize too much. In the case of your coworker, you might empathize by saying, "I hear you. It sucks to miss a kid's game. You must be dreading the hour when the game actually starts without you."

Strengthening the Link: GIVE

- *Get emotionally involved*. First, think about what is actually going on for the other and how you feel about it.
- *Develop Insight*. Have some good ideas about what the other needs or wants.
- *Verbalize*. Use talking as a way of giving, so that the linking is clear. Express your own feeling as a result of being emotionally involved. If appropriate, tell the other what you would like to do for him or her and ask if you can go ahead.
- *Empathize*. At every stage, try to observe your interaction from the other person's point of view.

Linking by Receiving

Linking is usually thought of as active. You have to like, learn about, and help the other. But to be skilled at linking, you must also allow yourself to be liked, understood, and helped. You have to enjoy having your needs met, too. It sounds easy, but when you undervalue yourself, you often feel that you do not deserve such kind attention. And in a culture that emphasizes ranking, receiving linking can be viewed negatively as "being dependent" or "acting like a baby." There are plenty of words for giving to another: being kind, altruistic, devoted, generous, loving, or concerned. But only the Japanese have a good word for receiving: *amae*.[7] It roughly means that one can "depend on or presume another's love," "bask in another's indulgence," or "feel cherished."

If you doubt your own worth, *amae* may seem even more challenging than giving; paradoxically, you will have to work actively at passively receiving. And caution is okay. But at the right time, even small doses of feeling cherished can work wonders to alleviate the undervalued self.

It is easiest to receive when someone simply treats you with loving kindness. But sometimes the person offering help in a general way needs to hear what you specifically need right now. Try asking yourself the following three questions to assess whether it is appropriate to relax and receive or ask for help:

• Is the offer right for you? Is this the right place, time, or person to meet your need? For example, your brother may be excellent for helping you move but not the best person to turn to for emotional soothing.

• Is it right for the other person? Or is your friend preoccupied with a need of his own today?

• Is it your turn? Although in linking relationships keeping score is taboo, there is still a rhythm to it, and asking yourself this question can help you realize when your own giving has been more than adequate to allow you to receive now.

Imagine meeting a friend for dinner. As you approach the table and hear him humming to himself, you reflect on how cheerful, kind, and full of good energy he always is — "unlike you," your undervalued self says. Especially tonight, you are glum, irritable, and exhausted, and you feel that you will bring him down. In this situation you need to feel that your current mood is okay and that you don't have to change it to be accepted.

He says, "Hi! How are you tonight?"

Rather than brushing off the question with "I'm okay," you decide to be more intimate by expressing some of how you feel. "I'm exhausted."

Your friend looks sympathetic, so you say a bit more. "I think I've felt this way the last couple of days." You have a sudden insight. "Maybe it's about my dad."

Your friend asks you to sit down and tell him more. "What's wrong with your dad?"

"He called on Wednesday. He never complains to me, but he said he's got this cough that's not going away and they're doing tests. What's a cough, you know? But it didn't start with a cold, and he sounded worried."

Your friend now has a choice to continue empathizing or to end your sharing. You notice that he invites you to continue to receive. "Gee, that's a little scary. Why don't we order, and then we can talk about it?"

You agree. As you place your order, you notice that you are feeling a little better already.

This is what you have just done:

• Accepted how you are feeling.
• Revealed it.
• Noticed that your friend was in the right place to give to you and really believed it.
• Continued to reveal and receive sympathy until you were satisfied.

When the undervalued self is triggered by some situation, another way to switch to linking through receiving is to ask for input from friends or colleagues who will be truthful, but in general feel very positively toward you. How do they honestly view your situation? For example, you carpool to work with someone in the same department, and you know you are friends by now. One day things have gone badly at work, and on the way home you feel that you must be about the worst pharmacist on the planet. You accept your mood, reveal it, and hear from her that she thinks you are doing a great job. She's offered suggestions when you did need to improve, so you believe her when she says the two customers who were mad about waiting looked like people who would be mean to anyone, and the insurance rep who was sharp with you was just having a bad day. That's all.

Sometimes you can let your need be known through a third party. For example, Phyllis, who often felt the presence of her undervalued self, noticed that she was feeling especially unsure of herself at work. She feared that her boss, Houston, did not really like her. She knew her fear was irrational, but she could not help it. A few days before her birthday, John, a friend of Houston's, stopped at her desk. She and John had a good link. He knew her birthday was coming and said that he guessed Houston would be taking her out to lunch.

Phyllis decided to risk the truth, knowing full well that Houston might hear about it. Half-jokingly, she said, "No, he and I don't do lunch. I think he feels he sees too much of me as it is."

John was taken aback. "That's not my impression. He speaks very highly of you."

That afternoon her boss not only asked Phyllis if she would have lunch with him on her birthday but invited her to a small get-together at his home that weekend. They have spent many good times together in the years since.

It is essential to alternate giving and receiving, especially in a new relationship. If the balance is uneven, it starts to feel like ranking again: one gives all the time. Once a relationship is established, the giving and receiving can be decided by each one's level of need. Do not be in such a rush to give back to the other that you cut short your receiving. Thus, when the other says, "It sounds like you've had a terrible day," you do not have to respond immediately with "I know you've had an equally bad one." And if you are the giver, do not rush to share that you have had the same problem, which can seem like a need to receive rather than a desire to give. It also keeps the link superficial by cutting short deeper discussion. When the other says, "I'm worried about my mother—she's going to hear today about her biopsy," do not empathize by saying, "I know how that feels, because last year my favorite aunt went through the same thing." Rather, say something like "Oh, my gosh, you must be on pins and needles, waiting to hear." You can share your own experience later if it still seems relevant, which often turns out not to be the case.

HOW TO AVOID THE UNDERVALUED SELF WHEN LINKING FAILS

It is risky to link with someone you do not know well—especially if you reveal your own need to receive. But even trying to give can leave you very vulnerable to shame if the other does not respond. Suppose, in the example of your confession of being exhausted and worried about your father, your friend's response had been "Well, dinner should perk you up" or, worse, "It seems like you're always tired." Or suppose you agreed after dinner to meet again soon, and then months went by without hearing from your friend.

You need to try very hard to consider the legitimate reasons that might be behind a lack of empathy or an outright rejection. Sometimes, of course, the problems are practical. Perhaps your friend has too much else going on. So try to stay in linking mode and empathize with him.

Sometimes you cannot imagine any excuses for the other person. If you have an emotional schema around rejection, it can be especially hard to prevent ranking and the undervalued self from taking over. You need to become an expert on what might be going on inside others when they hurt your feelings or make you feel ashamed in some way. There are at least four possibilities: you are in a ranking environment, the other is using one of the self-protections, you are dealing with the other's avoidant attachment style, or you have triggered an emotional schema in the other.

Don't Let a Ranking Environment Get You Down

When you have tried to link and been rejected, greeted coolly, viewed with suspicion, or judged purely on your work abilities, think about whether you are simply in a ranking environment. Others may be so focused on ranking that they cannot see linking even while it is happening. In some cultures ranking is encouraged at all times, not just in some situations. Nations have cultures, and so do families, businesses, organizations, and schools. In some, success is determined mostly by your linking skills: your kindness, cooperation, politeness, teamwork, avoidance of conflict, and sharing of knowledge. Other cultures strongly encourage ranking-oriented social instincts: competition, efficiency, effectiveness, pride, and victory. Still others, of course, try to strike a balance.

In an overly ranking culture, others may be cool when you try to link because they are suspicious of your motives. At a party you may think you are linking, only to learn later that others were ranking you on your linking skills — "great networker" or "social dud." Or they may link only for ranking purposes. They form an alliance with you, then let you down later. Being rejected or allowing yourself to be fooled can lead you to undervalue yourself.

Worst of all, perhaps, your linking behaviors, such as offering a gift or a compliment, may be mistaken as a sign of low rank and submission, especially if a little of your undervalued self is visible in your tone of voice or body language. If you realize that your effort to link is only making you feel low in rank, it is time to stop and reassess your values versus those of the people around you. A desire to link does not make you inferior in any way. But stop offering your friendship. "Love conquers all" except when your offer becomes the other's conquest.

In a ranking culture you really have to work to appreciate what you are up against and not blame yourself, since this type of culture encourages you to do just that. Trust that real linking does exist somewhere, not just over the rainbow. Your best hope is to try linking elsewhere.

When You Encounter the Self-Protections in Others

If you have tried to link and suddenly felt your undervalued self taking over, you may have encountered someone else's shame and use of one of the self-protections. For example, through no fault of your own you arrive very late to do some shopping with a new friend. You apologize sincerely but your friend still feels, without being aware of it, that you were late because you feel superior—that your time is more valuable than hers. She is in a ranking mood. Unless she is able to figure this out and tell you, she may minimize with "I don't mind" or act like the saintly non-competitor: "Things like that never bother me." But then she is cool toward you for the rest of the day, and you feel rejected, a terrible person. If she is more volatile, she might say, "I can't believe you were so late—you've ruined the whole day." She uses blaming and you feel the shame.

However she handles her sense that you must not care about her, the shame ball is bouncing between the two of you, and since the other certainly does not want to feel discounted, defeated, and ashamed, the ball is being tossed to you. The answer, as always in a basically sound link, is knowing how to link your way through rather than being drawn in. Even if your friend cannot respond by linking, you will feel better if you continue to link, on the assumption that she is protecting herself from feeling that you are ranking her low. After ten minutes of the silent treatment from her, you might say, "I'm starting to wonder if you're a little angry after all for my being late. It would have bummed me out a lot. But I think we like each other enough that you could get mad and our friendship would survive it."

The six self-protections often crop up in small, fleeting ways that barely affect the conversation, yet you may feel a subtle shift toward feeling guilty, stupid, or impolite. For example, you say, "Congratulations on your award." The other, wanting to avoid the shame of seeming conceited, uses noncompeting: "Oh, well, they had to give it to somebody, and I guess this year it was my turn." Or you and a friend choose a restaurant, but as you enter you say, "This restaurant sure is noisy." Feeling that you are blaming him, he says, "Well, you were the one who said you liked the ambience." You let it go, but at least you understand what is behind the blaming tone of his remark.

When you do speak up, the very best approach is not only to link but to do so by addressing the underlying shame. You let the other know you are not sitting in judgment; you would have felt the same way. You show you still like the person, perhaps mentioning something you especially value about him or her. You indicate your mutual relationship and history. "We've been mad at each other before—we'll get through it."

So when your friend says, "Oh, well, they had to give it to somebody, and I guess this year it was my turn," you might say, "Don't worry, I won't think you're uppity for having a little pride—you really deserve this recognition. I'd certainly be bursting with pride."

When you say the restaurant is noisy and your friend blames you for the choice, don't accept the blame or hand it back. "Neither of us knew it would be so noisy, but it sounds like we agree we don't want to eat here."

Sometimes you will find yourself trying to link with someone whose entire life is based on one of the six self-protections, such as overachievement, noncompetition, or inflation. Such people are so stuck in ranking as they struggle to avoid the powerful pull of their undervalued self that they almost always bring out the undervalued self in others. Your best defense is to recognize what is going on and stay in a linking frame of mind, so that you feel sympathy for the other's "stuckness" rather than rejected and inferior.

Isabel Protects Herself Six Ways

Imagine that you and your partner are taking a hike with another couple, Pat and Isabel. Your partner knows Pat well from playing softball on the same team for years, and they have fallen behind as they talk over the last game. You know they hope that you and Isabel, Pat's new girlfriend, will bond so that the four of you can do more things together.

You have heard that Isabel is having a difficult time. Her mother died unexpectedly this year, and Isabel has recently been diagnosed with a heart problem that may require surgery. Since she has competed in triathlons for years, you know this must be an especially hard blow. You do not want to upset her if she does not feel like talking about all of this, yet you want to use GIVE if she is open to receiving. That is, you want to get involved, show some interest, and try to understand her. You hope to have some insight and verbalize it so she knows you care. Above all, you are all set to empathize. What you do not know is that Isabel hated her mother, and she competes in triathlons as part of an over-achieving self-protection. This makes her heart problem a source of deep shame. In the following conversation you will hear all six self-protections.

In all innocence you say, "It sounds like you're having a pretty rough year."

"Oh, it's not been so bad." (Minimizing.)

You are thrown off a bit, but then try for some insight: maybe Isabel is minimizing because she doesn't want to be a burden. Should you verbalize some of what she's minimizing? It could take her where she does not want to go, so you are especially gentle.

"I heard about your heart problem—that must take some getting used to."

"Everybody says that, like they expect me to get used to the idea of open-heart surgery. I hate pity." (Blaming you for showing pity, like "everybody" else.)

You say, "Yeah, I think anyone would," and try to continue linking. "I hear you have won two triathlons. What's that like?"

"I don't do things like that in order to win." (Noncompeting.)

You would like to empathize, to show some understanding of the feeling that might be behind these rather unfeeling words. "Sounds like you take some pride in that. For you it's more about fitness?"

"It's more about doing well at whatever I undertake." (Overachieving.)

"You take real pride in doing your best."

"I find pride a bit of a bore, actually." (Inflating: since you apparently get excited by pride, she's showing herself to be better than you.)

You are running out of ideas, so you try your wild card. "We have something in common, you know. I lost my mother when I was in college. It took me three years to feel anything like my old self."

"I'm sorry about your loss. I'm doing pretty good, actually, but it sounds like it almost killed you." (Projecting.)

By now you are probably feeling like a blob of sticky feelings that's been stepped on by a woman of steel. The self-protections were subtle, so mostly you would have recognized them in the moment only by how you felt—stupid for making a big deal of it when she was minimizing, blamed for your "pity," crass for bringing up ranking with someone who never competes, impressed by her overachieving in everything she undertakes, inferior for thinking of pride as anything but a bore, and bewildered by her projection that your mother's death has almost killed you. She threw you her huge shame ball, and you caught it.

Below are some suggestions for linking responses that keep the shame from bouncing between you, although these replies might be difficult to think of in the moment until you become more practiced. And with a tough case like Isabel, you may still be met with even more extreme self-protections. But at least you will be in linking mode throughout, which is the very best protection against shame.

When Isabel indicates that her year really hasn't "been so bad," you could say, "It would be okay if it were bad, wouldn't it?" You are allowing it to be normal to be distressed by this year's events, not ashamed.

When she says, "Everybody says that, like they expect me to get used to the idea of open-heart surgery" and "I hate pity," you did well by normalizing that too: "Anyone would." You could also try some gentle irony: "It sounds like it embarrasses you to have people think you'd be bothered by someone cutting into you."

When Isabel comments, "I don't do things like that in order to win," you could say, "That's a great way to look at triathlons. That way, if your body quits on you, you don't get mad when you've tried your best but still haven't come in first."

When she says, "It's more about doing well at whatever I under-take," you could respond to her overachieving with a glimpse of the love awaiting her in her new relationship: "What a great approach to life, although I can tell Pat would love you even if you were terrible at everything."

When she inflates herself by saying, "I find pride a bit of a bore, actually," you could say (if you still feel this warm toward prickly Isabel), "I think seeing you feel proud would be kind of charming."

And, finally, when Isabel claims, "I'm doing pretty good, actually, but it sounds like it almost killed you," you could reject the projection and invite her to feel the same as anyone else, no better and certainly no worse: "Well, some days I'm like you and I feel pretty good, but on others I'm probably like anyone—I feel horrible."

When the Other Has an Avoidant Attachment Style

As you learned in chapter three, those who are insecure in an avoidant way try to act as though they do not need anyone. Full of shame from not being loved in early childhood, they now need love desperately, although they are rarely conciously aware of this. Above all, they must avoid the pain of asking for what they need and being rejected again. Better to be indifferent or even in control, which is what they feel when others want to love them; they act as if they do not need any of that. When you try to link, you are stirring up both their deep need and the deep fear. In response they seem to be saying, "I see how desperate you are for love, but I'm never that desperate." That is, they're projecting.

If your undervalued self is easily activated, you may stop trying to strengthen the link once you recognize that someone is an avoidant. The resistance you encounter simply makes you feel too rejected. He's charming until he knows you like him, then he acts cool. You call a few times but he never returns your messages. You feel rejected, but on the very day you feel you are over him, he calls, acting like your best friend. You agree to get together for coffee. He forgets. When you call, he rushes over and you go out together. But in the café he sees another friend and talks to her instead of you. You vow never to go out with him again, but at the end of the evening he is so charming that you back down. He invites you out on Friday and says he'll call, but you spend Friday night waiting, with no word from him. Next day you get an e-mail saying how busy he is and that he just couldn't make it. In fact he stays busy for months. This would annoy anyone, but for you it is toxic.

Sometimes an avoidant is "in recovery" and wanting to link, or at least wanting to want to. If she has other qualities you find appealing, and many avoidants do, you can try linking with her, thinking of yourself as part of the team that is building her security. You cannot make an insecure person secure in a few linking conversations, but you can provide experiences of genuine caring, as you would for anyone. Be careful, however, for you may feel such a desire to help that you offer more than you can give and then later find that you need to take back the offer or sharply decrease it, which would only strengthen the other's fears. Remember that deep down she is searching for secure, consistent, unconditional love, but she will keep testing your love by sometimes rejecting you.

Protecting Yourself from Another's Emotional Schema

Have you ever begun to get to know someone and suddenly found that the two of you are in a huge conflict and that you are feeling attacked or just plain wrong, stupid, defenseless, and ashamed? For example, during a convention you go out to dinner with a group in your specialty area. Maybe you are already in ranking mode, worrying about what others think of you, but you are determined to link with the man next to you. All seems to be going well. He says he's married, has two kids. You ask about his children and, on learning that he misses them, you show empathy. He asks if you have kids. It's time for you to receive, so you reveal a little bit. You say no, but half joke that you sure miss your dog. He says, "Sounds like you treat your dog like it was your baby or something."

You recall training your dog to obey you. You do not think you treat Chicory as you would a child. Missing a dog has always seemed normal to you. You try to explain yourself without falling into a self-protection, saying simply, "Gee, I don't think I see my dog as a baby at all."

He ignores you. "I guess you women always need to have something to fuss over if you don't have kids. It really drives me crazy when people make a big deal over a dog."

You start to feel a little mystified. You were trying to be friendly, and now you are about to engage in a silly argument. And you feel a little embarrassed. What do the people overhearing this conversation think? Then you feel on the verge of shame. And *do* you depend too much on your golden retriever? Here comes the undervalued self.

The signs of an emotional schema are already familiar to you. The other's voice becomes highly emotional, too loud and strident or too soft yet intense. You hear dire threats and predictions. "Always" and "never" pepper the conversation. You may be blamed, labeled, warned, or diagnosed in a bewildering fashion. With very rational types, a discussion becomes a debate, then a monologue designed to prove you wrong. Sometimes the signs are more subtle, and you simply notice you are suddenly feeling guilty or stupid, or your heart is starting to race or your stomach clenches. If you don't realize what is going on, your undervalued self takes over.

When an emotional schema is triggered, linking ends, at least for the moment. You may never know the trauma behind someone's emotional schema, so you cannot discuss it rationally. If you will never see the person again, you should simply say as little as possible and look for an opportunity to get away and calm the undervalued self with your new understanding of what happened, perhaps talking it out with a friend.

If you still like the person except for how she behaves when you bring up certain subjects, you must do certain things to minimize the damage to you and to the relationship. In the long run, if you can sensitively handle the other's emotional schema, it may lead to a much deeper friendship. What do you do?

• *Don't argue.* Do not get pulled in. Keep talking, but try to keep some part of yourself outside of the conversation, as a witness. If possible, change the subject in a kind and gentle way.

• *Continue linking.* Remember what you like about this person. Her emotional schema is only one part of her. You are seeing a temporary loss of control resulting from some past trauma. Here you can learn something about her that will eventually strengthen your link. Whenever you notice during this eruption that there's something here that the two of you have in common, bring that up. "We can both agree on that" or "I've had the same problem."

• *Don't agree for the sake of friendship.* Some part of her wants you to stay firmly grounded rather than have you join her in the black hole of an emotional schema. Especially do not agree if she says, "I'm so stupid, so worthless." Say "I hear you, although I can't agree with that."

• *Don't stay silent.* Your silence will be interpreted according to the projections that come out of the emotional schema. She may assume you agree, disagree, hate her, adore her, are deceiving her, or whatever. So you need to say enough that she does not go too far off into fantasies of what you think. Aim for mild, friendly interest.

• *Listen for and respond carefully to self-protections.* (They will arise in you as well as in the other.) Gently align yourself with the underlying fear of shame in yourself or the other and try to reduce it. "I know you want to blame me — it seems like one of us has to be wrong here. But maybe we don't have to decide who's to blame. All we have to figure out is what's going on and how to avoid this happening again."

• *Remember the centrality of shame.* It is at the bottom of every emotional schema. Also, the other is feeling out of control and ashamed of that as well. Do whatever you can to reduce her shame.

• *Talk it over later.* Wait until the next time you see her. Talking it over later is essential if the emotional schema seems likely to come up again, or if your feelings were hurt while it was triggered. You will probably have to be the one to bring it up, carefully and without shaming the other. "We sure got into something last night, didn't we?"

If you do not have any idea what the source of the other's emotional schema is, you can try to probe gently for it. Discussing the original injury behind an emotional schema is the only way to reduce its intensity in the long run.

Josh Avoids Being Hurt by Paul's Emotional Schema

Josh and Paul worked together and had known each other for two years. When they shared their thoughts about work and marriage, they seemed to think alike. Josh felt that he and Paul were getting closer until one day, when he felt as if he'd hit a wall.

JOSH: How ya doing?

PAUL: Fine. Just my back acting up.

JOSH: I'm sorry to hear that. Anything I can do to help?

PAUL: No.

JOSH: How about I do the lifting today and you do the paperwork?

PAUL: No, I'll be fine.

JOSH: Then at least let me do the heavy stuff.

PAUL: *I'll be fine. Lay off.*

JOSH: Okay, I didn't mean to piss you off.

PAUL: You didn't.

JOSH: Well, you sound pissed off. Talk about biting the hand that tries to feed you.

PAUL: Well, I don't need *feeding*. You're driving me nuts. You're just like my goddamn mother.

Josh was feeling increasingly hurt because Paul has an emotional schema about being a weak man. It was triggered by his admitting to having a bad back and by Josh asking if he could help. First he used the minimizing self-protection ("I'll be fine," "You didn't [piss me off]"), which made Josh feel brushed off, as if offering to help were wrong. He fell into arguing with Paul and then was blamed for the fuss, told he was just like a "goddamn mother." After their exchange, they went on working together without talking for the rest of the day, but they slammed a lot of doors.

Josh found he just could not forget it. His feelings were hurt;

his undervalued self was making him doubt his worth in Paul's eyes and in general. He did not want to feel that way, however, and he did not want to have to be so careful with Paul, so he risked revisiting the incident over beer the next night.

JOSH [*jokingly*]: Hey, what happened yesterday when I offered to do the heavy lifting? We sure got into it.

PAUL [*sounding ashamed*]: Yeah.

JOSH: I guess we both have that thing of never asking for a break. "Suck it up. You can do it."

PAUL: Yeah, and it's a good way to be. I'm damn proud of it.

JOSH: Yeah, just like our dads. Real marines. Good ones. And both of 'em died because they wouldn't admit to a problem. As I recall, yours wouldn't get his prostate checked.

PAUL: Yours just drank himself to death.

JOSH: Couldn't ask for help with that or anything. "Suck it up" doesn't age too well.

PAUL: Yeah, but I just hate being treated like an invalid.

JOSH: Invalid? Hell, I'm the one looking like an invalid when you've got me playing basketball. Look, next time I see you busting your back when you could use some *temporary* help, what should I do?

PAUL: I guess I could let you do the lifting. Temporarily.

What Josh does this time:

• Avoids arguing.

• Is more careful with Paul's minimizing self-protection by dealing with the shame behind it.

• Sticks to the facts on which he thinks he and Paul can agree. This is their point of linking.

• Does not act as if he knows what is going on inside of Paul by saying, for example, that he must be afraid of what his father would think of him. Instead, he lets Paul express himself.

• Admits that they both have a problem with allowing someone else to help, further reducing Paul's shame.

• Touches on the history of trauma he knows about and suspects is behind Paul's emotional schema.

Notice that Josh does not try to go too far. He is not going to heal the trauma entirely or even very much. He is certainly not going to rid Paul of his emotional schema. He just wants to end the ranking by having Paul see that he, Josh, is not feeling superior and judging Paul for either his bad back or his touchiness about it. Rather, he wants Paul to see that they have a lot in common. During all of this Josh feels close to Paul, even though it takes Paul a while to come around.

Finally, Josh asks Paul to tell him how he should handle this emotional schema in the future, a good strategy. Throughout, Josh is focused on linking in a helpful way so that his own undervalued self is never triggered.

WORKING WITH WHAT YOU HAVE LEARNED
Practicing Linking

You may have already begun to apply the reminders of SEEK and GIVE as you link with others. Following are some specific exercises to strengthen these new skills.

1. Practice initiating linking with two different people — one a trusted friend and one a stranger. Remember that to initiate linking, you want to use SEEK: *Smile, make Eye contact, Empathize,* and *do something Kind.*

2. When you have established a link and have an opportunity to continue talking, use GIVE: *Get emotionally involved, develop Insight about what the other needs or wants, Verbalize what you are feeling or would like to do about those needs or wants,* and *Empathize.*

3. When you feel ready, practice linking by receiving with two people from different areas of your life, for example, a family member and a coworker.

4. Think of some attempts you have made to link that have failed and left you feeling bad about yourself. Was there one in which the other person was using one or more of the six self-protections and you ended up feeling ashamed? If you cannot think of a situation like this, imagine one that could happen. Now write in your journal an imagined dialogue or script of a scene in which you handle those self-protections differently, staying in linking mode and disarming the other's shame while avoiding your own.

Try to think of a friend, partner, or someone you have dated (someone from the past is fine) who has an avoidant attachment style. Choose someone who has made you undervalue yourself by first running warm, then cold toward you, while you feel worse and worse about yourself. If you cannot think of such a person in your life, imagine one. Again, write an imaginary dialogue or script in which you respond in ways that keep you in linking mode. Try to give the avoidant aspect of this person a sense of security about the link with you without accepting the low rank of someone begging for the other's love.

Think of a time that you were in a conversation with someone you thought you had a good link with when the other person was suddenly caught up in an emotional schema that made you feel bad about yourself. Maybe the person was arguing with you vehemently and you could not defend your perspective, or he thought you were doing something that you knew you were not doing, but you could sense your undervalued self taking over. If you cannot recall such a scene, imagine one. Again, write a dialogue or script in which you handle the situation in a way that keeps you in linking mode and out of your undervalued self.

CHAPTER FIVE

Linking with the Innocent

Although switching from ranking to linking is an invaluable tool for alleviating feelings of worthlessness, there will be times when you cannot do it even though you know you should. You might feel too inferior or afraid to take the risk, or you might not be able to see that it can be done. In this chapter you will begin to work on your deeper, unconscious obstacles to linking. This requires working to undo the effects of the traumas that cause your unconscious to decide it is safer not to link and to expect ranking and shame if you do.

It is possible to bring unconscious thinking to consciousness by attending to emotional and bodily states, interpreting dreams, using guided imagery, and engaging in an activity called "active imagination." These tasks are usually done in therapy, because it is still widely assumed that the unconscious wants to keep hidden whatever is in there and thus you need someone else to pry it open for you. However, an overriding part of the unconscious does want to communicate with you; we all have a force within us that is meant to heal psychological wounds, just as we have a force that heals physical ones. You simply have to learn the language of the unconscious, which communicates through the kinds of images and stories that are produced in your dreams. You might find these methods unusual, but trust me, they work, and they do so in ways that advice and suggestions cannot. One of the most important ways to access and heal the unconscious is by using active imagination to get to know the "innocent."

THE INNOCENT PART OF YOU TOUCHED BY TRAUMA

Most traumas, as I explained in chapter three, involve feeling defeated, powerless, or used by someone who did not have your interests in mind or was willing to harm you. We come into the world expecting linking from others, as well as expecting to take a rank within our group. But ideally that ranking occurs with people to whom we are linked, starting with our parents. You are born prepared for some defeats within your group but also prepared to receive security and protection from adults while you are a child and support from your peers in adulthood. When these expectations are not fulfilled, you are shocked, defeated, and often ashamed as well. What part of you is shocked? The innocent, trusting part.

While I will refer to the innocent as feminine, you may see it as either gender and any age, from infancy to your present age. Perhaps you will see her as being the age you were when you encountered the trauma of abusive power. The first trauma often happens in childhood, but for some it does not occur until adulthood. Someone might say, "I lost my innocence the minute I found out my wife was being unfaithful." Sometimes we lose our innocence simply because we are unprepared for the fact that the world is not always kind and just, nature is not always benign, a job can disappear overnight, health is not a right but a privilege, and loss and death are inevitable. Suddenly we are overwhelmed with unbearable fear or sadness, which indicates trauma, as I have defined it.

As I said in chapter three, almost all shocks and traumas, but especially the ones involving people, can lead to feeling defeated, ashamed, and depressed. But whether the trauma occurred when you were a child or in adulthood, you had to go on, even though you were overwhelmed by your feelings. You could not afford to dwell on what happened or be immobilized by distress. The feelings had to be hidden from yourself as well as from others. The innocent is the name we are giving to that part of you still distressed by that trauma and unable to move through it because you are unaware of it.

As a part cut off from the rest of you, however, the innocent is real and must be reckoned with if you are to heal the undervalued self. As soon as she thinks there's danger of more trauma, she employs those instinctual responses of shameful self-blame, which reset your overall sense of self-worth to zero and activate the involuntary defeat response of depression to keep you from challenging those who seem to the innocent far more powerful than you. Your goal now is to use active imagination to experience the full reality of the original trauma so that it is no longer cut off and then to slowly work with the innocent to let go of her outmoded instinctual responses and defenses.

USING ACTIVE IMAGINATION TO HEAL TRAUMA

Active imagination was first developed by the Swiss psychologist Carl Jung and expanded upon by others in order to help people reach the parts of themselves that were cut off during a trauma and have taken on a life of their own.[1] Active imagination is not daydreaming or ordinary fantasizing but a dialogue between your conscious mind and the part of the unconscious you wish to contact, in this case the innocent. While it may sound strange, it is best if you can start thinking of the innocent as a separate person dwelling inside of you. Once you get to know her better through active imagination, you can begin to integrate what she represents into your conscious life, where you can better deal with it. The first step is to invite her to come forth and then listen to what she has to say or see what she wants to do and then help her; basically you want to link with her.

For example, if a group of kids ostracized you as a child, now, when some friends at work go out to lunch without asking you, the innocent is quick to think that they are excluding you on purpose. In addition, she'll conclude that you must be worthless. As a result, you tend to go to lunch before anyone excludes you—but also before anyone can ask you to come along. This ranking response, derived directly from the past trauma, is completely disproportionate to the situation and causes you to miss opportunities to link. You can reach this cutoff part of yourself and change that response in a deep and lasting way through active imagination. The idea is to get to know the innocent's feelings, make them less overwhelming by understanding and accepting them, and thus make it less necessary in the future to avoid any situations likely to stir up those feelings. You will not need to undervalue yourself or use the resulting self-protections; the emotional schema the innocent represents will be triggered less often. You will see ranking less and linking more and be free to choose linking.

HOW YOU WILL HELP THE INNOCENT

The essence of active imagination is saying something to the innocent and then *really* waiting for her to respond. This is a dialogue between two "people," you and what is in many ways an autonomous part of you. Let's begin with an overview of what you will do, before we get into the details. You start by being open and patient, as if waiting for someone to appear on a stage and speak. When she does, she may not speak at first. You may see the innocent riding the bicycle she had when you were four, or you may see her at age two, crying in a corner, or at twenty-one, falling in love. Whether she speaks or is doing something, you respond with your feelings about what is happening. If she asks how you are, be very honest. If she is trying to learn to swim, you could say, "That looks frustrating—would you like some help?" Then imagine giving that help.

Next you wait and listen again. She might say, "Everybody's tried to teach me to swim. You can't either. I can't put my face under." And so on. The key is holding on to that empty stage, allowing the innocent to appear and speak or act however she wants, as an autonomous other.

If you do active imagination with the intention of healing trauma, you or she will eventually turn to that trauma or the feelings that resulted from it. What should you do with someone precious to you who has been wounded by abuse? Take her home to be with you, comfort her, listen to her when she is ready to talk, and eventually help her make sense of the seemingly senseless cruelty she has experienced. This form of love, something like the love of a parent for a child, is needed to restore the inner security that's so essential if you are going to throw off your shame, depression, overall low self-worth, and overuse of ranking. Even if the innocent is an adult, she needs to regress, to go home to Mom for a while. She (you) needs healing so that you can go back out into the world and try again.

Unfortunately, if your parents did not know how to comfort you and restore your security, you cannot be expected to know how to do this for yourself. But good parenting skills can be learned. Even in the last decade much has been learned about how to reestablish security and self-worth in a victim of trauma. In particular, the victim needs to talk about what she thinks happened, over and over, and also learn not to feel worthless and powerless. And this must be done in the company of someone who can reassure her and gently reinterpret the event if need be. This is what you will be doing with the innocent.

Reparenting Yourself Is Not Always Best

I want to be honest and say that sometimes you are not the right person to try to reparent the innocent, especially if you chronically undervalue yourself. In that case, trying to reparent yourself is like asking a very distressed young child to take care of herself. It's asking too much. Of course, the innocent needs and hungers for someone besides you to offer help, much more help. Further, you simply may not have a good parent inside of you. You may even be furious with the innocent for all the trouble she is causing you or for reasons you cannot explain. For example, one woman, in talking with her innocent, had fantasies of kicking and beating her for being so weak and causing so much trouble. This woman needed a therapist to take care of the innocent until they could discover why these inner beatings were happening and then resolve them.

You, too, may need to do some of this work with a good psychotherapist. (See Appendix I for advice on finding one.) However, some people have been able to overcome chronic undervaluation, at least to some degree, through a very close, loving relationship with someone besides a psychotherapist. This book will help you with that process, but it requires first making some progress on your own, which you definitely can do. So I will give you the methods used by the best therapists, but I also acknowledge that sometimes it is necessary to take the innocent to an actual therapist.

Your Goal for the Innocent

You want the innocent to stop seeing herself as worthless, of course. But the overarching goal is to bring her out into your awareness and allow her to express herself just as she is. To achieve this, you must link with her. Remember that linking with her means liking her—accepting her for who she is and what she feels. It means being genuinely interested in learning all about her and meeting her needs if you can. This unconditional acceptance will do far more good than lecturing her, trying to teach her new ways of thinking, or acting as if she is defective, which is already her greatest fear. When she feels safe and accepted, the natural healing process will begin to take over.

Remember that you are looking for emotions you once cut off for good reasons, so you may find that your innocent has some feelings that make you uneasy or even ashamed at first. Maybe she tells you that you have felt shy because she feels unlovable and just wants to hide or be held or to be seen and appreciated by someone wonderful without her having to say anything. Maybe you find those feelings are too needy or weak, but stay with them. Don't reject them; doing so would punish the innocent all over again. Instead, your acceptance of her feelings allows the innocent to see her worth to you, just as the love of a parent gives a child a sense of worth throughout life.

How to Provide What the Innocent Needs

Before you can help the innocent through a dialogue, you need to learn some of the current principles for parenting children and for helping adults recover from trauma without undervaluing themselves. As you apply these principles, think of yourself as a reasonable person who cares very much for the innocent. Keep yourself in that role and separate from her. You may not feel particularly reasonable before you start an active imagination, but you will be surprised to find that you know what a wise, kind person would say, and any specific skills you lack you can begin to learn now.

Attunement and Understanding

Attunement means being in harmony with another's emotions. It is much deeper than the sort of awareness that happens when we hear ourselves thinking "Oh, he must be angry." Unlike that sort of logical deduction, attunement comes from the right brain, the intuitive and emotional side, which works quite automatically. For example, when we are acutely attuned to another's feelings, or even hints of feelings, we intuitively grasp the reason for the anger, and we may feel angry, too.

A good mother tries to be attuned to an infant's every feeling. It is easy and natural. When the baby smiles and laughs, the mother laughs, too. If the baby cries, the mother is distressed, too. However, most of the time, a mother is not in perfect attunement with her baby. What matters is that she corrects her attunement as she goes along. For example, she may think a particular cry means hunger, but if offering milk fails, attuning to the baby's feeling will help her decide what to do next.

Mothering that lacks attunement is distressing to an infant. Sometimes a mother misattunes in a systematic way. Maybe she does not want a baby who is easily frightened, so she ignores or responds less to fear and more to boldness. Misattunement is not just a problem for infants, however. We are always getting messages that certain feelings are not all right. At work you may be tired of Joe Smartmouth, or the innocent may loathe him, but your boss says, "I know you want to see Joe here do well this month, so I'm sure you'll be glad to relieve him of some of his day-to-day duties." To help alleviate your boss's deliberate misattunement to what he knows you must be feeling, at least you can listen to the innocent's feelings about Joe Smartmouth, even though you may have to continue working with him and taking on some of his duties.

Being able to attune to and understand another's feelings is now known to be a basic requirement of emotional intelligence. To understand a feeling makes it real. To attune with your innocent, you must identify her feelings and reflect them back to her, letting her know that *you* know she has these feelings. It is your job to reattune with the innocent every time you sense she has a new emotion. Each feeling will be important. Watch especially for subtle shifts. This is how change occurs: feelings shift as they receive attunement. Hate gradually becomes understanding and perhaps forgiveness, shame becomes a fragile self-acceptance, and fear melts away, although we cannot be impatient for any of this to happen or we are not really accepting the feelings as they are.

During an active imagination, if the innocent does not seem to feel as much emotion about an event as you would expect—for example, when she talks matter-of-factly about the death of her beloved mother when she was seven and the subsequent reign of an abusive stepmother—attune yourself to what you think she ought to be feeling. Ask yourself, "Would this event be upsetting to most people?" If the answer is yes, try asking her about this hidden feeling in an indirect way, such as "I wonder if you're sad or angry right now as you tell me this."

Listen and, if necessary, ask questions, but in ways that show you are truly interested and curious, not just determined to see the innocent in a certain way. Assume there are good reasons for her feelings, complaints, and so forth. Tell her you would love to hear about those reasons. Then give them serious thought and add understanding to your attunement. For example, "So you can't help worrying. You worry mostly about someone breaking into the house, is that right?"

This last response begins to establish a connection to the cause of the feelings. But mostly it shows that you want to understand, and we all find it satisfying to be understood in a way that helps us be more in touch with ourselves and grow. We trust the person more right away, and that is what you want, for the innocent to begin to trust you.

Connecting to the Present Cause

The next step is to discover the deeper emotional reason for the innocent's intense feelings right now. For example, your imagined dialogue may start like this: "I can feel how sad you are. This is devastating." This shows your attunement.

Next you express understanding of her feelings: "You feel more sad and depressed than angry that someone else is getting all the credit. But it makes sense to feel depressed. You feel powerless, defeated. In fact, you wonder if this is what you deserve, because you never stand up for yourself."

Now you go on to connect to the present cause. If she has already told you the cause, then you just restate it. But sometimes she has not seen it or you have not thought about it before. "But you're really scared of what will happen if you say anything. Lillian has always scared you. Accusing her of taking credit for your work could make her turn on you. And not just Lillian but all of her friends could turn against you."

Connecting to the Past Cause

Next you connect to the past cause by asking, "Have you ever felt this way before?" Asking the innocent when she felt this way is important. Do not assume you know. Remember, although she is part of you, she is autonomous. She will at least have something new to say about what you think you already know, just as dreams can give you a new perspective. Once she does connect her present feelings to the past, stay with her as she enters into the feelings that happened to both of you then.

In this case, maybe she tells you something you do remember but did not think mattered that much—the time the other kids took her homework, the picture she drew of Columbus's three ships. It was a really good picture and she was punished for "losing" it. Someone else handed in her picture, and it was put up on the bulletin board. The teacher didn't believe it was hers because she didn't draw that well, and everybody laughed at her for trying to claim that it was. She tried to explain, but he said he didn't like liars in his class. He called her parents and they believed the teacher, not her. Naturally it would be frightening now to claim credit for what Lillian has claimed to be her work.

It is important to encourage your innocent to feel and say how awful this past experience was. She is telling you about your own split-off feelings. To keep her talking, say something like "How terribly sad. That must have made you feel *so* bad." Keep this up until it all comes out.

A Corrective Emotional Link

This phrase sounds pretty fancy, but making a "corrective emotional link" is really very easy. You simply provide the response that the innocent should have received in the past that could have prevented her from feeling defeated and ashamed. For instance, if she describes a time when she was afraid, tell her how much you wish you had been there to protect her (in contrast to the time she faced it alone). Returning to the example of the stolen homework, you could say, "I know you drew that picture, and it makes me so mad that you didn't get credit. I want to go in and talk to the principal and get your teacher fired." Your response reflects your love for her, so it is the linking that corrects and starts to replace the old, hurtful experience that could not be shared with anyone.

Sometimes the only corrective emotional link needed is attunement, acceptance, and understanding. At other times the corrective emotional link requires a more active image of what you would do for her. Maybe her parents went to the principal but got nowhere. Maybe she felt ashamed of them as well as herself. The corrective emotional link is hearing how it would have been if you had been there. However, be sure not to provide another scenario until you have given her attunement, understanding, and connection to the present and past causes. Also, do not discount her current feelings—for example, that she still thinks she deserved what happened to her because she is weak—worthless—and the other kids saw that. Instead, accept those feelings but provide your own more fair perspective.

Anything you tell the innocent must be honest, however. She will be quick to detect ulterior motives. She can't trust you if you exaggerate your sympathy just to get her to change more quickly.

Disagreement When It Is Needed

This *is* a dialogue. Emotions are never "wrong." They just happen, like the weather. But they can be based on inaccuracies about what is happening, so you must contribute your thoughts, too. However, if you can't accept her perspective, consider why you are disagreeing. Does it make you uncomfortable? Is it inconvenient? Is she using a self-protection while you are trying to give her information she needs in order to respond more accurately? For example, she may blame others, but you know this is a pattern that has to stop. She may say, "Tell them all off, quit the job, and never work again."

Knowing this is unrealistic, you can suggest, "You have been so afraid to speak up that the supervisors think Lillian, who is more assertive, did the good job that you actually did. You have to let them see a bit more of yourself, that you are a good worker, not worthless and already undervaluing yourself by accepting a low rank in everything."

Appreciation

Always thank the innocent for showing up and expressing herself. Tell her how much you are learning from her. When you are too busy to dialogue with her, explain why and apologize when you finally do speak with her.

It may seem silly to thank a part of yourself, but there are many advantages to keeping her separate. For example, she will continue to tell you her outmoded or surprising feelings if you continue to speak to her, and you will grow less and less ashamed of some of the feelings *she* has. By accepting these feelings in her first, you will eventually be able to accept them as part of yourself.

Gentle Treatment

The innocent has all sorts of feelings from which you had to dissociate when the trauma occurred. One of those feelings is probably self-blame, so she has to be handled gently. Even if she has helped you develop a blaming self-protection, deep down she has blamed herself. Don't you blame her too.

Above all, do *not* lecture the innocent, give her advice she obviously can't follow, criticize, insult, or hurt her feelings. These actions rank you above her. They repeat the traumas and reinforce the instinctual responses of feeling worthless, ashamed, and defeated. Acceptance is your foundation. Begin with it and return to it when you stray. Remember, you do not have to agree in order to accept. You can say, "Although I don't see it that way, I really see how you could." In this manner, the innocent begins to learn that how she feels does not cause you to fight her, withdraw your love, punish her, disapprove, or feel superior.

What to Provide the Innocent During Active Imagination

1. **Attunement:** Let her know that you know what she feels and are not imposing your own feelings. "It's awful, what happened."

2. **Understanding:** Let her know that you grasp *her* reason for her feelings in the situation. "When he spoke like that, it crushed you." If she says you got it wrong, let her correct you.

3. **Connecting to the Present Cause:** Try to see what caused her reaction. "It crushed you because you care so much about what he thinks?"

4. **Connecting to the Past Cause:** Ask her what all of this reminds her of, or try to guess yourself what in the past has intensified her present reaction. "This is so much like when your father used to criticize you."

5. **A Corrective Emotional Link:** React to the past event the way someone who loves her should have, which is not what happened. This teaches her how she should value herself and react for herself. "I can understand how you feel. But it makes me angry that they have made you feel this way, because you don't deserve that kind of harsh criticism. There is no excuse for that."

6. **Disagreement When It Is Needed:** Oppose her gently when she is seeing the situation wrong, uses a self-protection or an outmoded instinct, or asks you to act in a way that you know will not work. "I can really see how you feel, but I will not let you give up because you think you are totally worthless."

7. **Appreciation:** Show her you care in small ways, too. "Thank you for talking with me. It is so helpful."

8. **Gentle Treatment:** Remember that she is full of shame, so offer her love and respect even if you must correct her, too.

GETTING STARTED WITH ACTIVE IMAGINATION

Active imagination sessions are most successful when planned, although some will be spontaneous. Use the following guidelines to prepare.

• **Schedule a time.** You should aim for at least once a week, but three times a week or more will help you progress faster. Be sure to choose a time when you won't be disturbed.

• **Be flexible.** There are no rules about length, but active imagination can take time if you are new at it, and you do not want to feel pressured. While you need to try for only a few minutes at a time, once you are engaged, the dialogue may go on for a half hour.

• **Choose a quiet place.** Turn off the phones. If you like, have objects around you that help create a sense of safety and even sacredness.

• **Prepare to write down what happens.** If the active imagination becomes mostly action instead of dialogue, take notes afterward. But if it is dialogue and more than a few sentences, you will be more focused if you write it as it happens. Be sure to identify the innocent and yourself distinctly in the dialogue. An easy way to do this on the computer with one keystroke is to use CAPS LOCK for one and not for the other.

• If you become very upset, stop and seek professional help.
You are unlikely to become upset or feel out of control during
an active imagination. However, you are dealing with the unconscious mind so you cannot know for sure what will happen when
you invite emotions that have been kept away for a long time. Be
prepared to stop and seek professional help if necessary.

Your First Active Imagination

- Get comfortable. Aim for a state of mind that is quiet and inwardly
  focused. You can use meditation, deep breathing, or another technique to move deeper into yourself.
- In the center of your torso, imagine a place of welcoming. Perhaps
  a dark, empty stage. Invite the innocent.
- Often you will see her or hear her speaking immediately. If not, ask
  if there is something she would like to say or do.
- If there is dialogue, keep it a true dialogue. After you speak, let her
  speak spontaneously. Then feel free to respond to her.
- If she is not speaking but doing an activity, consider imagining join-
  ing in without speaking and see how she reacts to what you do.
  For example, if you see her hiding under a table, imagine sitting
  down quietly at a distance and wait for her to gather her courage
  to approach you. Speak only when your sensitive attunement suggests that she wants or needs you to speak.
- When your mind wanders — as it almost surely will at times — just
  come back to where you left off. Sometimes a wandering mind signals that a highly important but threatening topic is trying to come
  to the surface, so do not quit just because you feel distracted.
- You will learn to sense when it is time to stop, perhaps when the
  innocent withdraws or the dialogue stalls or starts to feel forced.
  Don't devalue what has happened just because it seemed flawed
  at the end. Thank her for coming to spend time with you and agree
  on a time to meet again.

Tricia Learns from Belle

Tricia has been quite depressed lately. She knows she has been operating too much from the standpoint of the undervalued self. So she decides to check in with her innocent, Belle, which was her mother's nickname for her. The following dialogue has been edited and the parts numbered, so that you can see clearly how Tricia provided each of the elements Belle needed, but in fact her dialogue was not so trim and orderly, and yours will not be either.

To begin, Tricia sits at her computer, her preferred way of doing active imagination. (If you do this, and your journal is handwritten, you can later print out the dialogue and staple it into your journal.) She keeps the list of eight things to provide right beside her, her "cheat sheet," as she calls it, because this is still new to her. She closes her eyes, uses deep breathing to settle her body, and finds that quiet dark place in her stomach area that feels like a stage. Then she invites Belle, who appears front and center and says, "I'm not depressed like you. I'm just scared. So, so scared." Tricia begins to put her skills to work. (I've used names to indicate who is speaking in the following dialogue, but again you may find it easier to have CAPS LOCK on for one and not for the other.)

Attunement
TRICIA: Scared? I had no idea. I'm so sorry. What are you scared of?
BELLE: I don't like going to your new job. I'm scared there all the time. All the time.

Understanding
TRICIA: Gee, I'm glad you told me. I understand. It must be very hard for you to go someplace you're scared of. What's happening to you when we go?

148

BELLE: I don't like your boss, Mr. Barth. He makes me feel bad, like I'm no good.

Connecting to the Present Cause

TRICIA: He does criticize a lot. Are you afraid of him because you're afraid of feeling really bad again and again?

BELLE: I do feel really bad. Everything I do is wrong. He hates me. He thinks I'm stupid. But maybe he's right. I'm a loser.

More Attunement Because These Are New, Strong Feelings

TRICIA: It all feels pretty hopeless. You're feeling pretty bad—stupid, a loser. These are terrible ways to feel all day.

BELLE: He knows I hate him. But he started it. Now he's going to make it harder and harder for me.

Connecting to the Past Cause

TRICIA: Does Mr. Barth remind you of anyone, Belle?

BELLE: Daddy. And Mr. Wrong, the math teacher. And that first boss, Mr. Fathead. Daddy used to stand me on a chair to do the dishes. He'd inspect everything. I always missed some speck, and then he yelled at me. The more he yelled, the more I shook, so then I'd drop something and then he would really yell. He'd say he was going to help me with homework, too, and then he'd say I was dumb. I was so scared of him. Even if I got almost a perfect score on a test, I'd be spanked and shut in my room because it wasn't perfect.

Corrective Emotional Link

TRICIA: I wish I could have told Father how to treat you. You would have learned so much better if you had been praised for all that you did well. Well, I'm very proud of how hard you are trying at work even though you are scared.

BELLE: You are? You're proud of me? I've never heard you say that before. But look how bad I'm doing really. I'm gonna lose this job if I keep on like this. I'm so stupid.

Disagreement When It Is Needed

TRICIA: I hear you. I really do understand how bad that is, feeling stupid. But I can't agree with you. You definitely are not stupid. I think you feel stupid because of all those years with Father, and then Mr. Wrong and Mr. Fathead. Father especially—he didn't have a clue about how to raise a sensitive little girl. You were always doing the best you could. Always.

BELLE: I want to quit this job. I hate it. I hate how I feel there.

TRICIA: But I need this job. And I think we need to face together this problem of feeling afraid of men like Father. It will just keep happening.

BELLE: But what can you do? It's hopeless.

TRICIA: I guess I could start by just watching to see if he really dislikes me or if I am seeing ranking when it isn't there. Maybe I'll try to be friendlier. Maybe he thinks I don't like him.

BELLE: I hope you know what you're doing.

TRICIA: I will look after you. And if I find he really is just a mean man like Father, I will take care of you by quitting.

BELLE: I guess I could let you try, if you do not forget how scared I am and you're very careful to watch for him just being a bad, bad man.

Appreciation

TRICIA: I will take care of you, because I value you very much. You know, you've taught me a lot today. [Tricia imagines Belle looking brighter.]

Gentle Treatment

TRICIA: I'm glad to see you feeling better, but are you really doing okay? You were feeling pretty bad about yourself a few minutes ago.

BELLE: I guess so. I still don't like myself. I cause a lot of trouble, don't I? I mean, I'm such a scaredy-cat, and I don't have any self-esteem or self-confidence.

TRICIA: I'm so very sorry you still feel that way. I love you very much. It's hard enough to feel stupid and all that. But please don't feel ashamed of not feeling better about yourself too. You can't help it. You were not born this way. And you are doing all you can to change. Just keep talking with me. You'll feel better if you do. Okay?

What Tricia Did for Belle, and Belle Did for Tricia

Notice what Tricia does in this dialogue:

• Stays completely in the mode of speaking to someone else.

• Shows she is attuned to Belle every time Belle expresses her feelings.

• As part of the corrective emotional link, reduces Belle's shame by feeling proud of her. Tricia is not just saying this; she truly feels it. She also could have reminded Belle of her good grades in school and all the teachers who liked her, as well as her many past bosses and coworkers who have gone out of their way to praise her work.

• Continues to provide a corrective emotional link by showing Belle how she should have been loved and protected and makes clear that she, Tricia, plans to do so from now on.

• Accepts Belle's feelings of worthlessness but does not consider them to be based on fact.

• Stays in her role as a reasonable person who cares for Belle, a role Tricia can imagine if she tries, and she does so even at those times when she begins to feel more like Belle, scared and hating herself. By doing this, she goes deeper into the feelings that were too overwhelming for her to face when she was innocent and young.

• Keeps working gently on the problem of the undervalued self and offers Belle hope that this will change.

By linking with Belle, Tricia has linked with feelings, memories, and defenses that had been cut off from her awareness to some degree. Not only is she more conscious of these now, but her view of them has changed through the corrective emotional link she provided Belle (and that she failed to receive in the past). How could she do that for herself? She did it by playing the role of a reasonable person who cares for Belle, a role she has been able to play with another person, so why not with herself? It's one part of her brain helping another part.

As a result of this dialogue, Tricia began seeing her situation at work more clearly. She actually began to feel a little sorry for Mr. Barth. He was clearly overworked, as her father had been. The company was going through restructuring, and he was tense about his own rank.

Tricia decided to try linking with her boss. When she used GIVE, he actually lit up like a little boy. She realized that he had probably felt quite alone with his career problem and was delighted to receive her empathy. Not only did he begin to turn to Tricia for emotional support sometimes, but he became good at noticing when she needed support and providing it. Tricia's depression lifted. She knew her job was secure and often found herself looking forward to going to work. Most important, she began to undervalue herself much less.

If You Are Resistant to Active Imagination

While healing trauma, you need to do active imagination at least once a week, and more often when you are especially undervaluing yourself; new brain patterns are not built overnight. But sometimes you will not want to do it. One reason might be that you get frustrated. Active imagination can come with surprising ease, as if the innocent were waiting all along to speak. At other times you may have to be very patient. At these times a dream may help.

Clint was sitting quietly at his computer, eyes closed, feeling receptive to his innocent but getting no response. Then he remembered a dream from a few nights before. A Boy Scout was being shoved around by some bigger boys. The Scout was crying and then just flew away. The other boys were amazed. Clint decided to do active imagination with this boy as his innocent, and thus began Clint's long relationship with Scout.

It helps a great deal to pay attention to your dreams when trying to heal your undervalued self, because dreams put us in touch with parts of our brain that are normally closed off to us, such as parts sealed off by trauma. Waves of activation pass through the entire brain during the night, as if scanning for spots needing attention. A dream figure in trouble can represent the innocent.

It is also helpful to begin an active imagination right where the dream ends, as if the dream were continuing. Clint began his active imagination by flying beside the bullied Boy Scout and talking with him, eventually coaxing him down, returning with him to the bullying boys, and imagining himself driving them off while the boy glowed with pride that his new adult friend was doing this for him.

Even if an active imagination goes very well, you might still feel resistant. After Scout helped Clint see how he "flew away" from difficult situations because of his fear of being bullied, Clint began to link more. But then Clint went through a period of forgetting to have his conversations with Scout. Eventually he dreamed of a little boy who had been kidnapped and tied up with a gag in his mouth. Clint got the hint and returned to doing active imagination.

Resistance is natural. After all, the neural circuits in the brain that avoid these stored emotional memories of trauma are there for a reason, to keep you from being overwhelmed with bad feelings. Who wants to go back there? But if you want to heal, you'll need to go back.

If you are able to get started but find your mind wandering, just bring it back, again and again. If you keep forgetting to do active imagination, schedule it in your date book. Resistance can also prevent you from making contact with the innocent. You now have some ways to get around that problem. If you still can't reach the innocent, you can try the following:

- Picture yourself at an age when you were particularly vulnerable or troubled.
- Turn back to your list of childhood traumas from chapter three and imagine the innocent in one of these situations, perhaps one when you particularly "lost your innocence" about trusting people. This may stir the innocent to tell you how she felt.
- Imagine that your innocent is not speaking to you for a reason. Why? Is she afraid of something, angry, or feeling hopeless?
- If you *still* draw a blank, don't push it, but read the rest of this chapter and go on to chapter six, which will help you better understand what might be happening.

Even those who think they are very dedicated to the process encounter resistance to active imagination. If it happens to you, do not give up. Above all, do not treat it as a failure. Everyone has trouble with resistance.

Don't Forget the Body

The innocent's physical appearance and actions are significant. For example, you may see her as exactly nine and realize that you were nine when your parents separated for a few months. You were so worried that you did poorly in school, and now you see the parallel to your current worry and poor performance on the job. If the innocent's bodily appearance stands out in any way, for example, if she is a young woman with a broken leg or a teenage boy with acne, you could think about what that might tell you.

As an alternative to dialoguing with the innocent, you can imagine engaging her in some activity. If she starts to cry, simply hold her. She might appear playing in an empty field, dancing at the prom, lying in a darkened room petting a dog, giving a lecture to a large audience, riding a pony across the moors, or holding a baby. You might ask if you can join her or help her.

To imagine being with the innocent physically is more than another way of communicating with her. Emotions originate in the body and may still be stored there as bodily memories. Some of your first and most important experiences of linking and ranking may have occurred before you could talk. At a time of trauma in later childhood or adulthood, you may have had physical reactions that you were not aware of. This kind of information may show up as bodily states and symptoms, such as a headache whenever you go to see a doctor or unexpected tears when you hear a certain song. Bodily images in dreams might be, for example, flying or having no teeth. All of this is wordless but as real as anything you could put into words. While you are dialoguing with your innocent, you may have a strong emotional reaction to what she is saying; for example, as she tells you about her best friend rejecting her, you start to tremble. That tells you how much this memory still affects you. Take your bodily reactions seriously, for they may be the only way to know about certain past experiences.

For example, Clint's dream of Scout flying off was exactly what Clint had felt as a boy: so scared he wanted to fly away, to leave his earthly body and its painful emotions. When Clint and Scout talked about those times, Clint felt his stomach tighten and his fists clench. Scout was helping Clint relive the experience of being bullied, linking up the memories and feelings.

The Innocent and the Six Self-Protections

Mostly the innocent simply feels her feelings—your cutoff feelings—especially worthlessness and shame. But she may also employ the self-protections now and then in a very adamant way. By observing her, you may realize that you use the self-protection in ways you have not noticed before. Your awareness of them was cut off as long as you were cut off from the innocent. For example, at one point Belle switched from feeling ashamed to blaming Mr. Barth: "It's all his fault; he started it." From this Tricia realized how much she really did blame Mr. Barth, even for things he was not responsible for.

Tricia also discovered that Belle was especially evoking her minimizing and noncompeting. Tricia had simply thought she was being good-natured when she had said things to Mr. Barth like "Don't bother, I don't mind" or "I don't really care what he thinks." But as she learned more about Belle's fear of criticism or of making people angry, she realized that the innocent part of her was constantly avoiding the shame of defeat by not asking for what she wanted and not speaking up when someone was unfair to her.

Noncompetition may be an especially valued self-protection for the innocent because she would like to restore the world to the way it was before there was any abuse of power. She thinks she can do this by pretending that ranking just does not exist. You can help her accept that ranking is normal, that she cannot escape it, even in herself. In fact, she might even enjoy being the best now and then. As part of a corrective emotional link, give her what she should have had all along—a realistic sense of her abilities in areas where she should be competitive and of her rights in various groups.

Another favorite self-protection used by the innocent is over-achieving. She feels so inferior that she is never satisfied with herself and thinks others feel the same about her. Her solution is to want to be perfect. But tell her, just as anyone who cared for her would, that you value her for who she is, apart from all that she does. You might encourage her to admit how tiring her efforts are. Appreciate her when she does complain and ask her to do it more often. When you are overworking, she can help you find balance in life by insisting that it is time to play.

The innocent less often uses blaming, and if she does, you must seriously consider whether she has a justified complaint. She may be telling you something true that you never noticed before. Otherwise, a good response is "I understand your anger at Sally, but I'll bet you can be even harder on yourself than you are on her."

The innocent rarely uses inflation, but in her effort to avoid further hurt she may decide she does not need anyone else, or she may entertain you with her fantasies of greatness, which counteract her sense of powerlessness and shame. In this case you need to get at not only her feelings of worthlessness but her denied longing for love and acceptance. If she feels shame about being weak or too needy, always explain that these feelings are understandable and normal for someone in her situation and that you like her ability to admit to them.

As I said in chapter two, catching yourself at projecting can be very difficult, but you will see the self-protection better when the innocent does it. You will notice her saying things about others that are almost absurd. Maybe an active imagination will remind you of a time when the innocent was defeated by another kid, felt ashamed, and then started grabbing all the toys and ran off. In your active imagination you can hear her parting shot to her enemy: "I won't play with you—you're greedy and bossy." Did this accusation come up because lately she's being greedy and bossy? The fear of defeat and shameful humiliation can make any of us act that way. You know she is projecting if what she so dislikes in others could be very true of her. Whatever the flaw, you want to help her accept it and feel less shame about it. You can say, "We're all greedy now and then," or "Your friend is bossy, and sometimes you are too, but is that so terrible?" It can be especially helpful to connect to memories of people in the past who judged that certain feelings were very bad or who were so highly critical of everyone that the innocent had to deny having any faults at all in order to escape their judgments.

To help the innocent (and therefore you) stop using any of the self-protections, you need to get down to the underlying feeling of worthlessness and accept whatever she feels so that she can stop feeling ashamed. If she can stop feeling this shame around you, she can try dropping the self-protections, at least when the two of you are speaking. For example, at first Belle felt worse about herself during the dialogue and had to blame Mr. Barth, but as her shame lessened, the self-protections decreased.

Reviewing an Active Imagination

It is crucial not to forget about an active imagination after it is done. Ponder what you heard the innocent say and plan what you will do as a result. Forgetting or ignoring what happened can be another way that your old defenses protect you from planning anything that might put you at risk of further trauma, such as linking with someone new or speaking up.

It is possible that you will feel more upset after an active imagination, perhaps because you are now identifying more with the innocent. This feeling may be a necessary temporary result of integrating a cutoff aspect of yourself. If it lasts, then you should consider seeing a therapist who understands active imagination.

You may also simply feel dissatisfied with the dialogue. "This is all a waste of time" or "I'm just making this up." This response is part of your unconscious resistance to allowing cutoff feelings from the past to become conscious and possibly overwhelm you as they did in the past. Your active imagination is not at all a waste of time. And, yes, you or some aspect of you did make it up, just as some aspect of you makes up your dreams. But no one else would imagine or dream what you have. Even something "just made up" reveals much about your inner life.

You are going to have to handle your resistance on your own, but knowing what is really going on should help you ignore those negative feelings.

WORKING WITH WHAT YOU HAVE LEARNED
Deepening Your Relationship with the Innocent

You may have already begun your relationship with the innocent earlier in the chapter. If not, start now. Give the innocent a name if you have one in mind. Otherwise you can wait until a name comes to you. Remember, the innocent can be male or female.

Imagine a situation or a way in which you undervalue yourself and invite the innocent to talk about that experience, using the steps in this chapter. If something else is on her mind, however, attend to that instead. You should give her whatever she needs. If she needs soothing or comforting, be sure to give it, even if she is an adult.

During the next seven days, check in with the innocent daily. This does not always have to be a full active imagination, but be sure to talk with her if you are distressed or feeling down. These will usually be times when you are undervaluing yourself. Find out what is going on with her. You may be quite surprised. Remember that as a somewhat autonomous part of you, she often has a different perspective. You may find that she can explain right away those feelings that have seemed quite baseless or mysterious to you.

CHAPTER SIX

Dealing with the Inner Critic
and the Protector-Persecutor

W e each have an inner critic, and many of us have a protector-persecutor as well. The inner critic is the part of you that constantly comments on your appearance, performance, and general well-being. He — I use the masculine pronoun, but the inner critic could just as easily be a she — intensifies the undervalued self. Worse, he focuses on ranking. Still, over three million years the inner critic has evolved some effective instincts to keep you in good standing in your group, which is an important function. He wants to help and can be retrained.

The protector-persecutor, on the other hand, does not want to help you get along better in any area. If you have experienced serious or repeated trauma too early in life, it wants you to be nowhere, doing nothing. Its goal is also to protect you, but by keeping you out of life and its dangers, and it will persecute you if necessary to make sure that you are never traumatized again.

RETRAINING THE INNER CRITIC

The inner critic develops in childhood. As a child, you were far less competent than adults, and so was your inner critic, but that didn't stop him from pestering you to try harder to improve, to be as good as the grown-ups. The inner critic also had to see that you did not break the rules laid down by adults. But most likely he has not kept up with your development. He is too conservative for the adult you, who needs to be more free to make decisions.

Your inner critic has to be retrained to acknowledge your ranking today and to be less harsh. No more name-calling or global statements like "You're worthless. Better start changing. You have to work much harder, you idiot."

Identifying Your Inner Critic's Voice

Use the following checklist to help you recognize the voice of an unhelpful inner critic. Place a check mark next to each statement that sounds like what your own inner critic would utter.

- Your work is flawed.
- Your manners are never good enough.
- Be more careful—you always make mistakes.
- You will look foolish if you do what you just thought of doing.
- You are not dressed well enough.
- It is your fault that your child [partner, friend, or person you supervise] is not behaving well.
- You are not being kind or generous enough.
- If you don't call home more often, your family will not forgive or love you.
- Someone might be upset with you if you do that.
- You ought to work much harder than you do.

- You're lazy.
- You are not smart enough for this.
- You're a quitter.

If your inner critic makes even one of the statements above or others like them, he is at least guilty of bad coaching. The more statements you checked, the more of a hindrance your inner critic is.

Teaching Your Inner Critic How to Speak to You

Once you recognize your inner critic's voice, you can begin to have dialogues with him, much like those you had with the innocent. (You may want to review the steps in chapter five on how to do an active imagination.) In this case your goal is not to integrate a cutoff part of yourself but to tweak one you are all too conscious of. You want to appreciate the inner critic's good intentions but insist on better methods. To do that, you need to think about what you would ask a good coach — someone in your corner, not a tyrant — to do for you.

In particular, what you want the inner critic to learn is what you would want anyone around you to learn about communicating criticism:

- Use "I" statements, which take this form: "If you don't sing that song well, I worry that you'll be upset with yourself. I want to protect you from that." *Not* "You're going to be a total failure tonight."
- Make specific suggestions: "I'd feel better if you practiced the song three more times." *Not* "You sang that terribly, as you always do, and you'll probably never get it right."
- Use no general statements, labels, or name-calling: "You sang that like an amateur. You're such a neurotic — the more you practice, the worse you get."

• Aim for accuracy about how you actually rank. "I'm better than most singers, but I'm not a professional like Frank is (and that's okay—I don't have the voice or the time to practice that Frank has)."

• Accompany every criticism with four comments on what was good: "You have the first and third songs down well. Your voice is in good form. You wrote some great lyrics. I'm pleased with your new style. It's just that when I hear that second song, it doesn't sound quite right to me."

Myra's Inner Critic

Myra is learning a program for making data-collection templates, but her inner critic is distracting her. At first she does not realize what is happening and goes on working, but she feels worse and worse. Then she realizes that her self-confidence is sliding and suspects that her inner critic is approaching this program with a negative attitude, so she stops and has this dialogue.

MYRA: There you go again, telling me I can't do something.

INNER CRITIC: It's pretty obvious you can't, isn't it? You've been working on it for hours. You're too old to learn this fancy new stuff. It was never your thing anyway. They'll see that. As they said in your performance review, you aren't up-to-date and you never will be.

MYRA: Wait a minute. This is not helpful. What's bothering you? Please respond with "I" statements.

INNER CRITIC: That stuff again. Okay, when you work for hours like this and get nowhere, I get scared.

MYRA: You're scared for me. You think I've really stuck my neck out this time. I appreciate that you want to help. But the fact that it is a stretch for me doesn't mean it's hopeless. Can't you see anything right in what I'm doing?

INNER CRITIC: Okay. Well, you are learning some of it. You're stick-
ing to it. You did not overstate what you could accomplish by
tomorrow. And at least you sounded confident that you could
do it, although that may have been a mistake.

MYRA: That helped, if we strike that last comment. What should
I do then? Be specific, please. [Give the inner critic time to
think this through.]

INNER CRITIC: Why not call the support line that comes up when
you go to Help?

MYRA: Now there's a plan. Thank you. That's really helpful.

Notice that Myra was linking with her inner critic as much as
she could, appreciating him and empathizing with his feelings,
but she also stood her ground, making it clear that she held the
upper rank.

When Your Inner Critic Won't Behave

If your inner critic is not improving, do not give up. Often it
requires many conversations. Just persist and try to be consistent
in catching and correcting him. You will also probably need to
get to know his past. Ask him, "When did you become so worried about me?" Identify the voice from the past that he sounds
like—Mom, Dad, your second-grade teacher, your first boss,
your ex-boyfriend? If he is truly worried about you, show sympathy. But be firm; times have changed, and you expect him to
change, too.

Myra's relatively good working relationship with her inner critic
did not occur overnight. First she had to identify her critic's voice
and his particular specialty, which was to make her worry too much
about mistakes and doubt her abilities and basic intelligence. When
she began dialoguing with him, he criticized her for that too: "You
try every new self-help gimmick. That's dumb. Besides, even if it
works for other people, you won't be able to make it work for you."
Early on, Myra had to have the following dialogue with him.

MYRA: I'm sick of you. Get out. You are ruining my life.

INNER CRITIC: You've done a pretty good job of that on your own.

MYRA: Why do you criticize me in a way that makes me doubt myself, like you just did?

INNER CRITIC: I'm just trying to help you.

MYRA: Well, this is not helping.

INNER CRITIC: The fact is, I worry about you.

MYRA: Worry about me? When did you start worrying about me?

INNER CRITIC: I suppose I learned it from Mom. She always worried about you doing well enough to get along in the world and support yourself. But then she worried over just about everything.

MYRA: So you sort of absorbed worry with Mother's milk. But she cared about me. She gave me confidence.

INNER CRITIC: What did she know? You were one of the last kids to learn to read. You weren't that good at math. You did not get into the college you wanted.

MYRA: That's quite a list. So you decided it was better to tear me down rather than build me up? How about just being accurate about how I'm doing?

INNER CRITIC: Hmm. Well, I guess I expect you to be accurate...

MYRA: Yes, and I'll bet you could be pretty helpful if you were accurate too. Look, I appreciate your wanting to help. I really do. But try to support me, okay? You make a great coach.

INNER CRITIC: Do you think so?

What Myra did:

- Began with anger to get her inner critic's attention.
- Used reasoning, which inner critics appreciate.
- Connected with the past — Mother's worry.
- Ended with linking in the form of appreciation and a compliment.

RECOGNIZING THE PROTECTOR-PERSECUTOR

In the example above, Myra's inner critic responded to her firm-ness and her intention to link. But what if he hadn't? What if her inner critic insisted on maintaining the upper hand by continu-ing to mock her and make her doubt herself even more? In that case she would be dealing not with her inner critic but with her protector-persecutor. This is a part of yourself you may not have heard of, but if it is operating, it plays the biggest role in main-taining the undervalued self.

In chapter three you acknowledged the traumas from your past and perhaps the additional impact of prejudice, high sen-sitivity, and an insecure attachment to others. All of these can contribute to the triggering of a special defense system known as the protector-persecutor, which can either keep you in a protec-tive sanctuary of fantasy or addiction or, if you try to escape that, it can persecute you until you give up. So the protector-persecutor has two faces but is one in its purpose. It is a deep, primitive defense, and some clinical psychologists now believe that it is the protector-persecutor that keeps some people who are in psy-chotherapy with the very best professionals from stopping their undervaluing of themselves, even after years of therapy.[1] This new understanding is part of the latest thinking about how to resolve the effects of trauma.

Everyone has an inner critic, but not everyone has a protector-persecutor. The inner critic basically wants you to do well, but the protector-persecutor does not. The inner critic can learn to give good advice; the protector-persecutor cannot. You can dialogue with the inner critic, but you should not try to dialogue with the protector-persecutor until you see it change in specific ways. A retrained inner critic can actually help you stop undervaluing yourself. It can coach you to be realistic about your worth in rank-ing situations, to stop seeing ranking when it is not there, and, above all, to link more effectively. The protector-persecutor does not want you to risk doing anything, so it needs and encourages your undervalued self. With your undervalued self at the forefront, you will doubt your ability to do those things the protector-persecutor considers dangererous.

Since the protector-persecutor's directives bubble up from your unconscious, you will know about them only indirectly. To help you identify whether or not you have a protector-persecutor, ask yourself if you do the following:

• Feel chronically shy, usually quite certain you will be rejected by others.

• Find yourself repeatedly in abusive relationships or work environments.

• Feel there is truly no use trying.

• Miss out on major opportunities because you forget, come late, injure yourself, or have a sudden illness.

• Often feel too tired to do anything, even if you have had plenty of rest.

• Have recurring nightmares that are far worse than simply replays of a trauma.

• Manage to meet a goal or take steps toward one and then feel inexplicably much worse or have crazy nightmares afterward.

• Have a fantasy life that takes up a great deal of time.

• Have addictions or compulsions that keep you from engaging in a full social life.

• Lack feelings just when you ought to have them.

If you have experienced severe or early trauma, along with an insecure attachment in childhood or the experience of prejudice for most of your life, this innate defense system is probably operating in you. If you are highly sensitive as well, you are very likely to have a protector-persecutor because you are more affected by trauma.[2]

Out of the Dark: Instinctual Solutions

The protector-persecutor and a highly traumatized innocent are an inseparable pair. The protector-persecutor arises out of the dark depths of the mind when the innocent has been so overwhelmingly shocked and hurt by a trauma that the usual self-protections do not work; the child is too young to have them or the adult is too numb. In such highly traumatic situations, it is impossible to have hope. It's also impossible to muster one of the six self-protections against feeling utterly powerless. Instead, a bottomless black abyss opens up, and you fall endlessly into darkness while whatever sense of self you had is shredding and blowing away.

If someone came to your aid in time to stop the extreme trauma, the abyss closed up again. Otherwise, there are literally no words to describe what unfolds, because the entire experience is never consolidated into accessible verbal memory. The brain has been too overstimulated. If the trauma is remembered, it is broken down into manageable pieces that are kept separate—some sealed off from memory, some kept but without the feelings associated with them—in order to avoid overarousal. Without your knowing, the protector-persecutor defense system has been triggered to take over and prevent anything like this trauma from ever happening again.

The Protector

The protector acts like a guardian angel. It spins a cocoon of fantasy to keep you in a safe haven far from real life. We have all seen protectors in action: unhappy children living entirely in a world of books, computers, or make-believe; adults holed up in a room writing the Great American Novel or out on the basketball court preparing to be discovered. Others sense that the person's frantic work is too self-absorbed and out of touch with reality—the book will never be published, the amateur will never turn pro.

We also see the protector when a person idealizes and fantasizes endlessly about a celebrity or someone else whose love will never be returned. The worshipper may not have even met his or her beloved, which is fine with the protector, who does not want the worshipper to enter a real relationship.

The protector may also seduce with an addiction, and in this form, it may act like a demon lover. "You want a good time? I can show you one. Let's get a pint of extra-fancy ice cream [or vodka] and have a lovely evening together." More than once I have seen a woman free herself from a bad relationship or do the necessary work in psychotherapy to get ready to date, only to gain so much weight that she can't view herself as dating material. The protector has her in his grip.

The difference between fruitful creativity or hope and protective fantasy is, again, that the fantasy keeps you out of the real world rather than leading you into it. The make-believe world of the protector can expand infinitely, yet it does not take you anywhere and is not shared with others, because that might entail the trauma of rejection or whatever else must be avoided.

The Persecutor

If you grow restive in your sanctuary and start trying to leave it, the persecutor takes over. You realize that something is wrong because you cannot carry out your plans. You notice how much you procrastinate. You realize that you can't stop drinking or can't exit an abusive relationship. Your sanctuary is now a prison. You hate yourself. The persecutor kills hope, willpower, self-worth, and whatever else might encourage your innocent to go out and run the risk of being retraumatized. If you do take a step forward, the persecutor strikes and does whatever it takes to make you lose interest, energy, confidence, or courage. No amount of work on the inner critic or anything else makes a dent in these attacks on your attempts to change.

For example, you have a great new friend. But she hurt your feelings by forgetting to run an errand she promised to do, and that has cost you considerably. For the good of the relationship, you know you need to say something, yet you fear bringing it up. A voice in you says you ought to. This might even be your inner critic, saying you are a coward not to. But you simply don't do it—you can't. No sound comes out when you try to speak, and this mystifies you.

If you keep trying to speak to your friend, you might begin to hear the persecutor's voice saying, "This isn't the right time." If you still insist that you need to speak to her, it might say, "It really isn't that important." So even if your friend asks if you minded her forgetting, you will hear yourself saying, "No, it's okay. I really didn't mind." Soon you are tired of the friendship and it ends.

Or you want to fall in love. You recite affirmations, you speed-date, you talk about love all the time with friends or in therapy. Yet you hear yourself responding to a potential date, "I don't know about tonight. I've got so much work to do." Or you go on a few dates and decide this one's not for you. This happens repeatedly, and repeatedly the persecutor foils your plans.

Paradoxically, the persecutor often keeps you in abusive relationships, whether romantic or professional. It can re-create the abusive situation from the past in the most uncanny ways. Some people claim that we stay in abusive situations because we can't help repeating the same mistakes over and over. But why? We usually learn from our mistakes. Usually the actual reason is that the protector-persecutor views it as safer for you to stay with a known danger that keeps you undervaluing yourself than to risk something new that will open you to hope and then even worse loss or betrayal. Last time it was overwhelming, so *never again*.

The persecutor can also be a source of intractable depressions and self-destructive behaviors. In extreme cases, the persecutor will even offer suicide as a "solution." It seems to prefer death to more trauma, as many tragic suicide notes proclaim. I've had patients who had no idea they had such a death-dealing voice until they heard their own persecutor during an active imagination in my office. Suddenly a part of them was saying, "You'd be better off dead," or "You're so worthless, you ought to just kill yourself."

The Attack on Linking

The protector-persecutor, either as a unit or in one of its two forms, tries to break down every link you make, both outer links with friends and inner links that would end the dissociation it wishes to maintain. Hence you can see why your attempts to dialogue with the innocent might lead to mysterious resistance.

Emotions, memories, current thoughts and behaviors, and bodily states related to a trauma can all be dissociated. Memories may be repressed, literally unlinked from consciousness. Or your emotions may not be linked to current memories or events. You may feel numb, lacking all emotion, or all too conscious of emotions that seem to arise for no reason. Your body may be unlinked from memories, so you remember the events of the trauma but have no idea what happened to your body during it. Your body may still be dissociated from your thoughts, with the result that you are hardly aware of its needs. Or the body does not link with your actions, and you feel unreal or detached as you go through the day.

Dissociation can also affect how you act. You do things that make no sense or are self-destructive because your behavior is not linked to its real causes. You may have stress-related illness because memories, feelings, or thoughts that are pushed down in the mind then arise in the body. Or you may have recurring nightmares that seem unrelated to anything going on in your life.

As for outer links, the protector-persecutor makes every linking situation seem to be about ranking, usually with you as the inferior, although it can also make you feel superior—"he's not good enough for me"—if that will keep you out of a real, close, lasting relationship. The protector-persecutor might allow you to link in a limited way with someone who likes you by creating a false self that adapts to the world, but you know you are not really connected or authentic.

One man with a strong protector-persecutor told me that he simply feels very uncomfortable around anyone who treats him kindly, as if there is too much to lose in such a relationship. With people who treat him with warmth and respect, he keeps everything very superficial and often "forgets" to return their calls until they leave him alone. Instead, he has always had friends who have controlled or betrayed him and bosses who failed to promote him. He has been kept safe in the wizard's lair.

The Tale of Rapunzel and Her Protector-Persecutor

The fairy tale "Rapunzel" describes perfectly the relationship between the innocent and the protector-persecutor. In the story the witch "protects" her daughter Rapunzel from all the evils of the world by planning to keep her in a tower her entire life. But the girl can see out a window, and she eventually grows up and sees a prince. Rapunzel uses her never-cut tresses (her natural growth and talent) to help the prince climb up to her; her hair becomes her link to the outside world.

But the witch discovers Rapunzel's aspirations and promptly becomes her daughter's persecutor. She cuts Rapunzel's hair, symbolically destroying her link, and abandons the girl in the desert, where she gives birth to twins. The witch then uses Rapunzel's hair to lure the prince up to the tower one last time. When the prince finds that it is the witch on the other end of the hair, he is so heartbroken that he leaps from the tower and is blinded by the thorns into which he falls.

After many years of wandering, the prince hears Rapunzel weeping in the wilderness. When they come together at last, her tears heal his eyes. The reunited family lives happily ever after. The fairy tale tells us in a symbolic way that linking has triumphed in spite of the witch's attacks on the natural links between a young man and woman, between a head and its hair, a father and his children, and the father's eyes and what he wanted so much to see.

Kurt's Protector-Persecutor

Kurt was a highly successful computer-security specialist. From the outside he seemed well adapted and, at thirty-one, a real catch. Inside, Kurt was a different story. His parents had divorced when he was an infant. His young father had been a day trader — really a compulsive gambler — who lost the house, the car, and his wife's inheritance. His mother had allowed this to happen and then returned home to her wealthy, alcoholic parents so they could raise Kurt.

Kurt's grandfather, an ex-marine, eagerly took over Kurt's upbringing. His idea of child rearing was to impose punishments appropriate to a prisoner of war (which he had been in Vietnam). He intended to toughen Kurt up so that he would not turn out like his deadbeat father. So Kurt learned to go without food and water while locked in a closet for punishment, to find his way home in the dead of night after being left in a strange place, and to live in terror of his grandfather. He retreated as much as possible to his room and his computer, adding marijuana to his sanctuary once he discovered it. Kurt's protector had taken over.

Kurt left home at fifteen with his grandfather's approval. "It will toughen him up." His mother had a new boyfriend and did not seem sorry to see him go. Given his talent with computers, Kurt found it easy to get work, but he hated his job. Alone in his apartment, he played video games and online poker. His plan was to win enough at poker to retire early. His protector was continuing to defend him by spinning a cozier cocoon.

Meanwhile, the persecutor would show up in Kurt's nightmares, with Kurt being tortured by a dark lord, abducted by aliens, or turned into a zombie. In fact, Kurt felt like a zombie. He had a few friends like himself, but he found no joy in life. Like Rapunzel, he was weary of being protected in a way that kept him out of the world. Life seemed to be something you survived, or maybe won if you got very rich. And then Kurt met Catherine and fell in love.

Catherine saw something in Kurt that she dearly loved, but she would not commit herself until he stopped smoking marijuana and playing poker and saw a therapist about whatever was causing his nightmares. This is how I met Kurt. He did not want to lose this wondrous girl, but he did not think he could give up his addictions either. Rather than tackling them first, we began looking for Kurt's undervalued self, which I knew had to be there, given his childhood.

Reluctantly, he tried an active imagination with the Little Boy, which to his surprise made him cry. After that his resistance was high. But he told me about his nightmares, which revealed his protector-persecutor to us. When Kurt began to focus on Catherine's flaws, he could see that his persecutor was getting mean, now that an actual relationship with her was more likely.

Gradually Kurt began to give up his addictions. He saw how much he had needed the protection of marijuana and the protective fantasy of becoming a multimillionaire poker winner. His efforts to give those up had brought in the persecutor. But now that he understood how all of this worked, he realized that he truly feared some terrible punishment, as bad as being locked in a closet, if he could not be the tough and highly successful person his grandfather had expected. He also felt his fear of being utterly powerless again, as when he was a child unable to escape from his grandfather or to keep his mother from abandoning him. With these insights, he was able to return to his active imaginations with the Little Boy. Now his healing speeded up, especially with Catherine, his greatest supporter, providing the secure link he had never had before.

Attachment Trauma and the Protector-Persecutor

A protector-persecutor that arises from an insecure attachment is often the harshest. In these cases the protector may replace the missing maternal or paternal presence with an addiction, whether to smoking, alcohol, work, or something else. Or it may create a vision of perfect love, the love the child never received. It encourages the unbearable craving and yearning while undermining or belittling things in the world that might actually satisfy some of the craving. It says they are not enough, or not real, just lies or illusions, or will not work out in the long run.

Still, usually it is love or the thought of love that lures someone out. After all, the yearning for love that provides a secure attachment is utterly natural and very strong in all of us. The possibility of love is what lured Rapunzel out, and it did the same for Kurt. You see the possibility of linking and say, "Look at this amazing person who speaks of love. Others in my place would return this love and live happily together. Why can't I?" Does love conquer all? It does if you are able to use it to fight your protector-persecutor.

Since attachment trauma often involves an unbearable separation, such as divorce or the death of a parent, the protector-persecutor very often rules out love because it brings the risk of loss, which, it supposes, you cannot bear, as you could not when it happened before. Until you work out your own answer to these scenarios, it's impossible to convince the protector-persecutor that you can live with the pain of separations and loss, that you can tolerate in the future what you could not in the past.

This is never easy, because losses are painful for everyone. In fact, you may still be convinced that you would literally not survive a loss, that you would suffer a psychological if not a physical death. You will have to work on this. Perhaps you can see that there will always be others with whom you can link in love. Sometimes the only answers are spiritual ones. The good news is that as you struggle to accept the fact that all relationships eventually end, you may become far more prepared for loss than those who are secure because they had good childhoods.

The other two attachment traumas you are being protected from, besides loss, are betrayal and abuse. As I said, part of an insecure attachment is that the child feels the parent has all the power and uses it without love. This can be deeply traumatic. As a result, we continue to expect betrayals and abuse in adulthood too. The protector-persecutor can make use of the fact that no one can read another's mind, so you can never know for sure whether a person is insincere in her words of love and is really plotting to betray you. We all have to assume the best, that people who say they love us do mean it. But the protector-persecutor will get you to continue assuming the worst. The only solution is to try to absorb the love another offers, the kind words and deeds that are meant for you.

When the protector-persecutor keeps you from being intimate with someone you love, do not give up. Freeing yourself to love is perhaps one of the greatest challenges a person with a troubled past can face, and even a partial victory must be acknowledged for the triumph that it is. Further, the undervalued self simply cannot be healed without achieving some freedom to love. It is linking and love that take you out of ranking and undervaluing.

Breaking Free from the Protector-Persecutor

Simply knowing about the protector-persecutor loosens its control. It is comforting to realize that all your failures to change and your unrelenting self-criticism and preoccupation with ranking are the result of this psychological defense. It is certainly better than thinking you are just self-destructive. Your first step is to begin to separate yourself a little from this defense by simply observing it.

Your second step is to break the protector-persecutor's rules, as Rapunzel broke her mother's rules. Third, you link, as Rapunzel did, to others and to your own feelings. Fourth, you use the inside information provided by your dreams. They will tell you what the protector-persecutor is up to during this process as well as provide hints about what to do next.

If you cannot gain the distance required to take the first step, seeing yourself as separate from this defense, or if your self-defeating behaviors do not lessen at all by knowing their cause, then it is time to see a therapist. Similarly, if it seems to you that something literally outside of you, such as a voice, is making you self-destructive, then you *must* see a therapist before proceeding with the advice in this chapter.

Observe the Protector-Persecutor

Go back to the list of the signs that you might have a protector-persecutor and think about each one. Consider the methods of your particular protector.

Especially, observe your links with others. The protector-persecutor is always bolstering the defenses associated with an insecure attachment. If you are anxiously insecure, you will dream of an ideal other and feel deeply inferior and afraid when someone loves you. If you are insecure in the avoidant way, you will pull back just when a relationship becomes more intimate or miss the person when he or she is gone but drive him off with your irritation or withdrawal when he is around.

You should suspect that the protector-persecutor is distorting things because of your insecure attachment at some specific times like the following:

• When you are frequently super-critical of the other, losing interest or thinking about breaking up, especially after something good has happened between you.

• When you have idealized a relationship so much that when something goes wrong, you see it all as a disappointing failure.

• When you mistrust the other and don't bother to get a reality check or talk it over.

• When you are furious or crushed that the other does not want to be with you all the time.

• When you look down on the other for wanting to be with you more than you want to be with him or her.

• When you decide "it's all over" as soon as there is the slightest conflict.

• When you are obsessed with concerns that one of you is too dependent, weak, or needy.

• When you cannot stop thinking about the other leaving you, not liking you, or dying.

• When you cannot see any flaw at all in the other, as if he or she is a god.

It is painful to see what the protector-persecutor is doing to you, but again, it's much better to understand it as part of a defense than to simply think of yourself as a loser.

Break the Rules

To break the rules of the protector-persecutor, you must first identify them. The traumas you acknowledged in chapter three will often dictate the specific unconscious rules you have learned to obey. Some of the most common are listed below. Read the list, checking off rules that you recognize. Then make a list of any additional rules from your protector-persecutor that you obey.

• *No intimacy.* Never ask or answer personal questions; ignore others' self-disclosures; be flippant or rude; leave if someone wants to be closer.

• *No arguing.* Always be nice; end relationships as soon as there is a conflict or the other is angry; walk out on arguments.

• *No growth.* Turn down opportunities or invitations to do anything new; do not aspire; act stupid so no one will think of you when an opportunity arises.

• *No dating or marriage.* Postpone; be unattractive; stick to crushes or fantasies; stay in a relationship with someone you would never marry; have affairs with people who are married; be forever young, a flirty bachelor or party girl long past the time for that.

• *No strong feelings.* Stay in control at all times; don't cry; don't show anger; be cool, always.

• *No sex or no enjoyment of it.* Avoid sex; be mechanical about sex; feel numb to sex; soothe yourself with sex without feeling any emotions.

• *No believing someone who says he or she cares about you.* Don't accept compliments or affection; or, if you do, don't believe they are authentic.

• *No asking for help.* Be suspicious; withdraw; never complain.

• *No honesty.* Just say whatever others want to hear. Be careful, especially when they invite you to "just be yourself."

• *No hope.* Don't expect help; don't think anything will improve; do not believe in anything or anybody.

• *No standing up for yourself.* Just let others say whatever they will; don't cause any trouble; expect no justice or fairness in this world.

• *No trusting.* Don't be fooled; they don't really care about you.

Once you have the list of rules your protector-persecutor has been enforcing, you can begin to try to free yourself from them. It is very important not to be discouraged if at first you cannot break a rule or if it seems that you are taking two steps forward and one step back. The protector-persecutor defense is strong. Worse, it will make you think that what you are doing is hopeless just as your efforts are beginning to work.

To guard against the protector-persecutor's sabotage, try working up some anger against it. If you cannot be angry, at least be persistent. Watch especially for the protector-persecutor's attack on your link with this book and with the tasks you are asked to do, such as dialoguing with the innocent. Undoubtedly the protector-persecutor would like to put this entire book off limits. In fact, one woman who was reading an early version of the book manuscript, just when she began to see how this chapter on the protector-persecutor applied to her, lost the manuscript. She lived alone, so she knew that she had misplaced it herself. Eventually she found it among some other papers on a shelf she never goes to. She had no memory at all of putting it there.

Link

Like a terrorist attacking rail or telephone lines, roads, and anything else that links people, the protector-persecutor must try to attack all your links and keep them out of order. You must forge and reforge these links. Eventually, seeing that you will not give up, the protector-persecutor will sit down to negotiate. The attacks may flare up again, but you will be more in control each time.

Outer links. It is nearly impossible to oppose the protector-persecutor successfully without the help of at least one other person who can see the absurdity of the rules that bind you and will support you as you try to break them. But the defense does not want you to have any allies. Very often one of the rules laid down by the protector-persecutor is not to believe that anyone loves you. People can say they love you over and over, and you still find it almost impossible to believe. This can be very frustrating to both your loved ones and you. It is important to let them know that the best proof of their caring is to be there for you consistently, even if imperfectly at times.

It helps to link with a person who can give the innocent some additional security beyond what you can provide. This might be a therapist or a person who loves you. But remember that the protector-persecutor can try a person's patience sorely, and the innocent may need an enormous amount of reassurance. Often therapists are better at withstanding these tests and maintaining a stable, secure place for the innocent. But someone who understands what is going on can be very helpful, too.

Keep a list of the people who have helped or could help you break the rules. Spend more time with them. If you think it would be useful and they would understand, tell them about the protector-persecutor. You can have them read this chapter or even this book. If you have a life partner, be sure to make this person one of your allies. Having the other see how the protector-persecutor steps in and tries to destroy your link will help your relationship.

Inner links. You must also reforge your inner links among thoughts, feelings, bodily sensations, memories, and what you do in current situations that seem related to the past. Remember all you can, feel all you can, and be present in the moment so that you can see the connections as they happen. Keep acknowledging the reality of the emotions you have cut off, because they are still there. They are usually very simple: fear, anger, sadness, and hopelessness. What is more difficult is to link the emotions that seem to arise for no reason to the trauma that required them to be driven out of awareness. Sometimes you can only guess from what little you know. At other times you will know perfectly well what happened but still have trouble recognizing your emotional response. For example, many people struggling with depression or anxiety have told me quite casually that they were sexually abused as children and had never seen any connection!

Learn to look for your buried emotions in your body, for that is where strong emotions express themselves. Maybe they are already presenting themselves as rashes, headaches, tight muscles, or weakness. They may show up in your eyes as tears, in your throat as cries, in your clenched fists, in your heart, pounding or feeling like a hard black rock, in your stomach as knots. Examine the causes of all of these sensations. If you are having trouble feeling your emotions in your body, you might want to find a body worker who is trained to help people express emotions stored in the body. Therapists often know who can help with this process.

Strong emotions can be scary, but nothing lasts forever, and their duration will be shorter if you do not resist too much. Try to set up a time to feel your feelings, perhaps after you dialogue with the innocent. You may want to be out in a natural setting, or safe in your own room with some candles and music that will either evoke the feeling, if you think you will have trouble accessing it, or calm you. If someone who understands can be with you, that is ideal. Emotions are meant to be shared.

The most important single feeling—the one that signals that you are on track to accessing buried emotions—is grief. You have to grieve for what was not and never shall be. For example, you may need to grieve over an early childhood trauma and the fact that your childhood was tragically different from others'. Grief, sadness, and mourning are quite different from depression. When someone grieves, they know why. There is a normal, natural link between the event and the emotions, and this is what you need, painful as grief may be. But since it is painful, talk about it with others. This is part of the corrective emotional link you need.

The inability to mourn is often the greatest problem with very early trauma. You do not even know what to grieve because you don't remember. And in the past it may have been dangerous to mourn because you needed to suppress the feeling in order to go on. If others had noticed you grieving, you might have ranked poorly among people who were feeling fine. "What's the matter with her?" Or your mourning might have made those in charge look bad. "Are you trying to say I did something to you?" Above all, it was probably useless to grieve at the time of the trauma, because grief draws others to us, and when the innocent's only other is someone who does not respond appropriately or does not respond at all, then the situation is beyond mourning. However, now you *can* mourn what you did not receive, which you long for still.

Most of this inner linking can be achieved through your dialogues with the innocent. Your dreams will also tell you what you are feeling. Because the protector-persecutor is opposed to your efforts, you will need to be systematic about your approach and very persistent, setting aside at least an hour a week to allow your emotions and remembered traumas to emerge. Once they do, they need to become part of your life story in order for complete integration and healing to take place, so write about them in your journal. As you do, those aspects of the undervalued self that are due to trauma will gradually lose their hold on you.

Use Your Dreams

Even if you do not have a protector-persecutor, learning to work with your dreams is invaluable. They will help you see the innocent's current form, the ways in which you undervalue yourself, what has traumatized you, and the quality of your links with others. In general, dreams reveal what you have not realized is manifesting in your life. They give "the rest of the story."

In the case of the protector-persecutor, dreams provide essential information for restoring the links it would like to destroy. Your dreams are aerial photographs, giving you a sense of the exact positions of yourself and your protector-persecutor and showing precisely how it is working against you.

The language of your dreams consists of images and stories entirely made up of symbols and metaphors, and the particular ones in your dreams are those most likely to speak to you personally. Every detail matters, and if a dream's meaning seems to be telling you something you already know, pay special attention to the details, particularly the unusual or unexpected ones.

Yes, the meanings of a few dream symbols may be universal, such as the ocean representing the unconscious. But if you are a sailor, the ocean will have other meanings as well. Likewise, if you dream about a bird or a taxi, you need to think about what a bird or a taxi means to you personally. While I don't recommend looking up the meanings of symbols in a "dream dictionary," I do recommend reading more about dreams. One of the best books is Robert Johnson's *Inner Work*, which is brief and also covers active imagination.[3]

The protector-persecutor cannot prevent you from having dreams, but it can tell you not to bother to remember them or take them seriously, especially nightmares. *Don't listen to it.* Protector-persecutor dreams are always unpleasant. But even "bad" dreams are helpful, because they all come from a part of your unconscious that favors growth, which is always there as your ally. So your dreams are something like an insider's tips as to what the protector-persecutor is doing or making you feel.

You can even find out what the protector is up to when you have "pleasant" dreams that do not seem quite right. One person dreamed of a sanctuary, a huge glass dome that kept out toxic gases, but the plants inside that were supposed to feed everyone were made of neon-colored plastic. Or you may dream of falling asleep, taking a drug, or fainting at a crucial point in a dream. These are all showing you that the protector side is drastically limiting your awareness of the dream.

The three stages of a protector-persecutor dream. Dreams about the protector-persecutor will go through three stages as you work with this book. During the first stage, these dreams may be especially horrific, evil-feeling, violent, creepy, or catastrophic. Even if you have had dreams like these for a long time, they will come more often when you are learning about this defense or trying to break one of its rules. These dreams tell you how the protector-persecutor is reacting. Unless a trauma is recent and the dreams are clearly about it, the violence in dreams does not usually represent something that actually happened to you. Dreams in which atomic bombs are falling randomly all over the earth or aliens are spraying cities with poison are showing just how badly the innocent suffered and how thoroughly the protector-persecutor is keeping you afraid of what can happen in the world, telling you the entire place is dangerous.

During the second stage, your dreams reflect the progress you are making with the protector-persecutor. Even if the horrors are as bad or perhaps worse, now in the dream you can do something or some help is available. You are terrified by a missile that has landed at your feet, about to explode. You look around and see that it was sent from behind the high walls of what you know is a defense facility. Someone standing nearby tells you calmly that the people launching these missiles are insane and someone has to break in and stop them before they destroy the entire world.

Note that the setting—a defense facility—is clearly a reference to the protector-persecutor. The dream says you know this now. Further good news is that some neutral part of you seems to know what needs to be done. You know this is not just the protector, because you are not being lured away from the problem by something that will not help. Rather, you are being informed to some degree about how to deal with this defense, although it still seems rather impossible.

During the third stage, the protector-persecutor appears as a person in your dreams. Even if that person is Hitler or a mother who murdered her children, it is in a human form and thus has human vulnerabilities. He can be locked up, she can be tried. Other signs of third-stage dreams are being rescued or being highly effective on your own, confronting or even defeating the protector-persecutor. If someone other than you is the victim, that means you no longer identify with the one the protector-persecutor can control.

These stages are not rigid, but knowing about them in general can help you see progress and understand why you might go back to having very bad dreams. Your dreams may revert to an earlier stage any time the protector-persecutor has been stirred up by your trying to break one of the rules.

Settings and ages. The settings of dreams and your age in them usually tells you about the general topic. A dream set in the house where you grew up is probably about your childhood and what happened in the house that affects you still. If you are an adult in that house, it probably relates to your adult relationship to your childhood.

In a protector-persecutor dream, the setting will vary according to the stage. The setting of a first-stage dream will be nightmarish and otherworldly. A second-stage dream will be set in a more human-created but evil place, such as a concentration camp. A third-stage dream will involve a place where you could, at least in theory, face down the forces against you.

The younger you are in the dream, the more likely that it is about the innocent, even if you normally envision her as an adult. If you are your current age, the dream is more representative of how the protector-persecutor is treating you now.

Emotions and people. In general, the amount of emotion in a dream is roughly equivalent to the amount of emotion you need to become aware of. When there has been trauma, and the links between emotions and their causes are broken, the unexpressed or unknown emotions in dreams can be very intense. The links were broken for this very reason — to keep you from being overwhelmed. Although nightmares are very upsetting, they are meant to help you by restoring the link between emotion and consciousness. The spell of a nightmare is best dissipated by describing it to someone — again, the power of linking.

The form the protector-persecutor takes in a dream tells you a great deal. Kurt dreamed that he had to fight a black knight. At first they both had the same equipment, suggesting a stage-three dream, but it quickly reverted to stage one: the knight became a giant robot, which multiplied and began killing everything — humans, animals, and plants. Kurt was learning that his grandfather's warrior perspective would have been fair if it had been intended just to teach Kurt how to fight, but there was something more behind it, his grandfather's lack of human feeling. Kurt's early experience of adults was, from the perspective of the protector-persecutor, a reason to destroy all links with the living world. (Much later Kurt dreamed of fighting a robot with a sword, which was able to penetrate the robot's shell. Human blood spilled out, and the robot died.)

Details of torture or suffering. When a protector-persecutor dream involves torture or suffering, the details of what is done to you or the innocent can be crucial information. Cutting off the head, hanging, or strangling can refer to being cut off from the body and its emotions. Someone mocking you probably refers to the persecutor's constant use of criticism to keep you out of action. Cutting off oxygen, food, or other necessities may indicate that the protector-persecutor is preventing you from taking care of your needs to a dangerous extent.

If you have many dreams about horrific sexuality—rape or the sexualizing of a child, for example—then the innocent probably experienced some kind of sexual intrusion, physical or psychological. For example, a father may have discussed sexual matters in great detail with his daughter because it gave him sexual pleasure. Never underestimate the impact of a sexual intrusion that is "only" psychological. Whether physical or psychological, incest in particular is an archetypal violation that is very damaging to most children.

Sexual attacks in dreams do not usually represent what actually happened but rather often symbolize something important that you might not have previously known. For example, the presence in a dream of numerous perpetrators might indicate the amount of trauma that resulted from the violation or intrusion. Sexual malevolence does not always indicate sexual intrusion. It may show what the protector-persecutor is doing now: raping you, treating you sadistically, demanding a deeply intimate and humiliating submission, or attacking your femininity or creativity.

Karen's Dr. Death

Karen was a highly sensitive, hardworking surgical nurse who came to see me because of the anxiety she experienced on the job, which gave the doctors she worked with the impression that she was incompetent. She was unable to sleep because she worried about making serious errors during a surgery. Her undervalued self ruled her days and her nights, which was exactly what the protector-persecutor wanted, as it kept her from feeling confident enough to seek what she wanted or needed in life.

On one particularly bad day, a doctor dismissed her from a surgery and officially cited her for not acting on his orders. Karen knew that the doctor was not up-to-date on the procedure and that his orders could be dangerous; she simply froze. That night she had a nightmare in which she was a deer, her front legs tied to one pole and her hind legs tied to another. She was strung up so that she could not move. A doctor appeared, and as soon as she saw him, she knew he had arranged this torture. Impressed that she was still alive, he cut her free but also cut off her front legs. She hobbled off into the woods, ashamed of her handicap.

The doctor followed and changed her into a young girl but made her a slave. Now she had to help him catch deer and string them up, tying them to the poles by their legs until they died. She was in fresh agony every time she did this, but she had to obey him.

The girl in the dream was eight, the age Karen had been when her mother died of cancer. Karen had always been a good child, and she behaved even better when her mother became ill. But she was only a kid, and just before her mother died she became friends with a far more rambunctious child. The two of them stole from the local grocery store. For Karen it was thrilling to share this secret danger with her brave, clever new friend, until the two were caught.

Karen's mother was devastated, fearing her daughter would "go bad" without her there to guide her. The doctor told Karen that her deed had made her mother much worse.

What were the emotions in the dream? Pain, helplessness, and shame about the handicap Karen would always have — the cutoff legs representing her cutoff life and her lack of freedom to choose to change. Above all, the dream revealed her terrible guilt about having to help kill the deer, as she thought she had helped to kill her mother.

The doctor in the dream was the protector-persecutor, whom Karen nicknamed Dr. Death. Karen's dream came out at that time because she was freeing herself in therapy, so Dr. Death cut her legs off to keep her hobbled. But by linking the trauma associated with the medical world in her past to the medical world she was in now, she began to push for her freedom from the protector-persecutor, speaking up with less fear at work.

Remembering Dreams and Working with Them

Dreams involving the protector-persecutor are often so violent and disturbing that they wake you in the night or rush back to memory in the morning. But not always. If a dream might be helpful, the protector-persecutor may make it hard to remember. Don't be too upset about forgetting a dream — you will have others. But you can make an effort to remember by staying in bed each morning for a few extra minutes until you have searched your memory for dreams. You can try stirring your memory by running through categories: did you have a dream set outdoors, at work, with animals, with people, at the beach? When you sense something familiar, stay with it. Write down in your journal any dreams you recall, and think about them during the day and before falling asleep that night.

Working with another person on each other's dreams can be tremendously helpful, especially once you both understand protector-persecutor dreams. You can help each other the most by simply asking specific questions about the dream. For example, "What does Hitler mean to you?" Or "How do you feel about parties?" Usually the person who had the dream will begin to make the connections without further help. But when you discuss dreams with another person, anything can come out, so be sure you feel comfortable revealing your deepest self.

Occasionally people with a traumatic past say they have no dreams. We all dream, so this is probably the defense at work, although chronic lack of sleep or certain medications can interfere with dreaming. Once you rule out a physical cause, be patient and reflect on the meaning of even the tiniest snippet of dream. This will start to build the link between you and your dreams.

Practicing with Your Own Protector-Persecutor Dream

Choose a dream in which you think you see the protector or persecutor—a dream in which, for example, something or someone caused you fear, suffering, imprisonment, or loss of awareness. Note the emotions and their strength. Consider why these emotions are showing up in dreams: Are they feelings you may be having when you are awake without being aware of their cause? Are they feelings you ought to be having, given a situation you have been in recently?

Decide what stage this dream represents, given how the protector-persecutor appears. Is it a machine, a monster, or a human being? Big enough to destroy the world, a town, or just you? What do your age and the setting suggest?

List the details of each figure and object and ask yourself why it might be there. Imagine describing a detail to someone who does not share your cultural or personal symbolism. What is the bicycle for you? What's a dog? If the bicycle is red, what does that color signal to you? Does red mean anger? Is blue depression?

Step back and look at the entire dream. See if you can understand what the dream says about how the protector-persecutor manifests in your life right now. Can you recognize specifically protective or persecuting actions? What might you learn from the dream that you can use to humanize your protector-persecutor or break its rules? For example, Karen's dream of Dr. Death showed her that she was a survivor—good news—but that she needed to break the rules at work among the doctors, whom she had allowed to treat her like a child or a slave.

Active Imagination with the Protector-Persecutor

Now that you are aware of the protector-persecutor in your life, you will begin to notice that you are a bit freer and are breaking its rules with good results. You are able to link with allies and reestablish links between past and present, mind and body, and emotions and memories. Your success will be recorded in your dreams, as you see the protector-persecutor taking on more human or natural forms. When this happens, it may be time to try to negotiate with your protector-persecutor through active imagination.

Your goal in negotiations is not to be rid of the protector-persecutor entirely, for it appears to be impossible to do that; the goal is to have it activated less often by your demonstrating to it that you are going to be all right, or even better than all right, out in the world.

Being Safe

Before negotiating, you have to make yourself safe. Even after the protector-persecutor has taken on a human form in your dreams, it is probably still an attacker or untrustworthy in some way. For your first active imagination, plan to talk with its mildest, most human dream form. Then focus on physical safety. If in your dream the protector-persecutor is a man trying to break your door down, you don't want to speak to him while your door is creaking and splintering. Imagine the police coming and taking him away, then speak to him only when he is in a jail cell. If you cannot imagine this—for example, if he gets away or shows his superpowers again, or if the police are not entirely on your side—do not continue.

Negotiating

Your goal is to convince the protector-persecutor that breaking its rules and taking risks is working out for you and that you want more freedom. Explain that you are enjoying some success at work or at least not experiencing anything that would warrant all those old rules: that you should stay unnoticed, never speak up about your needs, never show your skills, or whatever the protector-persecutor had you doing that kept you undervalued. Tell the protector-prosecutor about your good relationships. Don't assume it already knows, for it is autonomous, disconnected from you. This is what keeps the defense safely in place.

Listen closely to what the protector-persecutor says in response. Even if you disagree, negotiations will go better if you listen. Also, you will see what areas still trouble it or how it is still operating.

As you learn its strategies for protecting you, acknowledge its good intentions. Then quietly and persistently point out that you, too, want to keep the innocent safe, but you also want her to grow. The innocent can help you in this, if she is obviously enjoying her increased freedom and refusing to be "protected" by being kept behind walls.

An Active Imagination with Dr. Death

Karen had been taking more and more risks and breaking more of Dr. Death's rules, including accepting a promotion to surgical nurse manager, but she learned too late that the position had proved impossible for the three people who held it previously. Even though no one acknowledged her successes, she could see that she was doing more than all right. Her mistakes were being overlooked, and she was being given more and more responsibility. Clearly she was doing better than any of her predecessors. But she was also losing weight, losing sleep, and losing friends. On the job she was able to prevent chaos, but just barely. Off the job, chaos was winning.

Karen knew she should quit. She wanted to quit. She had exciting plans to go back to school and could afford it. But the foremost rule of Dr. Death was *Make no changes*, because in the past a small change—making a new friend—had seemed to result in terrible things. However, Karen had already made other changes. She had moved out of her father's house and ended two terrible lifelong "friendships" in which she had remained loyal in spite of being mistreated. As she made these changes, Dr. Death began to be more human in her dreams, no longer able to cast spells that turned deer into girls or girls into slaves. Encouraged by this, she decided to dialogue with the most human form of Dr. Death about resigning from her crushing job.

KAREN: Hello again, Doc. I think you are trying to "help" once again. I want to resign from this job, but I just can't do it. Is that your doing?

DR. DEATH: You don't want to be a quitter, do you?

KAREN: That's it! [Karen knew that her father hated quitters. He had never recovered from his wife's death, becoming a cold and cruel taskmaster, and he had called Karen a quitter many times.] Hey, when the *Titanic* was sinking, it only made sense to quit the ship. This situation is due to poor management, and I can't change that.

DR. DEATH: Quit, then. But right now you're being paid more than ever before. You'll never find another job like this.

KAREN: I would not have been promoted to this position if I had not been an outstanding surgical nurse. I can go back to that.

DR. DEATH: They'll want to know why you quit. If you say the management was poor, they'll see you as a troublemaker.

KAREN: My former supervisor will give me a good recommendation.

DR. DEATH: Your boss will explode when you tell him you want to quit. Everything depends on you. [This stopped Karen again. She was terrified of her boss.]

KAREN: I'll write a letter. A letter of resignation.

DR. DEATH: You had this great opportunity, but you messed it up.

KAREN: I did not mess it up. It was messed up before I came and will be after I go.

DR. DEATH: Just blame it on others.

KAREN: Stop it! I should have said no when they offered it. Okay? But I've done my best. And I'm not scared. I'll be okay.

What Karen did:

- Dialogued with Dr. Death's safest form.
- Watched for a link with her past—her father calling her a "quitter."
- Argued firmly.
- Got angry when she had had enough.

Active Imagination with the Protector-Persecutor Versus the Inner Critic

If Karen's inner critic had been speaking instead of her protector-persecutor, he might also have called her a quitter, thinking this would be the best tactic to get her to try harder and succeed at her job. She might have had to tell him the same thing, that she needed to quit. But an inner critic can be persuaded fairly quickly by reason. The motivations of the inner critic and the protector-persecutor are quite different: the inner critic hopes to help, while the protector-persecutor wants Karen to stay at a job she will fail at rather than make a change. It values most the undervalued self.

Since they serve such different functions, even if you have advanced far in the healing process, the protector-persecutor will not morph into the inner critic, will never become enthusiastic or helpful about your progress. At best it will be cynical. When you are doing active imagination, listen carefully to who is speaking. Are you hearing something that could be useful, even if the form or the details are off, or are you hearing something that is not helpful for meeting your goal or completely untrue?

WORKING WITH WHAT YOU HAVE LEARNED

In this chapter you have identified how your inner critic is contributing to the undervalued self. You have also decided whether you have a protector-persecutor perpetuating your undervalued self, and if so, you've developed a general strategy for regaining control of your life.

Forming an Agreement with Your Inner Critic

Make notes in your journal about how you want your inner critic to change, then write him a letter making very clear what you expect in the future. In active imagination, read the letter and see how your inner critic responds. Make changes in the letter until you and he come to an agreement. When you notice your inner critic slipping back into the old ways, bring out the letter. Like any good coach, he should be conscientious and able to admit he has slipped from keeping his agreement.

Facing Down the Protector-Persecutor

If you have a protector-persecutor, think very broadly about your dearest values and goals and how the undervalued self interferes with your reaching them. Then think more specifically about how the protector-persecutor has obstructed your progress and maintained the undervalued self and why. Consider both the protector and the persecutor aspects. What has been the strategy of each, and which one dominates right now?

If you have not already done so, make a list of the rules (no intimacy, no standing up for yourself, and so on) you need to break and your progress thus far. Now write a master plan for the strategy you will follow to better contain the protector-persecutor. This should include watching for it vigilantly; continuing to break its rules; increasing every kind of link, inner and outer; creating a schedule for active imagination with the innocent; watching your dreams to see how the protector-persecutor is operating; watching for the right time to dialogue with it; and documenting all signs of progress. Above all, if you put this book back on the shelf and ignore it, ask yourself why you're doing that.

CHAPTER SEVEN

How to Deepen Relationships Through Linking

Having worked with the innocent, the inner critic, and the protector-persecutor, which are the mostly unconscious factors that can keep you from linking, you can now return to consciously developing further linking skills in order to switch from linking to ranking when you want to. Chapter four gave you the fundamentals of linking, but it focused more on relatively new links as well as those you want to maintain but in which you do not want or need deeper intimacy.

This chapter will help you move a new friendship or casual dating relationship to a much deeper level, to the point that you both "commit," in the sense of agreeing you are close friends now or a couple. You want to be together more, know each other much better, keep up with what is happening in each other's lives almost daily, and meet each other's needs as much as possible, especially during crises. Although sometimes this depth of closeness grows naturally, you do not have to leave it to chance. There are skills you can learn that almost guarantee that it will happen when you wish it to.

Close relationships provide you with more opportunities to

link rather than rank, but they help you avoid the undervalued self in other ways as well. In a close relationship you will know that the other knows most of your quirks and still loves you. You can heal traumas by talking about them together. If you tend to feel insecure in your attachments, this will lessen, and you will have a place of sanctuary in a world of ranking.

How Close Are You Now?

Although you could take a long test to find out how close you are to a particular person, this one, which my husband and I developed, is as accurate as any of them and captures the feeling of a close link. Simply circle the picture below that best describes your relationship with the other person. If you want to do this for several relationships, write the names of each person under the picture describing that relationship.

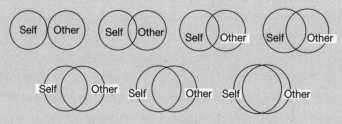

The more a pair of circles overlaps, the more you view the other person as a part of yourself. In our research studies, we have found that the degree of inclusion of the other in yourself determines how much you like the other and enjoy the relationship, are willing to meet the other person's needs, and generally treat the other as if the two of you are almost the same person.[1] This is not an unhealthy merger — each of you is still a separate "circle." To treat someone as you would treat yourself requires that you have a self of your own. But the two of you do share resources, viewpoints, and emotional support. This is the essence of linking.

ACTIONS YOU CAN TAKE TO DEEPEN A RELATIONSHIP

Although we deepen a link mostly by talking, it is good to remember that linking also happens when you skip the words and take action instead. In chapter four you were reminded about offering food, gifts, and kind acts. The more you offer these, the closer you will be. When the link is casual, you offer a cup of coffee. When it is deeper, you invite the person to dinner. Instead of sending a postcard while on a vacation, you bring back a handwoven blanket. Instead of offering to take your friend's shift at work when she is having outpatient surgery, you take her to the surgery, wait for her, bring her home afterward, and stay with her until she feels better, fixing her meals and reading or watching movies with her.

It is also well known that friendships and romances often deepen when the two people have gone through an intense experience together.[2] Think of the friends you have developed this way, perhaps by studying together for do-or-die exams, being in the armed forces together, or raising children of the same age. (In this chapter most of the examples will be of friends and relatives, but everything in it applies to deepening romance as well.) Some people have become friends for life after being stuck in an elevator together. You can also strengthen a link this way intentionally. You know you will intensify your intimacy when you decide to travel together and certainly if you decide to live together. This is not just because you will have a lot of time to talk but also because you know that unexpected situations will arise and you will have to do things for and with each other and see each other at your worst. Consider deepening a link by learning to sail together, going backpacking, or working in a homeless shelter side by side.

Researchers have found that they can turn strangers into close friends by having them face a common foe or work together.[3] Sometimes you can apply this knowledge, too. When you are worried about the rising water in the creek and you have a neighbor you like, make your sandbags together. When each of you is planning some remodeling, suggest helping each other with the decisions. Intense shared pleasures have similar effects. If you both like the same team or enjoy the theater, get season tickets together. Something thrilling is sure to happen during the season.

In general, when people do something exciting together that "wakes them up" to life, in large or even small ways, they feel more attracted to the person who is with them at the time.[4] Instead of dinner and a movie, suggest a moonlight hike. Instead of doing lunch, go Rollerblading, bird-watching, have a rooftop picnic, or volunteer at a soup kitchen together. Of course, you should not be insistent, and you must choose something you think the other will like and definitely not plan it as a surprise unless you are sure it will please. But just giving so much creative thought to your time together is a gift the other will appreciate.

CREATING A CONVERSATION WORTH HAVING

The better the link, the more responsive you will be. Each of you is alert to trying to understand each other and meet each other's needs. Most of this happens through talking, whether for fun or to get to know each other better or to be helpful. Even when you are helping a close friend move, a lot of the pleasure is in talking while you do it. Some of that might be playful. "You have more stuff than my parents! You even have stuff for keeping stuff." Some conversation may lead to getting to know each other better. "So it's that hard for you to throw things away?" Some might be a way to help the other. "I see moving from here is really hard for you. Want to talk about it?"

Conversations for Fun

Take a lesson from the French and many other Europeans, who love conversing and have a different philosophy about it from Americans.

First, they generally would not meet a friend in a dull state of mind. So be enthusiastic about your encounter. If you are naturally reserved, you may have to remind yourself to turn up the energy and the volume. Then, after checking that each of you is doing okay, instead of asking "what's new with you?" and listening to the other give a long news report, as Americans tend to do, try for some repartee, or playful back-and-forth. Think of it as a friendly tennis match; as in tennis, you will get better with practice. Here's an example:

"I just saw this great movie."

"Ah, you and movies. I'm sure it's something I'll *have* to see."

"So next time come with me rather than waiting for my review."

"No, half the time your reviews are better than the movie."

"You really want to hear about this?"

"I've stopped reading the menu, haven't I?"

Does that seem like too much work? A close friend, a strong link, deserves effort. And if you are going to play tennis, the better you play, the more fun you will have. If you want stronger relationships—and you do if you want to heal the undervalued self—then you need to put some effort into your conversations.

Conversations about What Is Inside

"Intimacy" comes from the Latin word *intimus*, meaning "innermost." To make a relationship more intimate, you have to disclose your innermost thoughts and feelings, especially your feelings. Think of the content of your conversations progressing on a continuum from least to most intimate, then move along that continuum as you and your friend are ready.

You might start by simply exchanging thoughts and observations, then moving to a mix of ideas and feelings, and then expressing almost pure feeling or emotion, as when you are both laughing hysterically or crying together. The emotional moments usually do the most to enhance your link.

Sharing what is happening in the present usually deepens intimacy more than talking about the past. Look at the difference between "That reminds me of the other day, when I saw this guy on a unicycle doing all sorts of stunts" and "Hey, look at that guy on the unicycle. He's amazing. Want to go watch him?" The second situation is more likely to draw you close in a shared moment.

A conversation can be entirely about someone else, about you and someone else, about your friend, or about you and your friend. The most enjoyably intimate conversations are usually about what you are feeling, not thinking, about each other. For example, "I just love getting together. I'm so glad we could meet for lunch today. I've been sort of down and I really needed some cheering. But you know what? I'm feeling better just seeing you."

Linking is usually strengthened *least* when you use words with little feeling to describe something that has no relevance to your relationship or common interests. For example, "I went shopping yesterday and had to return a dress, and the person waiting on me..."

These are not rigid rules. Sometimes you feel very close to someone while exchanging news, and you sense the other is feeling close to you as well. People who love each other also love to hear each other's ideas, life stories, recent experiences, and even just their wandering thoughts. Under the right circumstances, any of these can create intimacy. And, of course, sometimes the focus should be just on the other: "You seem preoccupied today." Or the past needs to be acknowledged: "I was really proud of you the other day when I heard you won the mayor's award."

My Friend Who Does It All

To some degree, what defines intimacy for the two of you is a matter of your personalities. I have a close friend who, besides listening without rushing in with her opinions, being skillfully attuned, and generally taking care of me when I need it, also asks thoughtful, penetrating questions that always take our conversations deeper. This is just her personality, but it certainly works to bring us close. These are questions you might not ask someone whom you felt less close to. "Is there anything you would regret not doing before you die?" "What's your earliest memory?" "If you had to change careers and could do anything you wanted, what would it be?" "What do you think happens after death?" She also has us reflect on our friendship. "What do you suppose our relationship will be like in ten years?" "Let's talk about the most valuable things we've learned from each other."

We get to our latest, deepest experiences by talking about our dreams. If we spend the night somewhere together, the first question every morning is "Did you have a dream?" Then we talk about it. I love her constant interest in this, and as I said in chapter six, discussing a dream with another person can reveal more than you ever imagined.

Finally, I don't know if she is aware of the power of discussing a relationship as it is happening in the moment, but she does this, and it always draws us closer. She will say something like "I'm so glad you said that—it's really helping me." If we are talking on the phone, she will say, "I'm even taking notes as we speak." Or she will ask, "Doesn't it seem like we are closer today than we have been in a long time?" She will also ask the all-important "I get the sense you are annoyed with me—is that true?" Or "Elaine, we have to talk, because I was really upset when you …"

As a result, every conversation I have with her deepens our link.

Match the Other's Pace

As you disclose your feelings, you want a balanced engagement in the conversation. When you share something, soon afterward the other does, too. If that does not happen, one of you may feel either overexposed or left out. (Of course, if one of you needs to talk about a problem, balance is not your goal.)

To even out an unmatched pace, it helps to gain a feeling of the other's state of mind. Is your friend preoccupied or agitated by something, and do you feel like an observer? If so, you may want to help him or her calm down by slowing your own pace. For example, you meet your friend for a drink after work, and he rushes into a torrent of conversation about struggles going on in his office. When it's your turn to share, you consciously speak more calmly. Eventually the pace of your friend's sharing slows down and you see him relax.

If you feel that your friend is sharing more personal feelings than seems appropriate for your current level of intimacy, you can slow him down by revealing a little less yourself or changing the subject just slightly. You certainly do not need to match his pace of self-disclosure. To do so could leave you feeling bad later because you said more than was comfortable for you. For example, if your friend begins to discuss his latest sexual adventures, which is more information than you want, it isn't necessary to share your own sexual experiences.

If your friend is talking less than you are, and you think it might be that he is still not sure of your interest or caring, you can try encouraging him by sharing just a little more about yourself than you have so far and then pausing to let him share something similarly intimate. But again, be careful not to share so much that you later feel embarrassed or ashamed. And if your friend stays reserved no matter how open you are, you can either let it go or try asking why, without prying. "You're being quiet tonight. That's okay, but if there's something going on that you want to talk about, I'm all ears." This caring, linking approach will help you avoid having your undervalued self triggered because of perceived ranking.

WHEN THERE IS SOMETHING WRONG BETWEEN YOU

Nothing is more intimate than daring to express your inner feelings about something the other has done that you do not like. But if you have an undervalued self, such a conversation can quickly lead, or seem to lead, to ranking. You are afraid of a fight in which you will be defeated or an accusation in return that will make you ashamed. If you expect something like that before it even happens, you may speak in a tone or manner that communicates ranking. You may fall into the self-protection of blaming or projecting. Above all, you fear that by bringing up a problem you will be rejected and destroy your link. But in the long run it will be far better to speak up. It is hard to love someone when you are feeling resentment or lack of respect because of something the other has done, but once you are able to say what bothers you, your undervalued self will see that there is nothing to fear.

Before you speak up, be sure you do have a legitimate complaint. You're getting closer to your cousin, and then she jokes that "you're no fun—you're a complete fanatic about carbs." Are you still feeling bad about her comment the next morning, or does it all seem trivial after a good night's sleep? If you still have that negative feeling, wait for the right time to speak—not when she's rushing off to work or exhausted. When a suitable time presents itself, begin your conversation by pointing out at least four positive things—seven is better—about your cousin before you gently and lovingly express your problem about her comment. The idea may sound silly, but it works.

Do not forget the problem of shame—don't judge or criticize what you see as the other's character flaws. Stick to the one time the other did something you did not like and express how it *did not work for you.* "When you jingle your keys I get nervous that you're about to go." You are suggesting that the problem might be yours, but because you feel this way it affects your relationship, and therefore you must bring it up. So rather than "Being late is rude," use "I" statements: "You're late and I'm really irritated" or "I get angry when you're this late."

Even with "I" statements, tackling one event at a time is far less shaming than discussing a category of events. "I was really upset when you were late today" rather than "It upsets me whenever you're late." You can discuss it again if it happens again.

You also need to speak up when you are having negative thoughts about yourself generally or else doubting the other's investment in the link. This can be equally challenging, since it is so easy to feel ashamed of the undervalued self. But the other has probably had similar moments. You can strengthen a link enormously by expressing these fears and negative feelings about yourself and allowing the other to support you, as you would support her. In this way you are rescuing each other from the suffering and harm that comes with an undervalued self.

MEETING THE OTHER'S NEEDS IN TIMES OF STRESS

Sometimes a link is strengthened most with an even exchange of dialogue, like the witty conversation or mutual self-disclosures I have already discussed. But there are other times when one of you has emotional needs that the other can meet. When you are the one wanting to meet the other's needs, the best way to strengthen the link is to hold the space for those emotions by being responsive and changing to listening mode. You learned about attunement in chapter five, when you were helping the innocent part of yourself during active imagination. You can attune to another with equally healing effects. Attunement means fully understanding another's feeling state, sometimes to the point of being in that same state. In other words, it is empathy in its most intimate form.

You meet a friend who is obviously distressed. He tells you that his parents are going to divorce after thirty years of marriage. Your first instinct might be to ask questions: "How did you find out? What did they say? Is this really a divorce or just a separation?" Or you might even ask, "How do you feel about that?" But for some people, direct questions about feelings can be uncomfortable. Instead, simple listening and attuning—feeling or trying to feel what the other is feeling—almost guarantees a deeper conversation.

The ways you are learning to help a friend in times of stress can sound like psychotherapy. While it is true that you are learning what skilled therapists do, there is an important difference. You do not have to do any of it. In fact, to push yourself to be attuned when you do not feel like it would only weaken a link. Nor do you have to be outstanding at this. Sincere caring is at the heart of it, and your linking instinct will see to that.

The Dos and Don'ts of Attunement

- Do try to share the mood. "Yeah, it makes me sad, too, hearing you tell me about them splitting up."
- Do reflect the other's feelings by stating what emotions were expressed verbally or nonverbally: "I can tell this is a big loss for you."
- Do show your interest and attunement in a nonverbal way as well. Lean forward and look at the person. If the other is saying something important, stop whatever else you are doing. If the other is sad, let your body and tone of voice express that you share his sadness. Cry if you feel like it.
- Do use comparisons to illustrate your understanding: "You're feeling like an orphan?" Metaphors are often the best way to capture a feeling in words.
- If you get it wrong, be a good sport. Your friend might respond, "No, not an orphan. More like I'm dead." Even if the correction seems inaccurate, when he moves in a new direction, stay with him. This signals that you want to help him sort out his feelings rather than tell him what they really are or ought to be.
- Don't try to talk your friend out of his feelings. "You shouldn't feel guilty."
- Don't come back with your own experience. "*I* was really angry when my parents got divorced."
- Wait awhile before giving other emotional reactions. At first stay with comments like "I can feel how worried you are, having to split

yourself between them from now on." Even "I'm so sorry to hear this" can wait. Of course you are.

- Don't give advice before understanding the entire situation and knowing your friend would like your opinion.
- Don't go off into intellectual ideas. "Yes, parents divorcing can have a major impact on a person's life."
- Avoid clichés, such as "Time heals all wounds," or generalities, such as "Life is rough."
- Minimize questions. Questions can be distracting or hint at what the other ought to feel, so ask a question only if some important omission has left you confused. Even questions about the other's feelings are less helpful than attunement and reflections.

Being attuned requires giving your friend your fullest attention so that he knows you care. You are listening for the feelings, no matter how buried they may be in his story. He says, "Yeah, my parents told me about the divorce last night. They took me out to dinner. I mean, I thought they were doing fine. What did I miss? I couldn't believe it. Maybe I should have called home more, had them here. Separately, you know? Seen what was going on."

You hear both his shock and his guilt. You can feel it as if it were your own. You then put your attunement into words that accurately reflect your friend's feelings, not just his thoughts. (Follow the dos and don'ts listed in the box.) For example, you might say, "You're really reeling from this. Yeah, sure, you wish you'd been able to stop it somehow." The effect of this attunement is to put your friend even more in touch with his feelings, which can be very healing. He will also feel your acceptance, which protects him from seeing your conversation from a ranking perspective and feeling ashamed of how he feels.

Your friend replies, "Yeah, reeling. And guilty. I just want them to stay together. I want my home to be like it was when I left it." As he continues, he realizes that he is feeling sadness for a past that is gone forever and knows that his parents may have different feelings that he will have to accept.

Linking During a True Crisis

When you and another have a close link, you inevitably will share some major crises in each other's lives. How you manage these events often determines whether the link grows stronger or is forced to end because one person cannot handle what is happening. It can be difficult to be present when a friend is in crisis; sometimes it is heartbreaking. But if you use linking skills to help the other weather a crisis, you will not only strengthen your bond but will bring healing to each other's undervalued selves.

In a conversation about something deeply painful, attunement remains the key to being helpful. See how it works in the following conversation. Notice that at the start the problem seems to be fairly minor, but in fact Sandra's friend is in real trouble, which she discovers because she is attuned and responsive.

SANDRA: How's work?

PAUL: Lately I've been feeling like quitting.

SANDRA: That bad?

PAUL: It's my boss.

SANDRA [*hearing a catch in Paul's voice*]: Sounds like you're feeling really beaten down by this guy.

PAUL: Yeah, and the worst part is, I'm stuck. I can't quit.

SANDRA: You're feeling trapped? That sounds scary.

PAUL: Yeah, and I sincerely worry that I can't get another job.

SANDRA: Finding something else seems almost hopeless?

PAUL: My skills are rusty. I'm not going to be a hot item on the job market.

SANDRA: Boy, you truly are feeling down on yourself.

PAUL: Yeah, really down.

SANDRA: Depressed, too?

PAUL: Depressed? I guess so. Can't sleep. Can't eat. On top of that, I'm having trouble with Phyllis. I think she's going to leave me. Sometimes I just want to give up.

SANDRA: You're at that giving-up point.

PAUL: Yeah, honestly, I don't really want to go on very much — you know — living. I can't believe I'm saying that though. It's so stupid. Let's forget it.

SANDRA: You sound ashamed that you're that down. I guess I can understand that. But anyone would be down with these burdens, wouldn't they? Honestly, I'm so glad you're telling me all of this. I mean, what would our friendship mean if you couldn't?

PAUL: I guess I am ashamed. And you're right; we've been through a lot together. It's just that... I feel so worthless.

SANDRA: Sounds like you're turning in circles in your mind and not finding anything good anywhere. I'm really, really sorry to hear that. It must be a terribly hard place to be.

PAUL: At least I have you to talk to. Thank you.

SANDRA: "You're welcome" doesn't quite do it. I'm really touched. I'm so glad you're talking, so glad to listen, and so glad it helps.

PAUL: It's people that matter most, I guess. I should see if someone knows of a job.

SANDRA: Ah, a tiny, tiny hope?

PAUL: Maybe. Yeah. I should try to find something before I quit, start asking around. How are you doing?

SANDRA: Nice of you to ask. But is that to change the subject for my sake?

PAUL: Well, it's not polite to monopolize the conversation.

SANDRA: Do you remember last March when I was breaking up with Pat and falling apart? You helped me tremendously then by just listening. So talk all you want. You're not down that often.

Notice the following about how Sandra helps Paul:

- She does not respond at the outset with something like "Yeah, sometimes I feel like quitting, too." She listens to find out more.

- Almost everything she says is about a feeling. Although she keenly wants to know and help, she stays away from surface facts ("What did your boss do this time?"), advice ("I'd quit if I were you"), or ideas ("It's amazing what companies can get away with these days"). Staying with his feelings quickly deepens the conversation, reaching what is happening inside Paul.

- Her listening has brought out his thoughts of suicide, which should never be ignored, but she does not jump on this. She can explore it later and perhaps recommend that he get some professional help. Sometimes we say we want to die because it is our only way to express our hopelessness and extreme undervaluing of ourself.

- She reassures him three times that his feelings are okay and she wants to hear about them. Life truly feels hopeless when you feel ashamed, so that it seems that your links with others are falling away, too.

- She adds her own feelings occasionally, but only so that he knows she is not judging or abandoning him.

- She does not miss his shift to some optimism, but she doesn't inflate it either.

- She does not let him move the subject away from himself out of shame.

Receiving Attunement

Allowing someone else to help you when you are distressed is just as important as helping the other when trying to strengthen a link. If you withhold what you are feeling, the relationship does not simply stay the same. It becomes less close for you, because even though you trust this person, you do not risk opening up, and it is less close for the other, because he or she senses your mood even though you do not share what is going on. So do not think of yourself as being selfish or a nuisance when you are the one in need of another's attunement. If you enjoy being attuned to your close friend, why wouldn't he like being attuned to you? If you care about each other, sharing your feelings will feel right for both of you and enhance your closeness.

Some friends will sense right away that you have something on your mind, but others will need prompting. Do not automatically take a missed cue or wandering attention as a lack of interest. Some people are simply more sensitive than others. Give the other a chance by saying, "I really need to talk about something." And if he offers advice too quickly, you can say, "I appreciate what you're saying, but I think I just need you to listen right now. That would mean a lot to me." Also, *do not hold back tears*. Crying is the clearest signal that you are in distress, and letting a friend comfort you, even if it is a little awkward, can be a great testament to the trust shared between you.

Above all, if part of the distress is that your undervalued self has been activated, try to absorb the fact that your friend cares about you. If you have any doubts, you can ask how she is feeling about the conversation or about you. You will probably receive instant reassurance, and part of you knows that, but the undervalued self still needs to hear it. And if you do not believe the reassurances, admit that you don't. They might not be sinking in because your inner critic or protector-persecutor is preventing it. If your friend understands about the protector-persecutor and your undervalued self, explain what she is up against. And try to break the protector-persecutor's rule that you should not believe it when someone seems to care.

Sharing Successes

Research shows that the strongest relationships are those in which each fully celebrates the other's successes.[5] This is what Geri did.

MAX: I can't believe it. I got this great performance review, a promotion, and a *raise*. With all those layoffs. I guess I've been doing something right.

GERI: You say, "*Something* right"? I guess. That's amazing. What terrific news. I'm so *happy* for you. You must be flying high.

MAX: I am. I'm just amazed. I've been working so hard for this. Still...

GERI: You've been working your butt off. What's the "still"?

MAX: You know. A lot of my friends got the sack.

GERI: Feeling guilty?

MAX: Maybe. No, not really. [*Laughs.*] I'm just blown away.

GERI [*laughing too*]: I can imagine. This is simply great.

Dwelling on a friend's success is like feeding a relationship the most nutritious food. However, what if you also feel a little jealous and undervalue yourself because your friend seems better than you now in some overall sense? Or what if you use the inflating self-protection and see your friend's success as trifling? Research shows that when two people do not see themselves as competing in the same area, they can enjoy each other's successes more.[6] When your husband is feted at a banquet for being the best salesman, you can imagine his award hanging beside your "Best Dancer" plaque.

Remembering the Details and Being Affectionate

Before you meet a friend, say for lunch, think back over what has been happening with him. Is he looking for a new apartment?

Nursing a sick mother? Recovering from an injury? Did he announce last time that his wife was pregnant? Some people who know they will forget such details even make notes after a conversation to remind them of what was said. Being remembered in this way makes the other feel your interest and really strengthens a link.

Also, be affectionate. Say whatever is in your heart, such as "Now I have ten more reasons to value this friendship." If you like being with the other, say it as often as the other seems to enjoy it. "You know? I just love talking to you." Or "I really look forward to seeing you." "I just want you to know how much I care about you." And, if it feels right, "Good-bye—and I love you."

Finding Time for Deeper Links

You absolutely must allow time for linking in a relationship that is important to you. I cannot emphasize enough how healing strong, rich, rewarding relationships are for the undervalued self.

Make appointments. If you are insecure in the avoidant way or held back by a protector-persecutor, you must be proactive about making regular contact with friends. Discuss together how frequently you would like to meet. Then make a note in your calendar for your next meeting.

Make your do-or-die list. If you want a link to be strong, it's important to go to events that are significant to your friend: weddings, graduations, or other celebrations that you've been invited to. You have to interrupt your schedule when a friend needs your help, even if it means a flight across the country. Don't automatically give so much weight to what's going on in your life that you allow inertia to win. Of course, you can't do this for everyone. The decision is quick and easy if you have a mental list of those people for whom you would drop everything if one of them needed you or was having a major life event. Keep the list up-to-date. This is not a ranking of your friends but an acknowledgment of your deepest links.

When Links Do Not Work Out

In chapter four you learned not to take it personally when you attempt to link and are rebuffed. This is a very important lesson, because trying to establish a link and failing can feel like a defeat. The undervalued self is likely to be triggered, returning you to ranking mode, and you might assume you should never try anything like that again. Because you have been rejected, you think you are not as good as others. You may not even notice all of this, but some part of you will probably decide to watch out more closely in the future for people who might reject you.

When you are trying to deepen an existing link, the effect of rejection is more subtle. Maybe you want to be closer than the other does, or you think you have completely misread the other's feelings. This can be far more painful than a rebuff by a stranger or acquaintance. You may resolve to be less involved, less caring than before; from now on you'll "keep it all superficial," but the undervalued self will still have gained power.

Simply assuming that you are the reason that the attempt failed ignores the fact that the problem may lie entirely in the other. Suppose a new friend turns down your second invitation to dinner. Perhaps she has decided that she simply does not have time for another close relationship but does not want to say that because she does like you.

When you try to move a relationship to a deeper level, you may encounter all sorts of unconscious obstacles in the other that sound like a rebuff but are something else entirely. Without knowing it, you may trigger one of the other's self-protections. For example, your brother discusses a problem he is having and you try to be attuned, but he feels ashamed of the feelings you are reflecting back and says, "It didn't really bother me that much" (minimizing) or "There you go, trying to be a therapist again" (blaming) or "It wasn't a big crisis for me, but it sounds like it's turning into one for you" (projecting).

215

You could be dealing with the other's avoidant attachment style, which can sound something like "I don't need any sympathy" or "Let's just change the subject." In that case the two of you may disagree fundamentally on how close a "close relationship" should be The avoidant wants the security of commitment but not the intimacy that goes with it.

You could also come up against an emotional schema in the other. You are very aware of how much a friend is distressed by a call from his mother, and you try to help him talk about it, but you get a surprisingly hostile response. "Why do you keep bringing up my mother every time I'm a little anxious? You seem to think she was some kind of a monster just because she beat us kids every day."

Finally, you could even be dealing with your friend's protector-persecutor, who will do anything to keep her from entering into a close relationship. When you are rebuffed as you try to get closer and then realize the problem is in the other person, rather than undervaluing yourself it may actually be you who decides not to try to take the relationship further. Do not let the undervalued self blind you to the many reasons another person may not want to get closer, other than your not being good enough.

WORKING WITH WHAT YOU HAVE LEARNED

This is a long list, but you do not have to do all the steps at once.

1. Decide whom you wish to strengthen your link with. Go back to the overlapping-circles exercise at the start of this chapter. Pick someone with whom you would like to increase that overlap, whether a new acquaintance, a first date, a relative, or a longtime friend you'd like to be closer to.

2. Plan something to do together. Try to choose an unusual activity or a shared challenge that will draw you closer.

3. Have an energized conversation. Keep the remarks bouncing back and forth like a tennis ball. If the other is not as skilled as you, slow down so he or she does not feel unequal, keeping in mind the goals of energy and wit.

4. Have a conversation that draws you closer through intimate sharing. Move along the continuum from talking about your thoughts about someone else toward the goal of disclosing what you are feeling in the moment about the other; that is, take the next of these steps: talk about your past feelings, then your present feelings and thoughts, then feelings about the two of you in the past, and finally, thoughts and feelings about the two of you in the present.

5. Be attuned the next time the other is stressed or upset. Follow the Dos and Don'ts of Attunement (pp. 207–08).

6. Be attuned the next time the other has a success. Watch out for any envious ranking on your part and try to stay with linking.

7. If the other has done something that irritated you, talk about it. But try not to create shame for either of these.

8. Next time you are struggling with a distressing situation, talk it over. Keep the person on track if you need to, and stick to your feelings. Perhaps share the Dos and Don'ts of Attunement.

9. Reflect on a relationship that failed and added to your undervalued self. Do you now have a different understanding of what might have been the reason? Can you stop ranking yourself so low when you think about it now?

CHAPTER EIGHT

A Sustained Close Relationship:
The Final Step to Healing
the Undervalued Self

In the last chapter you learned to strengthen the commitment between you and others to the point of deep closeness—to the point of love as defined in this book. This chapter helps you sustain that love. However, even if you are not now in a loving, committed relationship, this chapter is still important for you. There are degrees of commitment, and you are probably on the way toward greater commitment with someone, using the methods you learned in chapters four and seven. I define committed love as living together, or staying in very close contact, and intending to help each other through any life crisis or problem between you. Keep in mind that, while this chapter focuses on couples, it can apply equally well to close friends or relatives.

This chapter is the final step in your journey because love, besides its other rewards, has a profound effect on the undervalued self. It is there to turn to when you are awash in ranking. It helps heal trauma as nothing else can. And committed love is the only thing that can give you the security you may have missed in childhood because it assures you that you are valued and that you will receive the other's support through thick and thin. You have not been abandoned or abused so far, and you can begin to believe that you won't be. All relationships have problems, but you are learning to work them out in ways that increase linking rather than ranking. Even when you are not together or even thinking of the other, this person is part of the reality of your life. The other's love is a fact.

PROTECTING LOVE BY STRENGTHENING THE LINK

Paradoxically, a committed relationship can do more to intensify the undervalued self than a less close relationship. The more closeness and commitment you have with another, the more reasons there can be for conflict, self-protections, insecurity left over from childhood, triggered emotional schemas, and the protector-persecutor defense. All of these problems increase ranking, and the more ranking there is, the less true linking your committed relationship will have. No matter how many times you say "I love you" to each other, your relationship can become a fight over who controls whom. That is definitely an unhealthy place for you, with your easily activated undervalued self. So let's begin to understand how you can protect love. The best solution in most cases is to increase linking. Think of the link as having a bank account. Problems require withdrawals to pay for the inevitable conflicts and ranking struggles. But along with minimizing the need for withdrawals, you can also stay wealthy by making deposits.

Using the Expansion That Comes from Feeling Love

The best way to make deposits, according to extensive research done by my husband and myself, is to increase the sense of self-expansion that you find in your closest relationships. While self-expansion may sound selfish, it refers to the fact that when you are with the person you love, you feel bigger, expanded.[1] You share the other's perspective, treasured thoughts, status among others, and, in times of need, resources. When lovers feel "on top of the world," it is not about rank. It is about this wonderful sense of expansion, as if you could see in every direction. You walk taller and have a stronger sense of your own strength as a person. And your undervalued feelings are gone. This is linking at its most powerful.

When a relationship is beginning to deepen in the ways described in chapter seven, there is a strong sense of excitement as you experience this expansion with and through the other, especially if it happens rapidly. As you become more familiar with each other, the rate of expansion naturally slows. There's less to learn about each other. You might begin to associate the relationship with a comfortable status quo, which is a lot less exciting than expansion, or you may even become bored with each other. The undervalued self may arise again if you begin to blame yourself for being dull. You may "rank your link" because it seems less exciting than others' links.

Expansion Through Conversation

One way to preserve that sense of expanding together is to share daily experiences, focusing on those that are unusual or especially interesting. You could even ask each other, "What did you learn today that you never knew before?" It may sound a bit forced at first, but think of the alternative, the self-shrinking effect of responding to "How was your day today?" with "Oh, another frustrating day" or just "Same old same old."

You can make a conversation self-expanding at any time. I'm sure you can think of conversations you have had with an old friend or a longtime partner that seemed to revitalize the relationship, making it deeper, broader, and more alive. Think about what happened in those conversations and see if you can replicate some of the most effective elements, the ones that left you feeling most expanded.

Most often these conversations will involve intimacy and emotions, usually having to do with the two of you in the moment, and you developed these conversation skills in chapter seven. But even if you both prefer intellectual conversation to talking about feelings, you'll discover that this type of conversation is far more stimulating if you are both interested in or, better yet, passionate about your subject. My husband and I usually begin a day off together by just talking in bed. We're waking up and catching up. Often we find our way to some new idea that has excited one of us during the week. It is usually something from psychology, of course, and off we go, having tremendous fun discovering new insights. It would not be intimate or fun for everyone, but for us it renews our love because it reminds us of how much we expand from just knowing each other.

Expansion Through Activities

Talking is not the only way to expand a committed relationship. Indeed, it is probably better not to rely on it constantly. My husband and I have done a great deal of research on the effects on couples of doing novel and challenging activities together. In our laboratory we have asked pairs to do something as simple as trying to beat a timer in a silly contest of physical agility in which the two are tied together at ankles and wrists and have to push a ball back and forth over a barrier. Other times we have asked them to spend two hours a week doing something novel, exciting, or challenging together; the couples in a control group spend the time doing something pleasant. In all cases, those doing the exciting activities felt closer, more satisfied with their relationship, and more loving toward each other. They also felt better about themselves; that is, these experiences kept the undervalued self at bay.[2]

You have to choose an activity that is right for both of you, of course. Some pairs might want to learn to hang glide or scuba dive. Others might choose going to the opera or to an amusement park for the first time. Look at your committed love relationships and consider what would be an exciting, novel, or challenging activity that both of you would enjoy trying.

Physical Intimacy

We all instinctively want to be near someone we love. We want to know where the other is when he or she is not with us. We want to touch and be touched by the other at least now and then. Linking is so much more satisfying when it includes comfortable touching of some sort.

When sexual intimacy is appropriate and desired by both, it can strengthen a close relationship more than anything else. We tend to like sex most when there is maximal love—wanting sex only with each other, wanting to know each other sexually, and wanting to meet each other's needs. Being sexually active together can help heal the undervalued self because sex is a splendid shame reducer. Like most people, you may have developed a sense of shame about your body, your sexuality, and any impulse to take something for yourself. All of this inhibition contributes to the feeling that there must be something wrong with sexuality. Comfortable, loving sex reduces general shame by giving you a sense that your body and your sexual desire are wonderful in the other's eyes. And during an orgasm, there is usually a moment when you forget everything but your own needs and pleasure, and the other accepts and likes that you do so.

Being patient when one of you wishes to be sexual and the other does not also strengthens your link. In contrast, being sexual when the other wants to be and you do not (or when you do and the other does not) is rarely a good idea. Although it seems to meet the other's needs and be a sign of love, it usually turns sex into a ranking matter in which you feel you have to do what the other wants. Further, your partner becomes the pro-sex person, and you lose touch with your sexual desire because sex is too frequent or at the wrong times for you and thus is not so pleasurable. You may even begin to think something is wrong with you. Meanwhile your partner begins to feel you do not desire him or her sexually, and you both are in the grip of the undervalued self.

If this is happening, it is very helpful to agree that the one with less frequent sexual desire should be the one who initiates sex. If this is you, this arrangement will allow your natural rhythm of sexual desire to return. Your partner will probably like this idea because when you do want sex, he or she will feel your real love and desire rather than a reluctant giving-in.

Loving Communication

Two people who have grown close may say "Love you" to each other when getting off the phone or in an e-mail. We may proclaim "I love you" regularly to a partner. Two gruff guys might risk saying "I love our friendship." Yet we often forget to say what we *like* about each other. Sharing what we like is a direct way to strengthen a link as well as to help heal each other's undervalued self.

On a long road trip my husband and I once entertained ourselves by listing the ten things we most liked about each other. This led to a study in which we asked people exactly what made them fall in love. Some mentioned the other's good qualities, but a surprising number said it happened at the moment when they found out that the other liked them.[3] Besides signaling that the attraction is mutual and the relationship can proceed with less risk of rejection, the discovery that another likes us helps heal the undervalued self. Our good qualities truly come alive for us only when someone else notices them, not to rank us on the degree we have those qualities but to love them and us for having them.

SEEING RANKING WHEN IT ISN'T THERE

A constant threat to a committed loving relationship is the undervalued self's habit of seeing ranking when it is not there, especially when the other seems to be looking down on you or controlling you when that is not the case. For example, you are in love with a guy who never returns your messages. He assures you that he never returns anyone's messages, and you know that is true, but you do return his messages. He says he loves you, and he seems to mean it and show it in every other way. Still, when you want to talk to him and leave a loving message, and you get nothing in return, it is difficult not to feel that he is controlling your access to him and assuming that his time is more valuable and his rank is higher.

What can you do when the other's actions put you in ranking mode? Checking with the person is the first step. Say what you feel as well as listening to what he intended you to feel. If he keeps up this behavior, ask him at least to do it less often. If your request leads to conflict, ask him if he is willing to follow the steps for dealing with conflict given later in the chapter.

When You Feel Used

You might see ranking when it isn't there if you have been giving more than receiving. At the outset of a relationship, you try to keep the two in balance. But commitment, even in friendship, means being there for each other "for better and for worse, in sickness and in health." When the other needs a lot from you over a long period of time, you may begin to feel used. You should not feel ashamed of this, but you also should avoid talking about your ranking feeling directly. A direct statement will surely make the other feel ashamed and stir up self-protections such as blaming: "I never asked you to do all of this. You never should have agreed to help me if you were going to resent it."

Sometimes you can dispel the sense of being used by thinking about what the other has done for you in the past. If the feeling remains, you do need to have a talk about the situation. The best approach is usually to ask, "Do you still need my help in this way?" Perhaps you will find that you have been doing more than you need to do. Or you may be much needed, and when you hear the other's gratitude the ranking mood melts away. If that fails, then you probably have to express your resentment, but with gentle "I" statements like the following.

"Since the break-in at your house, you've been calling me to come over in the night when you've heard strange noises. I've been so glad to be able to help and you've been very appreciative. You say you feel a little less scared, and thank goodness for that. But last night for the first time — it's hard for me to say this — I started to feel a little put out, only because I have to get up so early for work. How can we work this out so you feel safe, which I still want as much as you, and I get enough sleep?"

Notice the four reassurances: I've been glad to help, you've been appreciative, thank goodness you're less scared, and I still want you to be safe. Be sure to say you have only just now felt the resentment. People can feel deeply ashamed at the thought that all along the person helping them really did not want to. Acknowledge the other's gratitude and continuing need, yet add your need too.

When You Feel Inferior

You might see ranking when it is not there if you fall into a competitive mood or feel unworthy of the other's love. You think you are not as smart, as popular, as mentally healthy, or whatever as the other. If this state of mind goes on too long, it may even become self-fulfilling, in that you become overly anxious and fail at things or, without realizing it, you cause the other to view you as inferior. The purpose of this book is to reduce just that feeling, and you know what to do: try to switch to linking. After all, one of the things the other probably likes best about you is your love. Can you see its worth? If you cannot do that, discuss your feeling of worthlessness as a problem you know about, rather than as if you really are worthless. That is, do not let your undervalued self speak for you. If you feel you would hear only reassurances you could not believe, also discuss your inferior feelings with someone else you trust.

One of the greatest obstacles to equality in a couple's relationship can be inequality of income.[4] Whether it is an obstacle depends on the reason for the inequality and how your culture views it. In the past it was the norm for a woman to be a homemaker and full-time mother without an income of her own, but it rarely led to a sense of equality. Many cultures view a man "living off a woman" as not only inferior to her but not a real man at all. If you and your partner do have an inequality in earning, usually even today, in this culture, you will both have to work very hard to counter the tendency to rank each other.

Another way that you may rank yourself as inferior to your partner is if you have a temperament that is unusual, at the extreme of normal, or not encouraged in your culture. There is a wide range of normal temperament variations. I mentioned one trait, high sensitivity, in chapter three, but some people are naturally highly distractible, for example, or energetic, orderly, easily bored, emotionally dramatic, or emotionally self-contained. Every culture favors some of these traits and not others. If you are different in some way, it does not make you inferior.

When a relationship begins or is not yet close, differences or "eccentricities" may be charming and even the basis of attraction. Perhaps one person even completes the other in a certain way. People whose work requires a great deal of cool logic often enjoy spending their time off with someone who seems deliciously irrational and impulsive, while the volatile one is grateful for some calm reasoning when problems arise.

With time, however, the differences between you reveal their disadvantages, the quirks that annoy or inconvenience the other. If yours is the less moderate or socially accepted style, both of you may see you as the problem. Learn more about your trait, convince yourself that it has advantages as well as disadvantages, and then point these out to the other, emphasizing the advantages. Since you are implying that the other person has been wrong, however, be careful how you express this.

When You Feel Superior

It may sound nice to feel superior, either generally or in some specific admirable way, but it is still ranking and not helpful when you want to link. Further, if you feel superior in all ways, not simply that you read maps better or are not color-blind, it usually means you do not respect the other person, and it is hard to love someone whom you do not respect. You may feel that you are faking your love, having to do everything for the other, or wanting to get out of the relationship but unable to because it would hurt the other person so much.

You might think that if you undervalue yourself you could never feel superior. But remember, if you undervalue yourself you are in ranking mode, and in that mode it is not hard to flip positions and feel superior, particularly if you use inflating as a self-protection, by thinking or saying, for example, "Well, he's just lucky to have me" whenever you feel inferior. It can also happen simply because you compare yourself to others besides your partner much of the time. If you are in the habit of ranking, you will be quick to pounce on your superiority whenever you can actually see and claim it, and with someone you know well it is easier to find flaws and then feel superior for not having them yourself.

Try to banish most comparisons in your closest relationships, even the ones favorable to you. Focus on whatever makes you love this person. As for those real or seeming flaws in the other that can make you feel superior, it helps to allow the other to have some quirks—you have them too—and to be different. When the two of you are out with others, avoid feeling that the other's flaw reflects on you.

DEALING WITH CONFLICT

The closer the linking relationship, the more potential for conflict over how you spend the time, money, or those possessions you have agreed to share. Plus, the outcomes of these conflicts seem to be about who ranks higher or has more influence in this relationship. Feeling that you lost can stir up the undervalued self more than it might in a less intimate relationship.

When There Seems to Be No Conflict

What if there is no conflict because one of you voluntarily gives in most of the time, and this person is you? Even if you are long used to it, you'll have to stop, because giving in feeds your undervalued self. Further, doing so makes you rank lower, which affects the amount of real linking in the relationship. You must learn to resolve conflicts while staying in linking mode. That requires you to respect your own needs. You have to learn to decide whether to give in according to which person's needs are greater in this particular situation rather than always giving in because you feel you ought to.

Too often those who undervalue themselves use the noncompeting self-protection in close relationships. They expect a shameful defeat, or they fear that winning could cause the other not to like them or even leave. If this describes you, and too much inequality has slipped into your "loving" relationship, you may have to correct this by engaging in some ranking for once. You need to establish your boundaries—"I'll give this much but no more"—before you can have the mutual respect needed to use the methods of solving conflicts that I provide.

Avery Makes a Decision of His Own

Avery and Louisa have been married for almost forty years, and Louisa has made almost all of the decisions for both of them.

Avery has been satisfied with this arrangement because he sees his wife as smarter and because he knows she loves him very much. Alas, a wealth of "I love you"s does not always mean that a close relationship is mostly based on linking. In this case, Louisa is very insecure because of her childhood and has needed to control Avery in part so that he does not "run off with someone else." As she has gotten older, she has been certain that some younger woman would catch her husband's eye.

Unfortunately, neither one realizes how dangerous it is for a close relationship to be based so much on ranking. Recently Avery was laid off from his job of thirty-five years. Louisa was still working and doing well, so she wanted Avery to "retire, relax, and let me support you." That sounded very loving to Avery, and he accepted that decision. However, a few years earlier, during a leadership training, Avery discovered that he had a strong artistic side, so after he retired he took up photography. This was fine with Lousia until he found he had a true talent for it and decided to take a serious photography class. His loving wife strongly opposed that, but he really wanted to take the course and stood by his decision. At that point Louisa became a regular demon. Indeed, upon reflection he saw that he had been giving in to her on almost everything, believing that this is what you do when you love someone. But he realized he was sick of giving in.

Eventually the two came to couples counseling, and Louisa confessed her conviction that in a class like the one Avery wished to take he would meet some woman who was more artistic and prettier than she. This confession eventually strengthened their link, but if Avery had not come to understand the root of his wife's dominating behavior, this conflict could well have ended their marriage.

Giving In Begins So Naturally

Most of us learned at home that the polite and caring thing is to let those we love have their way. And I have said that linking means meeting the other's needs as much as possible. What is confusing for a person with a strongly undervalued self is knowing whether the other really needs something or just wants it. A need usually refers to something that you both agree is serious. If one of you is sick, out of work, injured, or in some other crisis, there is no conflict. The other person gives. The importance of a want is less obvious. Wants have an *emotional reality*. You are pulled toward something, you desire it a lot or a little.

Conflicts occur when two people want different things. But with an undervalued self, you tend to see your wants as less important. Maybe you even truly need something, but you see it as only a want and let it go.

This confusion arises easily, especially when you have a persistently undervalued self. For example, say you have become close to someone very quickly. The two of you agree on almost everything, and when you do not, you enjoy each other's differences. So you try living together. One night you want to go to a classical music concert, but your new love is not interested. You could go alone, but he doesn't want to spend the evening without you. That's reassuring, at least, so maybe you say, "The concert's not that important to me anyway," and you stay home. But all evening he is enjoying himself and finally asks, "Why so gloomy tonight?" You hardly realize it, so you do not say it, but you are sad because this concert was one you had been looking forward to all year. That was the emotional reality of the matter.

Your love grows and you are now engaged. The two of you started living together on the West Coast, where you were born and which he enjoyed. However, he grew up in New England and wanted both of you to move back there. You did, but after two years you still miss California terribly. That is the emotional reality, but by now you have given your fiancé the habit of getting his way on most issues, so when you bring up moving back, he does not offer you what you gave him two years before.

You feel depressed and maybe anxious, but you only vaguely

know why. In fact, you have accepted defeat in order to keep his love, whether or not that was necessary. You do not see the ranking you created, nor do you realize that the loving thing to do now is for the two of you to go deeply into this conflict in order to decide the relative strength of each one's desire. The emotional reality is that if we put your own and your partner's wants on a scale of one to ten, your wanting to move back is a ten and his not wanting to move is a three. Fortunately, your fiancé has also read this book and wants to switch back to linking too. But you both know he can be very eloquent, persuasive, and logical, which is partly why it has been so hard for you to be his equal in an argument. You need to even things up.

What if both people give in to the other? The result is no better. Neither one voices a strong want, and the relationship becomes bland. On the other hand, when you decide to go along with the other's want or at least listen to it, you will sense that the relationship is expanding you. You may even be glad you tried something different.

How to Work with Conflict

A structured format is the way to maintain equality and love while resolving major conflicts caused by wanting different things.

1. Make an appointment to talk about your disagreement. Do not expect a resolution in one session, although it may happen. (But if you have to make a decision by a certain deadline, your appointment should be well before that deadline.) Choose a time when you will both be rested and not distracted and will have some free time afterward to regroup. One hour is a good length of time, so you neither exhaust yourselves nor cut off a conversation just when it is going somewhere. As for the place, being outdoors can help give you both a bigger perspective, without interruptions.

2. Start by having one of you take a turn, perhaps for five or ten minutes, depending on the urgency and importance of the issue. If you go first, express your feelings about your side of the conflict. Be honest. Do not hold back or exaggerate. It is okay to cry. Say how it makes you feel to imagine not having what you want. That is the emotional reality, and you need to hear each other's feelings in order to take them into account.

3. During this time the other person mostly listens, never interrupting to disagree and always following the Dos and Don'ts of Attunement in chapter seven. Going back to the East Coast–West Coast preference, your partner might listen and say in response, "So you've been suffering more than you've told me. You want to go back, not only because it's your home state and has warmer weather. You miss the greenness, the aliveness." You talk about how the winter affects you. Again he acknowledges what you said: "It's farther north here, too, so the days are darker. Cheerless for you." The listener can also take a few notes—very few—to help him remember how he wants to respond to a point, but these should not distract from being attuned and cannot be used until his turn to speak.

4. The other takes a turn, in this case talking about his home state and all the feelings he has about being there. You listen without interruption, staying attuned. Again, you can make a note or two about your reaction to be used later, but keep it to a minimum.

5. Add two minutes to his time so that he can also respond to what you said while he was only listening and acknowledging your words. He might say, "I enjoyed California too. You seem to think I didn't." Or, "I would miss the change of seasons. And my family. You say you would miss yours, but I'd miss mine too. You know how close we are."

6. Now you take two minutes to express your reactions to what he just said, while he goes back to listening mode. "I hear you about your family. I'd miss them too. But my parents are in California and getting older, and I won't have them much longer."

These few minutes of response by each of you is *all* the back-and-forth you allow yourselves. This sort of highly controlled argument takes some willpower.

7. Separate for twenty minutes. After you both have spoken, it is time to be alone. Reflect upon what you have said and heard. Think about how much each of you wants or needs to have your way—do not worry too much about the distinction between want and need.

8. When you return, see where you are at. Sometimes one or both will come back with a changed mind. "Obviously it's time to move back to California. I can fly home every fall to see the family and the leaves." If this isn't the case, repeat steps two through eight, but shorten the times: perhaps five minutes each, plus two minutes each to respond and fifteen minutes to reflect. But do not fall into arguing with faster responses.

9. If at the end you are still polarized, stop. Do not do another round. Set up another appointment and do not discuss the subject until then. This will contain your conflict to a specific time, so that in the meantime you can focus on linking. If you continue with this process, you will find a way to resolve the problem or at least live with it in a new way.

KEEPING THE SELF-PROTECTIONS FROM SPOILING LOVE

As you learned in chapter two, when you use one of the six self-protections you are in ranking mode, trying to avoid the shame that comes with a defeat or failure. Shame in a committed relationship has its own flavor, and so do the self-protections.

You could say that committed love does not begin until you have seen each other at your worst and still love each other. Shame is intensified when you dread having your partner see a flaw in you that perhaps no one has seen before. But once your "worst" has been accepted, often the shame goes away entirely.

A few things, however, may continue to make you ashamed even though they should not. Usually these have to do with your insecurity or emotional schemas, so you may use the self-protections in a close relationship more than anywhere else.

It is important to acknowledge that even when you have done something that really is shameful, such as lying to the other, there is always an explanation in your personal history, and that can reduce your shame. The trick is to hold the tension of the two opposites: you are a person who can be loved, yet you have a problem to work on. When both of you have that attitude toward the other's weaknesses, the need for the self-protections can gradually fade away.

HEALING THE EFFECTS OF AN INSECURE ATTACHMENT

Insecure attachment is the enemy of long-term relationships; where love should be, ranking exists instead, without either of you knowing it. You have lived so long with your insecure view of close relationships, which began when you were very young, that now of course you unconsciously repeat the same patterns. If you are anxiously insecure, you feel lower in rank, powerless to stop the other from abandoning you, or you feel you cannot stand up for yourself out of fear of abandonment. If you are the avoidant type, you work to stay in charge and rank higher than the other to keep from realizing how attached you really are, which leaves you feeling unbearably vulnerable.

Fortunately, a committed love relationship is the very best place for healing an insecure attachment. Your early attachment relationships, like this one, involved trusting one special person to stay near and love and take care of you as much and for as long as possible. So if things went wrong in that first relationship, you will feel increasingly uneasy as your adult relationship approaches committed closeness. But when things go right in this relationship, you will gradually feel more secure than ever before.

Unfortunately, however, a new insecurity arises—that this loving relationship must end when one of you dies. We all must face that ultimate separation. Even temporary separations can be hard for two people who love each other. The need for physical proximity is one of those innate emotional realities. It is painful to be apart from each other, unable to see or touch the other and not knowing where the other is at any given moment. No wonder we're all on our cell phones so much.

Separation is the downside of love, and there is no way around it. It is a high price but one shared by all of us. Alas, the insecurities from the past and for the future build on each other. So if you are an avoidant type, the very thought of separation really makes you try to act as if you don't need your partner, which does not promote love. If your insecurity is the anxious type, you think too much about when this relationship will end, which also interferes with feeling love right now, today.

An important way to link in a close relationship is to admit your distress about being separated and to support each other through it. But sometimes our self-protections do not allow admitting or even being aware of this fear. While I was in an avoidant phase—sometimes we go in and out of secure, avoidant, and anxious—I thought I was perfectly happy that my husband was spending more time than usual traveling. On the way to the airport one evening to pick him up, I was even thinking that I was a little sorry he was coming back. But as I watched him walking toward me, I started to cry. That was how I knew, on that night, how much I loved him, an emotional reality I was simply denying at the time.

Bottom line: If you are insecure, your heightened fear of separation triggers ranking. Your undervalued self makes you feel powerless about a separation, even when you are the one going away. This may trigger self-protections—in my case inflating and minimizing. Or you want to cry and beg the other not to let the separation happen, just as you wanted to in childhood. But it seems that to do so would lower your rank even more, so you say nothing and your unconscious finds a way to express itself, as when I finally did cry when I saw my husband.

An Argument Before Separation

People living together in a committed love relationship often plan trips away from their partners without realizing the emotional reality of what they are doing, the inner disruption those plans can create at a deep, instinctual level. If you are too insecure to talk about it, your undervalued self can cause the following type of conversation.

SCOTT: I don't have any clean clothes. I've got to leave early tomorrow and I've got nothing to wear. [*He's slamming doors and drawers.*]

WENDY: I suppose you expected me to wash them?

SCOTT: No. I never said that. I'm just mad at myself for forgetting. [*Now he's yelling.*]

WENDY: I hate it when you do that underhanded thing. Just be honest. You wish I'd done the laundry. [*She's getting loud too.*]

SCOTT: I don't. You're always trying to make me out to be sexist or something.

WENDY: Your mother did the laundry. To you it's a woman's job. Why shouldn't you expect me to do it?

SCOTT: Okay, you want honesty? I wish I were leaving tonight, right now, just to get away from your bitching.

WENDY: Go. You have no idea how much I would love that.

Ouch. Stop-action. No matter who is doing the leaving or how much they have agreed that the trip makes sense, people who are close do not want to be separated. It's that simple. But Wendy and Scott both have a history of insecure attachment, so they have buried their feelings even more and added self-protections to hide them. Scott has not planned well for his trip, unaware of how reluctant he is to leave her. She is furious that he is abandoning her and is blaming him by picking a fight.

They both do not want to be like their parents. Scott's mother died when he was twelve, and his father "went crazy with grief." His fear is about death—the other never coming back—so he doesn't want anyone to become as important to him as his mother was to his father and to him. In this instance Scott would like to leave earlier to get the pain over with, as if this separation from Wendy amounted to death.

Wendy's father left her mother. Not only did Wendy lose him, but her mother had to go back to work. Wendy spent much of the rest of her childhood with various babysitters or at home alone. Her fear is that Scott will be like her father, so she wants to abandon Scott before he can do that to her. Further, since her mother was not able to prevent her father from leaving, Wendy is worried about what it takes to keep a man and very angry that she has to be concerned about it. For her, separation amounts to losing a life-or-death fight.

Suppose Scott and Wendy were determined to get to the bottom of their true feelings? They would sit down, draw a deep breath, and say something like this.

SCOTT: What the hell is going on with us, fighting like this?

WENDY: Well, you're going away. And I guess I'm probably wishing you weren't.

SCOTT: Really?

WENDY [*starting to cry*]: I guess so.

SCOTT [*putting his arm around her*]: I don't want to go either. I hate to be away from you. I hate sleeping in a bed without you and going out to eat without you. I hate it all.

They both hug and cry. They set times when they will call each other. They also look more closely at their schedules to see if, when one has to take a trip, they can go together.

Getting Down to Basics

The following statements express the emotional reality at the foundation of long-term links: "I love you, and I'm afraid I will lose you. I'm afraid you'll die. I'm afraid you will stop loving me. I need you. I need your love." Though simple, these statements get to the heart of closeness. If two people love each other deeply, they can truly help each other bear these feelings, provided they can get past the idea that expressing them shows weakness or that they can make them go away by denying them.

Here is the ideal response when someone you love admits to the pain of separation: "I've got the same fears. I need you, too. I hate being apart. I get scared I will never see you again. I need to know I can reach out and find you here with me." Of course, two people who are close do not have to say all of this every time. But if you love someone and do not feel these feelings, you are almost surely keeping them out of your awareness to protect yourself from the pain they cause or for fear of sounding weak, clingy, or mushy. Express your feelings sometimes. It will strengthen the link, making both of you more secure and therefore helping to heal each other's undervalued self.

HEALING THE TRAUMA BEHIND EACH OTHER'S EMOTIONAL SCHEMAS

You learned in chapter three about emotional schemas in yourself, and in chapter four how to identify and handle them in someone you are getting to know better. Now you can think about healing them in each other. One of the very best ways to tame the undervalued self is to work on emotional schemas within a loving relationship, where you have the best opportunity for a corrective linking experience.

The downside of emotional schemas in close relationships is that you and your partner's emotional schemas can become intertwined. This is why schemas in close relationships show themselves in dramatic and devastating ways. If you ignore the role of your emotional schemas, you will have recurring fights that become loud and bitter or that end with one of you withdrawing, perhaps for days. The emotions can be overwhelming and remarks may be made that can never be taken back, creating fresh trauma. Intertwined schemas are undoubtedly the greatest threat to a close relationship, but becoming skilled at handling and healing them gives you the best chance of staying together.

When Emotional Schemas Intertwine

My husband tends to talk as he does something, providing a sort of play-by-play, and as a professor he has learned to speak with some emphasis. When we are making the bed, setting up a tent, or doing anything else that requires coordination, he tends to say things that to him are thoughts more than orders, such as "Put that down now," "Bring it over here," "Wait a minute, I'm not ready." Usually I have been smart enough to have already put it down, brought it over, or not rushed him, and it infuriates me when he makes these comments. I feel ordered around, as if he sees me as his slave or as a hopelessly stupid person. He then becomes very angry about my anger, since he did not at all mean to order me around. In fact, he is rightfully proud of our general lack of ranking, so this is a personal affront.

I react so strongly because being ordered around and treated as if I were dumb is exactly what I experienced from my older sister, with whom I was often alone when I was growing up, and it was very hard on me. My husband was an only child with gentle parents who rarely criticized him but often bitterly criticized each other, finally divorcing. He associates criticism with that painful event and all the arguments leading up to it. When he feels judged by me, he thinks that means our marriage is failing. So when I complain that he is ordering me around, making me feel unloved, he feels equally unloved. These particular emotional schemas would not be triggered in most situations, but in our very close relationship, this combination creates trouble. Fortunately, we have learned how to untangle ourselves, and you can too.

What to Do about Emotional Schemas in a Love Relationship

Remember from your work with the innocent that in order to heal traumas, the basis of emotional schemas, they have to be discussed again and again in the presence of love. What you learned to do for the innocent you will now do for each other. To begin, read again the discussion of emotional schemas at the end of chapter three and carefully consider what you wrote about your own schemas in your journaling for that chapter. When you love someone deeply, you can be sure that most of your schemas will eventually be triggered.

Also, reread what you learned at the end of chapter four about how to handle someone else's triggered emotional schema: do not argue; continue linking; do not agree just for the sake of keeping peace; but do not stay silent either, as that will be taken as either agreement or judgment. Especially if the other is being overly self-critical, rather than stay silent, say something like "I can really appreciate why you see it that way, but ..." Listen for and respond carefully to self-protections, and remember they cover up shame about something. Above all, talk afterward about what triggered the flare-up and how to avoid that happening again.

Triggered emotional schemas in a loving relationship deserve and require additional special handling. When you talk about the eruption afterward, offer to the one you love the kind of help you learned in chapter five to give the innocent. That is, provide attunement and understanding. Make the connection not only to the current cause—the trigger and how to avoid it—but also search together for the cause in the past. This will lead to the trauma behind the schema and to your opportunity to provide a corrective emotional link, the reaction from you that the one you love ought to have received from someone in the past. As you learned with the innocent, it is okay to disagree when you feel you must and can avoid retriggering the schema. Finally, be gentle and appreciative that the other has trusted you with these painful memories.

In addition, you will want to see how each other's emotional schemas intertwine. Does your childhood with a critical mother make it easy for you to feel criticized, and does her perfectionist father cause her to find you always falling a bit short? Did your controlling older brother make you sensitive to being dominated by men, while your partner has experienced so much prejudice that he, too, has a constant need to feel in control?

It is possible that you have even created an emotional schema in the other, for example, at those times when jealousy made you cruel. Heal this by admitting to what you did and saying what you now wish you had done and intend to do in the future. One couple in which one partner's emotional schema of jealousy created serious damage in the other decided to sign a contract that they would not betray each other, and, if one of them ever slipped, he or she would tell the other within twenty-four hours. Part of the deal was that this had to mean the end of suspicions and accusations.

You must handle emotional schemas compassionately and as objectively as possible. Doing so is a significant act of love and heroism, since you both may be facing down intense fears from past abandonment, abuse, separation, or other traumas. You each need to attune to the other whenever one of you revisits, perhaps for the hundredth time, the event that created the emotional schema. When you love someone, your attunement naturally leads to a corrective linking experience as you express your wish that it had all been different or that you could have helped or any other healing feelings and thoughts that come up naturally. If at first the other is not as good at attunement as you are, you will be the role model, or you can offer this book to the other to read.

Dealing with each other's emotional schemas sounds as if it requires Herculean effort. It does. Although it's easier once you learn the hard lessons about how not to handle them. As for the effort involved, what is your choice? Even the best love relationships come with their own set of problems. Most of us are never told this, but the loving intimacy we want in our primary relationship requires an incredible amount of work. You can't live well without this kind of love, especially if you have struggled with an undervalued self. So call it a labor of love.

WORKING WITH WHAT YOU HAVE LEARNED

1. Look back at the overlapping-circles exercise at the start of chapter seven. Consider your most committed love relationship. Do the circles overlap more as you apply the suggestions in this chapter?

2. Do you ever worry about being too close? Try to see why this might really be a ranking issue, in that perhaps you fear being controlled, or of being overwhelmed if you lose the other. Or is it that you sense your need to set boundaries so that your needs and wants are separate from the other's and made clear?

3. Think about the remaining obstacles to your being able to love the other fully by reviewing those discussed in this chapter. Write about the obstacles that apply to you, and when you are ready, discuss them with your partner.

4. Plan an exciting, challenging, novel activity together and have a wonderful time.

CHAPTER NINE

Breaking Free from the Undervalued Self

Together we have aimed to heal your undervalued self, and you are certainly much closer to your goal. But how can you heal what is built-in instinct? At the beginning of the book, I said that each of us has an undervalued self because it is natural to have an overall sense of self-worth that responds to defeats, and defeats happen to all of us. Your conservative built-in response, designed to see that you survive above all else, protects you from further defeat (or any shameful misbehavior) by lowering your self-worth more than necessary. This keeps you from challenging anyone about anything for at least a while, turning you over to your undervalued self. This is all part of your instinct for handling ranking situations. Of course, you also have a strong instinct to link, which you now see can overpower the ranking instinct.

If you've found that often you cannot switch to linking, you now know that this is because your overall low self-worth is not the result of just any sort of defeat, but of repeated or traumatic defeats, defeats that involved unbearable feelings of being emotionally overwhelmed, powerless, and ashamed. In that case, very likely the protector-persecutor defense described in chapter six was called upon to keep you safely stuck in ranking mode.

These traumas are what need to be healed, and just as you can heal physical traumas, you can also heal the psychological ones. However, in both cases the right conditions must exist. To heal, you now know that you need corrective linking experiences, both within yourself and with others. So it is true that we all have an undervalued self and it is also true that you can heal the damage that causes the undervalued self to exaggerate its natural response to defeat. Even when the healing is not complete, you can be more conscious of how the undervalued self tends to distort things, just as you might be aware of an old injury.

SIGNS OF PROGRESS

Look back over your journal (if you did not keep one, think about your life since you began reading this book). Make notes of the progress you have made. To help with that, write yes or no beside these signs of progress:

1. You are missing out on fewer opportunities, social and professional, because of undervaluing yourself.

2. You can tell more often whether ranking or linking is going on in yourself and others.

3. You rank yourself less often and do not automatically see ranking in situations where it is not helpful to you and is probably not happening.

4. When you do compete for rank, you enjoy it more and have more success because you are valuing yourself accurately, not competing when you would clearly lose or failing to compete when you know you can win.

5. You feel friendlier, and people may have commented on it.

6. You are closer to those with whom you have wanted to be closer.

7. You use the self-protections less.

8. You spend less time in the grip of your emotional schemas.

9. If you were insecure in your relationships, you now feel more secure in at least one.

10. If you have the protector-persecutor defense, at least you know about it and are free of it more often.

11. If you are in a long-term close relationship, there is more love, less ranking.

12. Above all, you are happier, because according to study after study, feeling good about yourself in a realistic way is probably the greatest single predictor of happiness.[1] If you are not there yet, you are on your way.

As you see more progress, you are freer to make real choices rather than being driven by fear, and that brings us to a crossroads.

THE CROSSROADS OF LOVE AND POWER

Since I first conceived of this book, I have had an image of a crossroads of ranking and linking, of love and power. My hope has been that at the end of our work together, when you find yourself at this crossroads you will be able to choose your way according to what is needed in the moment rather than feeling that your only choice is ranking. With an expert's skill, you will know which to use or how to blend the two.

I hope you are now free to link and love but also to use ranking to preserve good personal boundaries, as this serves linking best in the long run. I hope you can enjoy competition and strive to do your best while maintaining values of fairness and good sportsmanship and even linking with your opponents.

Equally important, I hope that your strong links have given you the confidence to assume a high rank when appropriate. You can use the power provided by a higher rank in the service of linking with children, students, patients, or whomever you are trying to serve through your influence. You can let ranking support your valuing of linking and love, so that no matter how much others pressure you, you stand by what you believe. You can encourage the use of linking rather than ranking in larger groups and among nations without denying the reality of ranking or the need to preserve boundaries. And you can appreciate why people so readily turn toward a deity who is both all-loving and all-powerful: we sense that these two forces should ultimately be in harmony.

Those are quite a few hopes, but I have one more, which is that you will continue to work with this book as you strive to find the right balance between linking and ranking. Each time you apply the ideas here, you will become more and more skilled at using linking to leave behind the undervalued self and the unnecessary ranking it creates.

Of course, linking is far more than a technique to feel better about yourself. Linking, coming together, is central to life itself. One-celled organisms linked to become simple animals; simple animals linked to form complex ones; and many of these animals formed groups to help each other. In all cases, they were attracted to, needed to understand, and helped one another — my definition of love. Now some of us aim to link with every other living being in peace and goodwill. Surely linking will evolve with us into stronger and stronger forms.

Now we come to the end. But we are still linked by having shared this journey. As I have worked, you have been in my heart as friends whom I can only imagine but know are there. So I will miss you, now that the last words are written. But I celebrate with you our having reached these final pages together. May your deepest self be removed from the scales that measure value and compare rank, and may your links be strong.

Acknowledgments

I wish to thank my husband, Art, who supports me, always. It was easy to know to whom to dedicate this book.

I am also grateful to my agent, Betsy Amster, who trusted me when she did not have to, after I said that what seemed then like an offbeat book was the only one I wanted to write.

Then my editor, Tracy Behar, took over in the trusting-me department, as this unwieldy material passed through draft after draft. At a crucial point an independent editor, Angela Casey, also stepped in with firm support. I wanted to say everything; she wanted to be sure you understood everything.

Finally, when I was first planning to write a book about power, a person who prefers to remain anonymous suggested that it should be about *love* and power. That has made all the difference.

How to Find a Good Therapist

Begin this important task by asking friends and medical or mental health professionals if they can suggest a therapist whom they know very well, paying particular attention to anyone who can tell you what it is actually like to be in therapy with that person. If your insurance includes mental health coverage and has a list of providers, show the list to those from whom you want suggestions. Often, however, the best therapists are not on these lists because of the drawbacks of participating in insurance plans.

I advise you not to see a therapist whom a close friend is already seeing, unless you can't avoid it because you live in a small town. Most important, do not have a professional therapy relationship with a friend or relative who is a therapist. If your partner sees a therapist, don't see the same one, and beware of any therapist who suggests that you do so. Also, watch out for feeling that you should see a certain therapist because you feel obligated to the person who made the recommendation.

IF YOU CANNOT AFFORD THE THERAPY YOU WANT

If you cannot afford good therapy, do not see someone unlicensed or poorly trained just to save money. It could cost you dearly in other ways. Aim for the best. Even if the price seems steep, it will be worth it. You might need fewer sessions with a better therapist, or you might make gains that truly change your life, including your earning ability.

Why are fees so high? Along with the costs of training, overhead, malpractice insurance, and the stress of life-and-death responsibilities, the reflection and consultation needed for most cases require good therapists to limit their schedule to no more than twenty patient hours a week. However, many therapists have a sliding scale, so about a quarter to a half of their patients pay well below their normal fee. Explain your situation and state what you can pay. If the therapist you have approached cannot offer a lower fee, ask if he or she knows someone who could — perhaps an intern or someone who is starting out in practice. These can be the best referrals of all.

Also ask schools that train therapists and professional organizations if they know of interns, low-fee clinics, or other low-fee opportunities. Interns may lack experience, but they are enthusiastic and up-to-date on the latest techniques. Those seeking the highest level of licensing usually need thousands of hours of experience and must be supervised by a highly skilled therapist, giving you the secondhand input of a true expert. Try to find an intern planning to start a private practice so that you can continue with him or her if you want to.

YOUR PARTICULAR PREFERENCES

Should you see a man or a woman? That is up to you, of course. Which would make you more comfortable? Do you need a male or female role model or perspective? For deeper emotional work, sometimes it is good to choose the same gender as the parent with whom you had the best relationship.

What type of therapy should you be seeking? Therapists fall on a rough continuum from methods that are conscious and rational to methods focused on the unconscious generally or on how it operates specifically in the therapy relationship. Cognitive behavioral and interpersonal therapies are largely rational. Others are in the middle, such as Eye Movement Desensitization and Reprocessing (EMDR). It is mainly used to treat recent traumas, such as witnessing a sudden death, but some practitioners use it to recover memories of trauma or for other, more general, purposes. Emotion-focused therapy and gestalt therapy are also in the middle of the continuum, as they aim to work with the emotions but do not delve systematically into the unconscious.

Psychoanalysis, Jungian analysis, and what is called self psychology (introduced by Heinz Kohut) best represent therapies that seek to access the unconscious as it appears in the therapy relationship and in dreams. Their aim is to go as far back into childhood as necessary to find where your development got off track and work from there. These approaches are best when you have an insecure attachment or a protector-persecutor or have tried more rational approaches without success.

Jungian analysts (those officially certified by Jungian training institutes) and Jungian-oriented psychotherapists (trained in Jungian methods but not through one of the institutes) also use dreams and other methods to access the deepest self and various archetypal symbols that your particular psyche brings up. To Jungians, the ultimate goal of all therapy is individuation—that is, living more and more in harmony with your life's unique purpose, as understood from the point of view of the psyche, not merely the conscious ego.

If you prefer one particular method, such as cognitive behavioral, interpersonal, EMDR, emotion-focused, gestalt, psychoanalytic, Jungian, or self psychological, contact an institution that teaches that method. Even if the teaching institution is far from where you live, it will be able to refer you to a practitioner near you. Be sure, however, not to place the particular method above the skill and personality of the therapist. In fact, you may want to find the very best therapist you can, then inquire about his or her method and consider whether it makes sense in your situation. Indeed, most therapists are eclectic and versatile enough to use the approach that will suit you best, and they can change approaches according to what is working. Perhaps bring this book along and specify what you liked about it. A good therapist will be interested in whatever you think will help you.

SETTING UP AN APPOINTMENT AND
THE FIRST SESSION

After you have assembled a list of therapists, you may want to visit the websites of those who have one. Decide whether you can reach the office easily and think carefully before committing to driving a long distance. Plan to see at least two or three on your list before deciding on one, so next call to find out if they have openings at the times when you are free. Ask about their fees, including whether they charge for the first session (most do). If you will have trouble paying that fee, tell them so on the phone. They may be willing to discuss a lower fee. You may not have a chance to talk more, but do ask as many questions as you can by phone. Most therapists, however, feel that the two of you need to meet in person for an hour at least once before deciding if it is a good match, so set up an appointment. To work well together, you have to like each other. There has to be some chemistry on both sides.

For the first session, allow time to find the office. Psychotherapy appointments, unlike medical ones, usually start on time. Plan to pay with a check and/or have your insurance card and referral ready. Also, be sure to space your introductory session with each therapist—remember, you want to see two or more before deciding—at least one day after the previous one. You'll need time to reflect and recover should a session become emotionally intense. In this first session, ask where the therapist was trained, how long he or she has been in practice, and what his or her specialty is. At some point, bring up enough of your deepest issues to gather whether this therapist will have some useful insights.

If you want to do dream work, you can present a recent, recurring, or disturbing dream. Or the therapist may encourage you just to start out and tell your story or discuss your goals and then hear how they will be achieved. Be a bit spontaneous for part of that first hour to see what happens between you, but also get your questions answered. You are the customer.

MULLING OVER YOUR EXPERIENCE

After meeting each therapist, ask yourself, "Did I gain something from the session? Was I engaged enough to want to return?" You should have felt that the therapist was kind and empathic. They are trained to be that way, so that quality does not in itself make the therapist special. But if one is not, don't go back. Also, do not go back to any therapist who pushes you to work with him or her, discourages you from interviewing other therapists, or makes you feel that his or her needs will get in the way of yours. For example, did this therapist answer a phone call during the session, use you as an audience for personal stories, or try too hard to impress you with his or her talents?

After seeing several therapists, pause for a few days to sort out your impressions; otherwise the last person may leave the strongest one. Don't ignore your reactions to details, such as the atmosphere of the waiting room and office, which reflects much about that person. Also, watch your dreams for your psyche's response to each therapist.

If you are planning to do long-term work, arrange to see the person you like most for four to six sessions, with the understanding that you will both evaluate how it is working after that time. For your next session, decide what else you need to know about the therapist, including office policies such as what happens if you have to cancel suddenly or how often fees are raised. How do the responses feel to you? Mainly, delve deeper into your issues, get the work started, and see how it goes.

Again, take time to make your decision. It may affect you for the rest of your life.

ONCE YOU DECIDE

Once you have made a choice, give the therapist a chance to work in his or her own way. Trust your choice through the ups and downs, but always discuss the downs. I cannot emphasize enough how essential it is for you to be honest. If you don't like something, talk about it. Therapy often leaps forward after these discussions. Above all, do not quit without discussing the reason unless something very unusual occurs, such as a request for sexual intimacy or friendship (absolutely unethical and wrong), a breach of confidentiality, or any other failure to maintain boundaries. Nice as it may sound, therapists should not be willing to see you for no fee, be inconsistent about the session length, or suggest you meet outside of the office unless for very good reasons.

Also, do not try to see two psychotherapists at once except when one has referred you to another, as for marital counseling. The patient-therapist relationship is a place to learn, and if you avoid difficult issues that come up between you by taking them to another relationship, you will not learn as much. It is usually best not to see the same person for couple and individual work. For a couples therapist, the relationship is the real client. The therapist's chief goal is having that work out, so it is a conflict of interest for the same person to have you, individually, as a client.

WHERE LINKING ENTERS IN AND TURNS TO LOVE

Some ranking is inherent in therapy—some power in the service of linking—but obviously you and your therapist should like each other and form a good link. I personally think that therapy, especially when the focus is on healing an insecure attachment, requires an experience of love. However, the love that occurs in therapy does not involve meeting the therapist's needs. Beyond paying for sessions and working honestly and diligently, you are there partly for what I said in chapter four the Japanese call *amae*—basking in another's caring, especially if you had too little of this in your childhood.

I thank Ellen Siegelman, a friend and Jungian analyst, for articulating the obvious role of the therapist's love. She writes that in the course of their work most therapists "come to feel a deep and un-invested love for most of their patients."[1] Notice the word "un-invested." The love must be sincere, not contrived, not even for the purpose of making the patient better. Siegelman is not alone in emphasizing the role of love. Carl Rogers, one of the great founders of modern psychotherapy, based his life's work on the simple idea that "unconditional positive regard" from the therapist is what heals in psychotherapy.[2]

Some psychotherapists, both now and in the past, were taught to feel only as much about their patients as a dentist would, keeping a professional distance and with only just enough warmth to have a good working alliance. We are now learning that linking, or even love (with good professional boundaries), is an essential part of providing patients the safety to explore their emotional schemas, develop a secure attachment style, experience the richness possible in very close relationships, and heal the undervalued self.

Trauma Charts

Childhood Trauma Chart

1	2	3	4	5	6	7	8
Childhood trauma	Before age four	Before age twelve	Received little or no help	Happened more than two times	More than one at a time	Life-altering or profound impact	Felt depressed or ashamed

Adult Trauma Chart

1	2	3	4	5	6	7
Adult trauma	Happened while still "innocent"	Happened more than twice	More than one at a time	Received little or no help	Life-altering or ripple effect	Felt defeated or ashamed

Notes

INTRODUCTION

1. J. V. Wood, W. Q. E. Perunovic, and J. W. Lee, "Positive Self-Statements: Power for Some, Peril for Others," *Psychological Science* 20, no. 7 (2009): 860–66.

ONE. RANKING, LINKING, AND THE UNDERVALUED SELF

1. R. Eisler and D. Loye, "The 'Failure' of Liberalism: A Reassessment of Ideology from a New Feminine-Masculine Perspective," *Political Psychology* 4 (1983): 375–91; J. Sidanius, B. J. Cling, and F. Pratto, "Ranking and Linking as a Function of Sex and Gender Role Attitudes," *Journal of Social Issues* 47 (1991): 131–49.
2. L. Sloman and P. Gilbert, *Subordination and Defeat: An Evolutionary Approach to Mood Disorders and Their Therapy* (Mahwah, NJ: Lawrence Erlbaum, 2000).
3. Ibid.
4. *Diagnostic and Statistical Manual of Mental Disorders*, 4th ed. (Washington, DC: American Psychiatric Association, 1994); J. P. Tangney and K. W. Fischer, *Self-Conscious Emotions: The Psychology of Shame, Guilt, Embarrassment, and Pride* (New York: Guilford, 1995).
5. P. Zimbardo, *Shyness: What It Is, What to Do about It* (Reading, MA: Addison-Wesley, 1977).
6. K. S. Kendler, J. M. Hettema, F. Butera, C. O. Gardner, and C. A. Prescott, "Life Event Dimensions of Loss, Humiliation, Entrapment, and Danger in the Prediction of Onsets of Major Depression and Generalized Anxiety," *Archives of General Psychiatry* 60 (2003): 789–96.

7. S. S. Dickerson and M. E. Kemeny, "Acute Stressors and Cortisol Responses: A Theoretical Integration and Synthesis of Laboratory Research," *Psychological Bulletin* 130 (2004): 355–91.

8. N. I. Eisenberger, M. D. Lieberman, and K. D. Williams, "Does Rejection Hurt? An fMRI Study of Social Exclusion," *Science* 302 (2003): 290–92.

9. A. J. Elliot and A. Moller, "Performance-Approach Goals: Good or Bad Forms of Regulation?" *International Journal of Educational Research* 39 (2003): 339–56.

10. E. Berscheid and H. T. Reis, "Attraction and Close Relationships," in *Handbook of Social Psychology* (4th ed.), ed. S. Fiske, D. Gilbert, and G. Lindzey (New York: McGraw-Hill, 1998), 193–281.

11. F. P. Morgeson and S. E. Humphrey, "The Work Design Questionnaire (WDQ): Developing and Validating a Comprehensive Measure for Assessing Job Design and the Nature of Work," *Journal of Applied Psychology* 91 (2006): 1321–39.

12. H. E. Fisher, "Lust, Attraction and Attachment in Mammalian Reproduction," *Human Nature* 9 (1998): 23–52.

13. A. Aron and E. N. Aron, *Love and the Expansion of Self: Understanding Attraction and Satisfaction* (New York: Hemisphere, 1986); A. Aron, E. N. Aron, M. Tudor, and G. Nelson, "Close Relationships as Including Other in the Self," *Journal of Personality and Social Psychology* 60 (1991): 241–53.

14. A. Aron, E. N. Aron, and D. Smollan, "Inclusion of Other in the Self Scale and the Structure of Interpersonal Closeness," *Journal of Personality and Social Psychology* 63 (1992): 596–612.

15. L. Tiger, *The Pursuit of Pleasure* (New York: Little, Brown, 1992).

16. B. H. Raven, J. Schwarzwald, and M. Koslowsky, "Conceptualizing and Measuring a Power/Interaction Model of Interpersonal Influence," *Journal of Applied Social Psychology* 28 (1998): 307–32.

17. B. H. Raven, "Power Interaction and Interpersonal Influence," in Lee-Chai and Bargh, *Use and Abuse of Power: Multiple Perspectives on the Causes of Corruption* (Philadelphia: Psychology Press, 2001), 217–40.

18. A. Y. Lee-Chai, S. Chen, and T. L. Chartrand, "From Moses to Marcos: Individual Differences in the Use and Abuse of Power," in

Lee-Chai and Bargh, *Use and Abuse of Power*, 57–74; I. H. Frieze and B. S. Boneba, "Power Motivation and Motivation to Help Others," in Lee-Chai and Bargh, *Use and Abuse of Power*, 75–89.

19. E. Sober and D. S. Wilson, *Unto Others: The Evolution and Psychology of Unselfish Behavior* (Cambridge, MA: Harvard University Press, 1999).

20. C. Boehm, *Hierarchy in the Forest: The Evolution of Egalitarian Behavior* (Cambridge, MA: Harvard University Press, 2001).

21. S. Chen, A. Y. Lee-Chai, and J. A. Bargh, "Relationship Orientation as a Moderator of Social Power," *Journal of Personality and Social Psychology* 80 (2001): 173–87.

22. E. S. Chen and T. R. Tyler, "Cloaking Power: Legitimizing Myths and the Psychology of the Advantaged," in Lee-Chai and Bargh, *Use and Abuse of Power*, 241–61.

23. E. Viding, R. James, R. Blair, T. E. Moffitt, and R. Plomin, "Evidence for Substantial Genetic Risk for Psychopathy in 7-Year-Olds," *Journal of Child Psychology and Psychiatry* 46 (2004): 592–97; T. E. Moffitt, A. Caspi, H. Harrington, and B. J. Milne, "Males on the Life-Course-Persistent and Adolescence-Limited Antisocial Pathways: Follow-up at Age 26 Years," *Development and Psychopathology* 14 (2002): 179–207.

24. P. Zimbardo, *The Lucifer Effect: Understanding How Good People Turn Evil* (New York: Random House, 2007).

Two. The Six Self-Protections We Use to Deny Low Rank

1. R. Mendoza-Denton, G. Downey, V. Purdie, A. Davis, and J. Pietrzak, "Sensitivity to Status-Based Rejection: Implications for African American Students' College Experience," *Journal of Personality and Social Psychology* 83 (2002): 896–918.

2. A. G. Greenwald, M. R. Banaji, L. A. Rudman, S. D. Farnham, B. A. Nosek, and D. S. Mellott, "A Unified Theory of Implicit Attitudes, Stereotypes, Self-Esteem, and Self-Concept," *Psychological Review* 109 (2002): 3–25.

3. D. Kierstead, P. D'Agostino, and H. Dill, "Sex Role Stereotyping of College Professors: Bias in Students' Ratings of Instructors," *Journal of Educational Psychology* 80 (1988): 342–44.

4. L. A. Rudman, M. C. Dohn, and K. Fairchild, "Implicit Self-Esteem Compensation: Automatic Threat Defense," *Journal of Personality and Social Psychology* 93 (2007): 798–813.

THREE. REASONS FROM OUR PAST FOR RANKING OURSELVES TOO LOW

1. J. Bowlby, *Attachment and Loss,* vol. 2: *Separation: Anxiety and Anger* (New York: Basic Books, 1973).
2. Sloman and Gilbert, *Subordination and Defeat.*
3. R. Janoff-Bulman, "Characterological versus Behavioral Self-Blame: Inquiries into Depression and Rape," *Journal of Personality and Social Psychology* 37 (1979): 1798–1809.
4. L. A. Rudman, J. Feinberg, and K. Fairchild, "Minority Members' Implicit Attitudes: Automatic Ingroup Bias as a Function of Group Status," *Social Cognition* 20 (2002): 294–320.
5. M. Guyll and K. A. Matthews, "Discrimination and Unfair Treatment: Relationship to Cardiovascular Reactivity among African American and European American Women," *Health Psychology* 20 (2001): 315–25.
6. E. N. Aron, *The Highly Sensitive Person* (New York: Broadway Books, 1997); E. N. Aron and A. Aron, "Sensory-Processing Sensitivity and Its Relation to Introversion and Emotionality," *Journal of Personality and Social Psychology* 73 (1997): 345–68.
7. J. Kagan, *Galen's Prophecy: Temperament in Human Nature* (New York: Basic Books, 1994). Kagan uses the term "inhibitedness"; the animal studies on "sensitivity," "shyness," or something similar are now too numerous to cite, but there is a partial review in Aron and Aron, "Sensory Processing Sensitivity," p. 345, and an interesting discussion of the overall theory in A. Sih and A. M. Bell, "Insights for Behavioral Ecology from Behavioral Syndromes," in H. J. Brockmann, T. J. Roper, M. Naguib, K. E. Wynne-Edwards, C. P. Bernard, and J. C. Mitani, *Advances in the Study of Behavior,* vol. 38 (San Diego: Academic Press, 2008), 227–81.
8. E. Waters, S. Merrick, D. Treboux, J. Crowell, and L. Albershein, "Attachment Security in Infancy and Early Adulthood: A Twenty-Year Longitudinal Study," *Child Development* 71 (2000): 684–89.

9. More precisely, research finds that children are insecure if their mother's description of her childhood is incoherent in certain specific ways, whatever the content of the description, suggesting a basic disorganization in her "internal working model" of attachment relationships. See I. Bretherton and K. A. Munholland, "Internal Working Models in Attachment Relationships: A Construct Revisited," in J. Cassidy and P. R. Shaver, *Handbook of Attachment: Theory, Research, and Clinical Applications* (New York: Guilford, 1999), 89–111.

10. The term "emotional schema" is currently used in many contexts throughout psychology to describe the cognitive organization that allows one thought or memory of a highly emotional event to activate a high level of emotional arousal about the more general idea or type of situation that originally created the intense emotion — for example, A. Neumann and P. Philippot use the term in "Specifying What Makes a Personal Memory Unique Enhances Emotion Regulation," *Emotion* 7 (2007): 566–78. My use of it here is most similar in details to Carl Jung's idea of the "complex" as found in C. G. Jung, "A Review of the Complex Theory" in vol. 6 of *The Collected Works of C. G. Jung*, ed. W. McGuire (Princeton, NJ: Princeton University Press, 1971).

Four. Healing the Undervalued Self by Linking

1. M. W. Baldwin, "Priming Relational Schemas as a Source of Self-Evaluative Reactions," *Journal of Social and Clinical Psychology* 13 (1994): 380–403.

2. M. Mikulincer and D. Arad, "Attachment, Working Models, and Cognitive Openness in Close Relationships: A Test of Chronic and Temporary Accessibility Effects," *Journal of Personality and Social Psychology* 77 (1999): 710–25.

3. M. Mikulincer and P. R. Shaver, "Attachment Theory and Intergroup Bias: Evidence That Priming the Secure Base Schema Attenuates Negative Reactions to Out-Groups," *Journal of Personality and Social Psychology* 81 (2001): 97–115.

4. T. Pierce and J. Lydon, "Priming Relational Schemas: Effects of Contextually Activated and Chronically Accessible Interpersonal

Expectations on Responses to a Stressful Event," *Journal of Personality and Social Psychology* 75 (1998): 1441–48.

5. M. Mikulincer, O. Gillath, V. Halevy, N. Avihou, S. Avidan, and N. Eshkoli, "Attachment Theory and Reactions to Others' Needs: Evidence That Activation of a Sense of Attachment Security Promotes Empathic Responses," *Journal of Personality and Social Psychology* 81 (2001): 1205–24.

6. A. Thorne, "The Press of Personality: A Study of Conversations between Introverts and Extraverts," *Journal of Personality and Social Psychology* 53 (1987): 718–26.

7. T. Doi, *The Anatomy of Dependence* (Tokyo: Kodansha, 1973).

Five. Linking with the Innocent

1. C. G. Jung, *Jung on Active Imagination*, ed. J. Chodorow (Princeton, NJ: Princeton University Press, 1997); R. A. Johnson, *Inner Work: Using Dreams and Active Imagination for Personal Growth* (New York: HarperOne, 1986); H. Stone and S. Stone, *Embracing Ourselves: The Voice Dialogue Manual* (Novato, CA: New World Library, 1989).

Six. Dealing with the Inner Critic and the Protector-Persecutor

1. D. Kalsched, *The Inner World of Trauma: Archetypal Defenses of the Personal Spirit* (New York: Routledge, 1996).

2. About patients most likely to have a protector-persecutor defense, Kalsched notes that they were "extremely bright, sensitive individuals who had suffered, on account of this very sensitivity, some acute or cumulative emotional trauma early in life." Ibid., 11–12.

3. Johnson, *Inner Work*.

Seven. How to Deepen Relationships Through Linking

1. A. Aron, D. Mashek, and E. N. Aron, "Closeness, Intimacy, and Including Other in the Self," in *Handbook of Closeness and Intimacy*, ed. D. Mashek and A. Aron (Mahwah, NJ: Erlbaum, 2004), 27–42.

2. A. Aron, D. G. Dutton, E. N. Aron, and A. Iverson, "Experiences

of Falling in Love," *Journal of Social and Personal Relationships* 6 (1989): 243–57.

3. E. Aronson and V. Cope, "My Enemy's Enemy Is My Friend," *Journal of Personality and Social Psychology* 8 (1968): 8–12; J. Strough and S. Cheng, "Dyad Gender and Friendship Differences in Shared Goals for Mutual Participation on a Collaborative Task," *Child Study Journal* 30 (2000):103–26.

4. D. G. Dutton and A. Aron, "Some Evidence for Heightened Sexual Attraction under Conditions of High Anxiety," *Journal of Personality and Social Psychology* 30 (1974): 510–17.

5. S. L. Gable, H. T. Reis, E. A. Impett, and E. R. Asher, "What Do You Do When Things Go Right? The Intrapersonal and Interpersonal Benefits of Sharing Positive Events," *Journal of Personality and Social Psychology* 87 (2004): 228–45.

6. A. Tesser, "Toward a Self-Evaluation Maintenance Model of Social Behavior," in *Advances in Experimental Social Psychology*, vol. 21, ed. L. Berkowitz (New York: Academic Press, 1988), 181–227.

EIGHT. A SUSTAINED CLOSE RELATIONSHIP

1. A. Aron, C. C. Norman, E. N. Aron, C. McKenna, and R. Heyman, "Couples Shared Participation in Novel and Arousing Activities and Experienced Relationship Quality," *Journal of Personality and Social Psychology* 78 (2000): 273–83; A. Aron, M. Paris, and E. N. Aron, "Falling in Love: Prospective Studies of Self-Concept Change," *Journal of Personality and Social Psychology* 69 (1995): 1102–12.

2. Aron et al., "Couples Shared Participation"; C. Reissmann, A. Aron, and M. Bergen, "Shared Activities and Marital Satisfaction: Causal Direction and Self-Expansion versus Boredom," *Journal of Social and Personal Relationships* 19 (1993): 243–54.

3. A. Aron, D. G. Dutton, E. N. Aron, and A. Iverson, "Experiences of Falling in Love," *Journal of Social and Personal Relationships* 6 (1989): 243–57.

4. P. Schwartz, *Peer Marriage: How Love Between Equals Really Works* (New York: Free Press, 1994).

Nine. Breaking Free from the Undervalued Self

1. P. Hills and M. Argyle, "Happiness, Introversion-Extraversion and Happy Introverts," *Personality and Individual Differences* 30 (2001): 595–608.

Appendix I. How to Find a Good Therapist

1. E. Y. Siegelman, "The Analyst's Love: An Exploration," *Journal of Jungian Theory and Practice* 4 (2002): 19.
2. Carl Rogers, *On Becoming a Person: A Therapist's View of Psychotherapy* (Boston: Houghton Mif 255flin, 1961).

Index

About the Author

DR. ELAINE ARON is a native Californian who graduated from the University of California, Berkeley, as a Phi Beta Kappa. She earned her MA at York University in Toronto and her PhD in depth clinical psychology at Pacifica Graduate Institute in Santa Barbara. She has also received training at the Jung Institute in San Francisco.

Dr. Aron has lived all over North America, from a geodesic dome on Cortes Island, British Columbia, to an aging mansion on Peachtree Street in Atlanta. She divides her time between New York and San Francisco, where she enjoys the opportunities for deep, inner explorations provided by her psychotherapy practice. She also writes, conducts research, and gives public lectures and workshops as often as her highly sensitive, introverted nature allows. She revitalizes herself through meditating daily, taking walking trips in France, and riding the trails of Marin County on a quarter horse named Annie.

In addition to her books and articles on highly sensitive persons, Dr. Aron has published widely in academic journals on the social psychology of close relationships. She and her husband, Art, are world leaders in the study of love and attraction and pioneers in the use of magnetic resonance imaging to understand the brains of sensitive persons and of persons in love.